From
Bobby and Barbara
Christmas 2001

Lady of Arlington

LADY
OF
Arlington

THE LIFE OF MRS. ROBERT E. LEE

JOHN PERRY

Multnomah® Publishers *Sisters, Oregon*

LADY OF ARLINGTON
published by Multnomah Publishers, Inc.
© 2001 by John Perry

International Standard Book Number: 1–57673–849–3

Cover design by Uttley DouPonce DesignWorks
Cover image by Virginia Historical Society, Richmond, Virginia

Multnomah is a trademark of Multnomah Publishers, Inc., and is
registered in the U.S. Patent and Trademark Office.
The colophon is a trademark of Multnomah Publishers, Inc.
Printed in the United States of America

For information:
MULTNOMAH PUBLISHERS, INC.
POST OFFICE BOX 1720
SISTERS, OREGON 97759

Library of Congress Cataloging-in-Publication Data

Perry, John, 1952-
    Lady of Arlington: the life of Mrs. Robert E. Lee: a biography /by John
Perry.
        p. cm.
Includes bibliographical references and index.
    ISBN 1-57673-849-3
    1. Lee, Mary Randolph Custis, 1808-1873. 2. Lee, Mary Randolph
Custis, 1808-1873—Religion. 3. Generals' spouses—Confederate States of
America—Biography. 7. Custis family. I. Title.
    E47.1.L4 P47 2001
    973.7
092—dc21

                                                        20011001645

01 02 03 04 05—10 9 8 7 6 5 4 3 2 1 0

This book is dedicated to my wife,
Susan Ann Pyle Perry,
whose love, patience, encouragement, and friendship
over twenty-four years
give me no cause whatever to be jealous of the general.

Table of Contents

PREFACE

*H*istory has given Mary Custis Lee a bad rap. I'm out to change that. When she's mentioned at all in books about the Civil War or in the many biographies of her famous husband, Mrs. General Robert E. Lee is almost invariably described as a whining, neurotic invalid whose weakness and selfishness made everybody around her miserable and held the general back from rising as high as he otherwise would have during his thirty-plus years in the United States Army.

These characterizations are based on the misreading of isolated quotations from her husband's letters, her son's memoirs, and a few other sources. They are, as I hope to show, entirely false.

The general was famous for his wit and the way he joked with correspondents in his letters. A single stray, teasing comment from Lee about his wife's "laziness and forgetfulness in her housekeeping" to a friend in 1834, when he had been married less than a year, has given rise to a tradition that Mary was a slob. Granted, there may have been a grain of truth in Lee's complaint. But Mary was away from her parents for the first time, keeping house for the first time, living without a retinue of servants for the first time, and living in the nineteenth-century version of government housing.

Mary was in fact a charming, gracious, attractive woman who turned heads in the Supreme Court chamber as a teenager and who almost certainly received a marriage proposal from Sam Houston. Over her sixty-five years, friends, relatives, and perfect strangers consistently described her as cheerful, smiling, welcoming, and industrious. She read Latin and Greek, and when she ordered a copy of *Les Miserables,* she wrote the bookseller to send it in either English or French, whichever was more readily available. She was an excellent painter, a published author, a tireless fund-raiser for charities, and the mother of seven children whose father was away from home for years at a time.

But if Mary seemed to fall short as a housekeeper in her husband's eyes, one might ask, "Who wouldn't?" Lee was an engineer, the son of a man who died disgraced and penniless—a heritage Lee was determined to live down. Again and again, people characterized Lee as the most precise and punctual man they had ever met. Mary, on the other hand, was what we today would call a "right-brain" person: artistic, articulate, gracious, literate, but not really too concerned about what time it was or whether a column of numbers added up.

There are numerous examples of historical misinterpretations of Mary's character that have gained a life of their own, as well as instances where historians have gotten the facts just plain wrong. This past year or so, I have felt more like a detective than a writer, and either in spite of or because of that, this has been the most enjoyable project I have ever undertaken.

Thanks to some very diligent, dedicated, and friendly people, I have been able to run down a lot of rumors, half-truths, and conflicting claims. Certainly the most exciting discovery was Mary's prayer journal at the Virginia Historical Society in Richmond. As far as I can learn, none of it has ever been published or even examined before. Filled with her innermost thoughts, hopes, and fears, it casts new light on every word we have from her.

Of the numerous people who labored to bring the real Mary Custis Lee into the light, a few deserve special attention.

I must offer a heartfelt word of thanks to Frances Pollard, Assistant Director of Library Services at the Virginia Historical Society, whose hospitality never faltered and whose staff was universally kind, considerate, efficient, and enthusiastic.

I'm also most grateful to Colleen Curry, curator of Arlington House, and to Mary Mallen, the site supervisor there, and their staff. They allowed me complete access to their archives and to Arlington House. When you are trying to understand how someone felt about the only home she ever owned, nothing compares with standing at her bedroom window looking out at the garden she loved—or crawling through her attic! I only wish the National Park Service had a budget commensurate with the level of dedication and enthusiasm shown by the people who are safeguarding our heritage there. They do a lot with a little.

Thanks also to Ruth Ann Coski and John Coski at the Eleanor S. Brockenbrough Library of the Museum of the Confederacy. Their efficiency and professionalism are testaments to their love of a legacy that remains a rich and important component of the American experience. And I must acknowledge the expert assistance of Holly Bailey at the Leyburn Library, Washington and Lee University, who gave me more useful information per research hour than anybody else during this whole operation.

Wes Driver served once again, as he has in the past, as my good right arm, soldiering on gamely with me day after day through letters, photos, newspapers, notebooks, maps, card files, and computer indexes; dealing equally well with gracious librarians and snippy bureaucrats; and eating in weird all-night diners without once complaining. From the familiar to the new, I extend my sincerest thanks and professional admiration to Judith St. Pierre, my new friend and editor at Multnomah, who has done so much to improve both this story and the telling of it and whom, like Mrs. Lee, I much admire but have never met.

And last but not least, I thank my dear wife, Susan Ann, and our children, Charles and Olivia, for their patience through all the absences, late dinners, and vacant stares this project has produced despite my best efforts to "keep things normal this time."

Getting to know this brave and magnificent woman, Mary Lee, has made it all worthwhile. And if this book succeeds in introducing her to a world looking frantically for heroes—especially female ones—the reward will be sweeter still.

Soli deo gloria.

JOHN PERRY
PALM SUNDAY, 2001
NASHVILLE

With patient mind thy course of duty run;
God nothing does or suffers to be done
But thou wouldst do thyself, if thou couldst see
The end of all events as well as He.

COPIED BY MARY CUSTIS LEE
INTO THE KEEPSAKE ALBUM OF J. E. B. STUART

Lord, let me suffer any thing
rather than have my heart turned away from Thee.

MARY CUSTIS LEE IN HER PRAYER JOURNAL
FEBRUARY 29, 1832

When through fiery trials thy pathway shall lie,
My grace, all sufficient, shall be thy supply;
The flame shall not hurt thee; I only design
Thy dross to consume and thy gold to refine.

FROM GEORGE KEITH, "HOW FIRM A FOUNDATION"
RIPPON'S *SELECTION OF HYMNS*, 1787

CHAPTER ONE

THE ROSE OF ARLINGTON

*S*pring was always magnificent at Arlington, and the spring of 1861 promised to be the most glorious ever. Standing on the great portico of the mansion, framed by its eight massive columns, a small woman in traveling clothes scanned the acres of rolling lawn between the house and the Potomac River, which flowed lazily through the verdant landscape from north to south in the middle distance. Ripples etched with shimmers of light glowed golden in the dawn. A soft breeze carried the rich fragrance of roses from the garden.

Looking beyond the river, Mary's deep brown eyes came to rest on Washington City, its buildings of sandstone and limestone and marble silhouetted against the rising sun, ruddy with the morning. The place had its detractors. Some said the political maneuvering there was as foul as the swamp it was built on, a waterlogged marsh that still muddied the boots of patrician statesmen from more civilized places like Boston, Philadelphia, and New York.

But Mary had never thought—could never have thought—such a thing about that imposing and important place, which she had watched take shape over a lifetime from the portico high on the opposite bank of the Potomac. The city was named after George Washington, Mary's paternal great-grandfather by marriage. Mary's father had grown up at Mount

Vernon. He had idolized Washington and had built Arlington, and the portico where Mary now stood, as a monument to him.

Mary saw another monument to Washington as she looked eastward. Even unfinished, the spare marble obelisk dominated the city. Begun in a burst of patriotic fervor in 1848, the Washington Monument had been abandoned six years later. Lack of funds and political squabbling among the sponsoring groups had left the stone column less than a third complete. Contemplating the unfinished memorial, Mary saw in it a metaphor for the world around her: plans halted, allies at odds, the future in doubt.

Servants passed back and forth between the open door behind her and a wagon in the drive, gingerly adding bundles and odd pieces of furniture to the growing heap of household goods. Mary had lived in many places and was used to moving. The wife of an army officer could expect to do that. But Arlington had always been home.

Mary's earliest memories were of this hillside, this view, this heady spring atmosphere infused with the smell of damp earth and flowers and apple trees in bloom. Her parents had begun the garden beside the house before she was born, and from the time she could hold a hoe, she had worked there, cultivating camellias, hyacinths, honeysuckle, gardenias, lilies, morning glory, dogwood, and roses.

Especially roses. For years, Mary and her many correspondents had sent seeds, cuttings, and pressed blossoms back and forth to one another. She herself had planted many of the roses, right up to the time her crippled hands could no longer grip a spade.

There was another garden in the back of the house, a large kitchen plot brimming with herbs and vegetables; stretching out of sight to the north, west, and south there were fields of corn, wheat, tobacco, and pasture. Nearby were fisheries and vast stands of timber.

Just over a rise in the lawn to the south, Mary could see the canopy of oak trees that covered the graves of her parents.

Inside, in Arlington's dining room, Mary had entertained presidents, generals, and foreign dignitaries—even the great Marquis de Lafayette. In the parlor she had refused one suitor and accepted another. And under the triple archway between the dining room and the parlor she had exchanged wedding vows with a young army lieutenant. Six of their seven children had been born upstairs.

Leaving this place was unimaginable. Yet here Mary stood in her bonnet and dark traveling dress, leaning on her crutch as she waited to be helped into her coach, not knowing how or when she would return.

Were the decision hers alone to make, she would stay at Arlington despite the ominous events of the past few weeks. But remaining only added to her husband's burdens. A month earlier it had seemed inconceivable that Virginia would secede. Now it had happened. Even so, here on her peaceful wooded hillside high above Washington, Mary could not believe that war and danger were so close.

Although the bustle and clatter of the city below had been replaced by "a deathlike stillness," to Mary the country had never seemed more beautiful—"perfectly radiant," she wrote her husband in early May. "The yellow jessamine is in full bloom & perfuming the air." From his vantage point in Richmond, however, his perspective was dramatically different. "I am glad to hear that you are at peace and enjoying the sweet weather and beautiful flowers," he wrote. But, "You had better complete your arrangements and retire further from the scene of war."

Mary had continued to delay her departure. Fact and fiction were so entangled in Washington City and Richmond that she scarcely knew what to believe. She did not want to pack up and leave as long as there was any chance of a settlement between the federal government and the seceding states.

In another letter on May 13, her husband made plain the chilling reality: "Do not put faith in rumors of adjustment. I see no prospect for it. It cannot be while passions on both sides are so infuriated. Make your plans for several years of war." But Mary had still refused to leave, even though the Washington press was lashing out at her husband and urging the federal government to seize Arlington.

Neither her husband's letters nor the incendiary newspaper coverage had spurred Mary to action. What finally convinced her to leave was the urgent plea of her young second cousin, who burst into her room one sunny afternoon and announced breathlessly, "Union troops are on their way. They're coming to take the house and property. They're going to fortify Arlington Heights to protect the capital. You've got to get out—quick."

The ironies could scarcely have been lost on Mary. Throughout her life, Arlington had been a constant reminder of General Washington's greatness.

The very walls before her had been built to honor the namesake of the city across the river where Union troops were now encamped. The bed in her daughters' room upstairs was the one in which Washington had drawn his last breath. There were roses from Mount Vernon growing in the garden outside. Mary had spent her entire life steeped in his legend, and her husband all but worshiped his memory. Anyone who knew him knew that. Now the country Washington had led to independence was unmaking itself. Now she was a threat to his army. Suddenly she had become the enemy.

Bowing to the inevitable at last, Mary had hurriedly crated her most valuable belongings and sent them to safety. Mercifully, there was a reprieve; her cousin returned the next day to report that the movement of Union troops had been delayed. The additional time allowed Mary to plan an orderly withdrawal. She sent two large wooden chests containing family silver, her husband's personal papers, Washington's letters, and other family documents by rail to Richmond.

Mary's aunt had invited her and the children to come to Ravensworth, the ancestral home of Mary's mother, and to bring anything she wanted to safeguard. On May 8, two of Mary's daughters had left for Ravensworth with wagons full of paintings, household furnishings, food, wine, and the family piano. Another daughter was visiting one of her brothers and his family at White House, the family plantation on the Pamunkey River. The two youngest children were away at school. That left only her oldest son to help Mary make the final preparations to leave.

Mary did not doubt that her homelessness would be temporary. Thinking she would be away from Arlington for only a matter of weeks, she left precious but cumbersome Washington memorabilia in the attic. Among them was Washington's campaign tent, folded, rolled, and stored in two large canvas sacks. Mary could not count the number of times her father had pitched that worn red canvas shelter for one of his celebrations. The tent and its happy memories stayed behind with the harpsichord that Washington had ordered from Europe, the blue damask curtains from Mount Vernon, an enormous wrought iron lantern that hung in the Mount Vernon portico, fine imported carpets, and more.

Other valuables were buried in the garden. Winter curtains and rugs that normally went into storage that time of year were rolled and packed away with extra care. Books were locked in closets, and Washington's china was crated and secured in the cellar.

Mary walked slowly back to the house and stepped inside the cool, wide hall that ran the length of it. To her right was the parlor where she had been married almost thirty years earlier. Across the hall to the left was a large, comfortable room where she had spent much of her time on the days she was able to come down the stairs from her bedroom.

This was the one room in the house that she and her husband had built to suit their own taste. Her father had designed it as a ballroom but never had the inclination or the money to finish it, so for years it was used to store treasures from Mount Vernon. Expecting her husband to retire soon, Mary had been pleased when he added marble fireplaces and other homey touches. *How long would it be before the two of them sat before that cheerful fire again?* she wondered.

From the spacious parlor, Mary walked down the hall and out through the conservatory to her large, meticulously tended flower garden. Her bedroom windows looked out on its luxuriant tracts of blossoms, vines, borders, and ground cover. Her children had had plots of their own there, and Mary's love for it had brought her outdoors to surround herself with its color and heady fragrance even when she had to be pushed in her rolling chair. As a young girl she had dug in the dark rich alluvial earth alongside her mother, and her children had dug the same dirt with her.

As she expected to be gone only a short time, Mary instructed the family's slaves to carry on as usual. According to the terms of her father's will, written years before, they were all to be freed in 1862, only a few months from now. Surely she would be back to help them make the transition. Though she thought it would be difficult, she was eager for all of them to have a fair chance to build a new life in freedom, and she felt a responsibility to do her part.

Mary handed her keys to her personal maid, whose mother had served at Mount Vernon. She was now responsible for safeguarding the household effects, while the overseer was charged with protecting the house and grounds. They bid one another a heartfelt farewell.

Mary turned toward the waiting carriage but then paused and walked haltingly back into the garden. There, as she had so often before, she bent over to cut her favorite flower. Of all those that grew on the estate, this was her favorite: the moss rose, fresh, fragrant, perfect, misted with morning dew—the rose of Arlington.

With her son's help, Mary settled stiffly into her coach and took a last look around. On the one side, she saw Arlington's majestic colonnade; on the other, the city of Washington lying in the distance. The sun was up, hovering a little south of a dark, spidery shape arching into the distant sky—the iron framework of a soaring new Capitol dome.

The coachman snapped his reins, the wheels turned, and Mary began the ten-mile trip to Ravensworth. As the house dropped from view behind her, she already longed for one more look—just one more—at those columns, those roses, and those two quiet graves under their gently swaying oaks.

CHAPTER TWO

LITTLE WASHINGTON

*I*n departing ahead of what seemed an inevitable war, Mary Custis Lee followed the historical trail blazed by her forefathers—more than two centuries before and half a world away—on account of another bloody conflict dividing a country against itself.

John Custis, the first to bring Mary's ancestral name to the New World, was born in 1630 in Holland, where his parents had fled, probably from Ireland, during the conflict leading up to the English Civil War. When he was twenty, John sailed from Rotterdam for Virginia, where he received a grant of 600 acres. He married Elizabeth Robinson, and in 1653 she bore him his only child, a son also named John. After Elizabeth died, he married three-times-widowed Alicia Burdette, whose second husband had built a large house on Plantation Creek near Cape Charles.

John II later bought the house and surrounding property from Alicia's son and received a royal patent on the adjacent land. The estate was known as *Accawmake,* an Indian word meaning "double purchase." Custis renamed it Arlington, after Henry, Earl of Arlington.

Widowed a second time, John I married Tabitha Scarborough in 1680. When he died at Arlington in 1696, he left all his property with the exception of Arlington to his son, John II. The Arlington plantation passed to his wife, Tabitha; when she died it was to go to John II's oldest grandson, John IV, who had been born at Hungars Plantation, on Hungars Neck along the Virginia coast, in 1679.

John IV was reared in the lifestyle of the Virginia gentry. In addition to the name of John Custis, he was expected to carry on family traditions of engaging in community service, running a profitable business, and enlarging the Custis landholdings. As was common for the sons of the wealthiest Virginia families, he was sent to England to acquire the education and polish expected of the ruling class. When he returned to Virginia, like his father and grandfather before him, he was elected to the House of Burgesses.

Reveling in the life of a young, rich, handsome, well-traveled gentleman, John IV lived part of the year at Arlington and part at the colonial capital of Williamsburg, where his fine clothes and freshly minted English affectations earned him a reputation as a dandy. Even as he began to make his mark in Williamsburg politics, he became known for his love of parties and his eye for young ladies. Eligible women, drawn to both his looks and his money, agreed that he was "a young man of parts and possessions."

In Williamsburg, John met Frances Parke, the beautiful and spirited granddaughter of the former royal governor of Virginia, Sir William Berkeley. Frances lived with the governor's widow and her husband at Green Spring, the Berkeley mansion in Williamsburg. Frances's father, Daniel Parke, was American-born, but bored with life in the colonies, he spent most of his married life away from his family. He eventually died in Antigua, the victim of a mob outraged by his policies as royal governor of the Leeward Islands. His death left his wife rich and his daughters, who scarcely knew him, with fabulous dowries.

Frances's fabulous wealth only added to her popularity among the highborn bachelors of Williamsburg. Her grandmother, Lady Frances Berkeley, had endowed her with beauty, charm, and wit; along with his money, her father had gifted her with curiosity, self-assurance, and a sense of independence remarkable for the time. All in all, it was a package John Custis found irresistible.

Although he was one of many who competed for Frances's charms, John soon outpaced the others. Their wedding in 1705 was one of the great social events of the year—the colonial governor's beautiful and vivacious granddaughter marrying the heir of one of Virginia's oldest and wealthiest families. For their honeymoon, the newlyweds embarked on the Grand Tour to visit the great capitals and attractions of Europe. Frances reportedly told her husband that she wanted to see the world "before you bury me alive at your Arlington."

Some months later the couple returned home in high spirits. They agreed that they had had a wonderful time on their trip—and that was the last thing they agreed on for the rest of their married lives.

It was a union of two firstborn children who were used to getting their way. Husband and wife alike were natural leaders, and neither wanted to follow the other. They argued at home and in public, often disruptively loud, and usually about money. Rich and generous as he was, John Custis was meticulous in his financial record keeping and insisted on budgeting every penny. Frances bristled at being held accountable that way—she considered herself accountable to no one.

According to tradition, one day the two were in a small hack with John at the reins. An argument began, and John headed straight for Chesapeake Bay. Furious, Frances screamed, "Where are you taking me?"

"To hell, madam!" John Custis shouted.

Frances settled back into her seat. "Drive on," she ordered. "Anyplace is better than Arlington." And the horse—with couple, hack, and all—plunged into the water at a trot.

The battle was never-ending. When Frances wanted to give a bolt of cotton cloth to charity, John refused to allow it. Frances accused him of cheating her in plantation accounts and withholding money. John accused her of stealing silver from the pantry. They fought over who had command of the slaves. They swore out depositions against each other in court. As their wedding had been the social event of the season, their marriage was the talk of the town day after day.

Despite their adversarial relationship, the two managed to become the parents of two children, a daughter and a son. The daughter was named Frances Parke Custis, after her mother. The son, born in 1711, was christened (one can almost hear the argument now) Daniel Parke Custis, after his long-absent grandfather, thus breaking with the tradition that called for each generation to produce a John Custis.

It was merciful, perhaps, that Frances died of smallpox at Arlington in 1715. John eventually moved to Williamsburg and lived a long and happy life, continuing his service in the House of Burgesses and serving other official duties. He died in 1750.

Frances and John's son, Daniel, grew up at the White House, a Custis family plantation along the Pamunkey River that encompassed some of the richest and most productive river bottomland in the region. The year before his father's death, Daniel married Martha Dandridge, daughter of John and Frances Jones Dandridge, a well-to-do but not wealthy Virginia family from New Kent County, where the White House was located.

If not extremely well off, John Dandridge was a respectable planter and a colonel in the militia, and Martha was one of the most charming and beautiful young ladies in Williamsburg. Still in her teens, she had an elegance and assurance about her that soon won over old John Custis's heart, just as it had his son's. John not only agreed to the marriage, but also gave the couple the White House plantation as a wedding gift.

After their wedding there in the summer of 1749, Daniel and Martha settled down to a life of managing large and profitable stands of tobacco, running a household, and raising a family. These happy years were darkened by the death of the couple's first two children. Their first child to survive was John Parke Custis, whose birth in 1754 marked the return of the name John to the Custis lineage. Two years later his sister, Martha Parke Custis, joined the family.

Martha Custis fretted over her children—what they ate, what they wore, what they did, where they went—and was always nervous about them whenever they were out of her sight. She had already lost two children, and little Martha always seemed to be in delicate health. "Jackie" and "Patsy," as they came to be called, were her constant concerns.

Then in 1757, Daniel Custis died unexpectedly, leaving Martha, not yet thirty, a widow with two young children and a plantation to run. Her assets included 15,000 acres of land, about 150 slaves, and £30,000 in cash from the Custis family, which in time would pass to her children. With the help of Robert Carter Nicholas, an attorney and family friend, Martha took over management of the estate as sole executrix, transacting loans, selling and exporting her tobacco crop, arranging insurance, managing bank dividends, and overseeing the property. All told, the widow Custis was one of the richest women in Virginia—and still one of the most beautiful.

After an appropriate period of mourning, Martha began accepting social engagements, and at the home of a New Kent County neighbor, she met a handsome young colonel who had just retired from the Virginia militia. George Washington had proved himself a brave, inspiring, and resourceful leader during the French and Indian War, but after nearly six years, he had grown disillusioned with the political intrigues of military service and resigned his commission.

Mrs. Custis and Colonel Washington were "mutually pleased on this their first interview," according to one account. They made a dashing and compatible pair: educated, intelligent, gracious, prosperous, and born within a few months of each other in 1732. Only a matter of weeks after their meeting, George called at the White House to ask Martha for her hand in marriage. She joyfully accepted, and on January 17, 1759, the two were married at the home of the bride.

The newlyweds spent three months at the White House before moving to Mount Vernon, Colonel Washington's home on the Potomac. At the time, the Mount Vernon estate belonged to the widow of Washington's older half-brother, Lawrence, and the colonel rented it for 15,000 pounds of tobacco a year.

Martha Custis Washington's new house was originally a well-built but modest one-story wooden building with four rooms and a central hallway, surrounded by more than 2,000 acres of picturesque farmland and forest. By the time she arrived, the colonel had added a second story and more refined decorations throughout.

Jackie and Patsy Custis were young children when their mother remarried, and they readily adapted to life at Mount Vernon. The colonel had no children of his own, but he cherished Martha's. They grew up surrounded by servants, wanting for nothing and having the best of everything. Their clothes, and even their toys, were imported from England. The colonel was often absent, and Martha indulged their every wish.

The children were so spoiled that by Jackie's fourteenth birthday, Colonel Washington viewed his foster son's development with alarm. Jackie was intelligent, and his morals and manners were excellent. But he was self-centered and indolent—disinterested in education, disinclined to take responsibility, and increasingly disposed to enjoy dogs, horses, guns, and fancy clothes. Washington worried that Jackie would not be prepared to carry out his duties as a man of property and the head of a leading Virginia family, and he tried hard to redirect Jackie's attention to his studies.

By the time Jackie turned seventeen, Washington had achieved some success and was considering sending his foster son on a European tour. But Jackie showed no enthusiasm for foreign travel. Furthermore, he was in love with a girl he had met in Annapolis, and he wanted to get married.

Eleanor Calvert, known as "Nelly," was a slim, beautiful young lady of sixteen. Her father, Benedict Calvert, was the illegitimate son of the sixth Lord Baltimore, who had died in 1771 without legal heirs. Calvert's inheritance more than compensated for the circumstances of his birth. He was a respected member of the community and the owner of an elegant estate, Mount Airy, near Upper Marlborough, Maryland.

Washington opposed the marriage because he thought Jackie and Nelly were both too young and that Jackie ought to finish his education first. But it was Nelly herself who convinced Jackie that it would be better for their future together if he were to continue in school. And so he enrolled at King's College (later Columbia) in New York, where the simple dormitory life and rigorous academic schedule further separated him from his past habits. He seemed happy at school, and his teachers reported that he was making satisfactory progress.

Nevertheless, Jackie left college abruptly and for good upon the death of his sister. Some sources identified Patsy Custis's illness as "consumption"—tuberculosis—and others as epilepsy. Whatever the cause, she died when she was only sixteen, the same age as Nelly. When the new term approached that fall, Jackie refused to return to King's College. His mother sided with him, Washington acquiesced, and on February 3, 1774, John Parke Custis and Eleanor Calvert were married in the great hall at Mount Airy.

Jackie was already a rich man, and he stood to be even wealthier in the future. In a letter to Nelly's father on April 3, 1774, George Washington noted that "Mr. Custis's estate consists of about 15,000 acres of land…several lots in [Williamsburg]; between two and three hundred negroes; and about eight or ten thousand pounds upon bond, and in the hands of his merchants. This estate he now holds, independent of his mother's dower, which will be an addition to it at her death…."

At Washington's suggestion that "middling land under a man's own eye is more profitable than rich land at a distance," Jack Custis moved to

Mount Vernon and began to consolidate his holdings, selling distant and less fertile property to buy farms that were closer together and more productive. He bought some Custis holdings from his mother and also received the £8,000 inheritance that would have gone to his sister.

A year later, the battles of Lexington and Concord marked the start of armed conflict between the British and the American colonists, and on June 15, 1775, the Continental Congress unanimously elected George Washington general and commander in chief of the army. Before he left to take command, Washington counseled Jack to stay at Mount Vernon and look after Nelly and Martha.

Nelly was expecting their first child, and Jack agreed to stay at least until the baby was born. They traveled to Mount Airy in hopes of enjoying a quiet time with the new arrival, but the baby died shortly after birth. To lift everyone's spirits, Jack suggested a trip to visit General Washington, and Jack, Nelly, and Martha spent the following winter in Cambridge, Massachusetts, near Washington's winter quarters. Custis family tradition holds that Jack served his stepfather as an aide-de-camp during the winter. But with the beginning of the spring campaign, Nelly was expecting again, and Jack and the ladies returned to Mount Vernon. On August 21, 1776, Elizabeth Parke Custis was born. Sixteen months later her sister, Martha Parke, arrived.

In trying to help Jack manage his affairs, General Washington advised him to buy more land. The war had sparked inflation, and paper money was rapidly losing its value. Washington urged Jack to invest in property while his Virginia currency still had significant purchasing power.

Jack set his sights on three adjoining tracts, nearly 3,000 acres in all, owned by brothers Robert, Philip, and Gerard Alexander. The land was convenient to both Mount Vernon and Mount Airy and combined rich river bottomland along the Potomac with rolling hills, much of it covered in fine timber. This property had originally been part of a 6,000-acre tract awarded by Governor William Berkeley, Jack's great-great-grandfather by marriage, to Captain Robert Howsing for carrying 180 colonists over from England. The Howsing Tract (also spelled "Howsen" or "Housen") was undeveloped wilderness, though there were two small Algonquin Indian villages on the property. Located at the head of navigation of the Potomac, the land had great potential. Even so, Captain Howsing soon sold it to a surveyor and planter named John Alexander for six hogsheads of tobacco.

Successive generations of Alexanders worked the land, leased some of it out to tenants, built houses, and divided and redivided the original tract. By the time three of his great-grandsons inherited their shares, there were numerous houses and cleared fields, as well as a mill and a warehouse.

Washington was pleased to hear that the land was so beautiful and so near Mount Vernon, but when he heard what Jack would pay, the general, ever careful and conservative in business affairs, was astounded. Jack gave Gerard Alexander £11,000 for his tract, due by the end of the year. For Robert Alexander's land, he agreed to pay £12 an acre plus compounded interest at the end of twenty-four years, which came to a king's ransom of £48,000. He did not buy Philip's tract.

In a letter to Washington at military headquarters, Jack explained, "Nothing could have induced me to give such terms but the unconquerable desire I had to live in the neighborhood of Mt. Vernon."

Though he thought the price too high, Washington's greater concern was that Jack would move too slowly, or that the Alexanders would stall, further devaluing Jack's money. He was doubtless relieved to hear that the two Alexander brothers conveyed their land to Jack on Christmas Day, 1778.

Robert's tract included a simple four-room frame house set in a grove of trees overlooking the Potomac. Though architecturally modest, it was roomy and comfortable, and Jack, Nelly (expecting again), and their two daughters moved in. Jack named his new home Abingdon; another daughter, Eleanor Parke Custis, was born there the following spring.

In 1780, Nelly Custis gave birth to twin girls, but they lived only three weeks. About the same time, Jack fell ill. He rallied but was ailing again when Washington passed through Mount Vernon on his way to Yorktown in September 1781.

It was the general's first visit home in six years. He spent much of his three-day stay dealing with estate matters and getting to know his new "grandchildren," particularly the youngest, who had been born at Mount Airy on April 30 of that year. He was the first son in the family, and his parents had proudly christened him George Washington Parke Custis.

Jack Custis again offered to serve as an unofficial aide-de-camp, and he accompanied General Washington to Yorktown, where the Continental army under the Marquis de Lafayette had the British backed up against Chesapeake Bay. When the British evacuation fleet failed to appear, Lord Cornwallis surrendered. By then, Jack had caught camp fever. Too sick to walk, he was carried into the field to witness the British surrender on October 19.

Jack was critically ill by the time Washington had him taken to Eltham, the home of a Custis relative thirty miles away. When Nelly and Martha came a few days later, Washington's personal physician told them that there was no hope. The general arrived at dawn on November 5, and that evening John Parke Custis died in his wife's arms. He was twenty-seven. Family tradition holds that while he was comforting the newly widowed Nelly Custis, General Washington announced, "From this moment I adopt the two youngest children as my own."

Within two years, Nelly Custis married Dr. David Stuart, a respected local planter, and the couple settled at Abingdon with Nelly's two oldest children, Elizabeth and Martha. The two youngest children, Eleanor, nicknamed "Nelly" like her mother, and her brother, whom the general fondly called "Little Washington," "Washy," or "Tub," moved to Mount Vernon. The general loved Nelly and Washy as if they were his own grandchildren.

Washy was only six months old when his father died, and so from his earliest years General Washington filled a father's role, both in his eyes and in his heart. When General Lafayette visited Mt. Vernon after a triumphal tour of America in 1784, he wrote about the handsome three-year-old who tagged along on tours of the house and estate, his whole hand grasping one of the general's large fingers. The general returned the affection of his young ward, often calling him his "son."

Washy moved easily among the distinguished visitors who came to Mount Vernon to pay their respects to the hero of the American Revolution. The boy mimicked the courtly manners he saw in his famous guardian's guests, entertained their children, and soaked up the atmosphere of refinement that permeated the house.

Those were peaceful, pleasant years for the family, marked by a consistent routine that had a comfortable predictability to it. The general rose and dressed before dawn to take a turn about the stables and then joined his family and any guests for breakfast. From then until midafternoon, he saw to the work on the family estates, which, in addition to Mount Vernon and Abingdon, included Woodlawn, Audley, and Tudor Place.

Promptly at 2:45 the main meal of the day was served, after which the general retired to his private study to answer letters and go over estate accounts. During the afternoons, he was strictly off-limits to the children, but he emerged early in the evening for tea and a light supper. Afterward there was more time for the children to play or to listen to the general read aloud until nine o'clock or so, when everyone went off to bed.

During these years, the mansion at Mount Vernon reached its final form. Washington added to it steadily after his return from the war, and in time it had a new master bedroom, library, piazza, kitchen, and office, as well as a large and magnificent dining hall featuring an Adam-style Palladian window. Everything reflected the taste of its owner: elegant and of high quality but never ostentatious. Work on the house culminated with the installation of a weather vane atop the cupola in 1787, decorated—at Washington's direction—with a dove of peace.

In 1789 the news that Washington had been unanimously elected president of the United States interrupted the famous general's retirement. The family moved to New York, then the nation's capital, where Washington was sworn in as chief executive. They lived in a house on Franklin Square, where Washy, an observant and impressionable boy of nine, drank in the essence of the place as thoroughly as he had Mount Vernon.

Washy loved accompanying the president on his Saturday morning drives around Manhattan Island, taking in the sights and smells of the various neighborhoods and the docks with their exotic ships and cargoes. He was not particularly diligent at his studies, but he loved the theater and took a great interest in painting after watching his sister Nelly work with her art instructor. He faithfully tagged along after the various portraitists who came to have the president sit for them.

In 1790 Congress transferred the national capital to Philadelphia, and Washington moved his family to a new presidential mansion on Market Street, one of the finest houses on one of the most fashionable streets in town. Again young Wash was immersed in the spirit of a city, this time the historic place where, almost fifteen years before, the Continental Congress had proclaimed the United States free and independent from Great Britain.

Like his father, Washington Custis was a handsome, witty, intelligent adolescent. Also like him, he was indolent, spoiled, self-centered, and disinclined to reach for his full potential. History had repeated itself: If Martha Washington had been overly worried and overindulgent with her son, she was even more so with her grandson after her son's early death. General Washington had been too lenient with Jackie, but Wash got away with even more.

Jackie had been spoiled by a houseful of servants waiting to carry out his every wish. Wash had all that and the trappings of the presidency besides: a mansion in Philadelphia, foreign ambassadors in the parlor every Tuesday afternoon, and familiar greetings from the most famous and respected men in the land. Jack Custis had died a rich man; when he came of age, Washington Custis would be even richer.

While he endured his classroom studies, Wash looked to the world of experience for his true education. It was a world few boys ever see. He listened as a distraught military commander reported to the president that Indians were ambushing his men in Ohio. He accompanied Washington to the theater and to concerts. He traveled with the president to Federal City, the new national capital under construction only a few miles by riverboat from Mount Vernon. And on September 18, 1793, he stood in Washington's shadow, watching proudly as the president laid the cornerstone of the Capitol on Jenkins' Hill, a high spot of ground not far from the marshy Potomac shoreline.

Had Wash looked directly across the river that day, he would have seen a beautifully wooded hillside on the Alexander property that his father had paid so much for—property that one day would belong to him.

In the fall of 1796, Wash began his studies at the College of New Jersey (later Princeton). His start was promising, but his final examination scores were a disappointment to the overly optimistic president. Master Custis promised to do better: "I will make a grand exertion and show you that your grandson shall once more deserve your favor. Could you but see how happy I now am, you would soon forget all that is past and let my future conduct prove the truth of my assertions." At the same time, however, he told his cousin, Eliza Law, that he was "very much dissatisfied" with school.

Wash began the new academic year on a hopeful note. Although he struggled with mathematics (as he later admitted, "because of the superficial manner in which I imbibed first principles"), he did well in geography, literature, and French. It wasn't long, though, before Wash was home again. Found guilty of unspecified "acts of meanness & irregularity," he was suspended and ordered to leave the college.

Returning to Mount Vernon after being expelled, George Washington Parke Custis was delighted to find George Washington Lafayette, son of the French general, staying there. They quickly became fast friends and had a wonderful time together before Lafayette left to rejoin his family. It was a memorable occasion for Wash, who vicariously experienced the life of a European nobleman only a little older than himself.

In February 1798, retired once again to his beloved estate, Washington decided to try yet another school for his wayward pupil and enrolled Wash at St. John's College in Annapolis. This time, Washington had no illusions that Wash would excel, and predictably the school year was not a success. Wash spent lavishly on clothes and entertainment—and announced his intention to marry.

Washington had regularly consulted Nelly about important decisions concerning her son. Though Wash had inevitably grown somewhat distant from his mother—especially after she and Dr. Stuart had started having children of their own—the president knew that Nelly Custis Stuart and her son loved each other deeply. Besides, the president, though a great leader of armies and hero of the nation, was flummoxed by the behavior of a teenage boy.

Now, appalled at Wash's plans to wed, Washington sent Nelly to prevent, or at least delay, the marriage—an ironic choice of messenger inasmuch as she herself had married at sixteen. Confronted with his behavior, Wash insisted he had told his young love only that he "hoped to marry her when he was old enough."

At the end of the year, Wash lobbied to leave school, though Washington thought he had made it clear that he was to return for the next term. In the end, Wash's lassitude wore down the general, and the young man came home to stay. That was the end of his formal education.

Not long after Wash returned to Mount Vernon, America was threatened with invasion by its old ally, France, and Washington was called out of retirement to head a new army. Wash was desperate to join the military. Of course his mother and grandmother objected. True, he was the last male of his line, but, as Washington reminded the women, "the same providence that would watch over and protect him in domestic walks can extend the same protection to him in a camp or the field of battle, if he should ever be in one."

Wash spent three months training, after which the general applied for his promotion to cornet (second lieutenant), saying that his "ample fortune, good education, more than common abilities and good disposition, free from vice of any kind" were worthy qualifications. Wash received his commission and proudly went to serve in a gunnery detachment up the Potomac River at Harper's Ferry. The war, however, never came. Custis was discharged as a brevet major and returned to Mount Vernon.

In the meantime Wash's sister, Nelly, had married Washington's favorite nephew, Lawrence Lewis. One crisp December day in 1799, Wash and Lawrence rode out to attend to estate business at the White House, the Custis plantation where dashing Colonel Washington and the beautiful widow Custis had met and married. They had hardly arrived when a messenger, exhausted from riding hard, came with the news: George Washington was dead.

Washington Custis joined the nation in mourning the loss of the greatest hero of the age. General Washington had claimed him as his own son on Jack Custis's deathbed, and Little Washington had assumed that identity in every way. Washington had truly been a father figure to him—hero, advisor, benefactor, protector, advocate. The greatest influence in his life was gone. Now Little Washington would have to grow up.

Having appropriated his father's old identity as "the child of Mount Vernon," Washington Custis dedicated himself to preserving Washington's memory and perpetuating his beliefs. Soon after the general's death, he wrote an "Address to the Youth of America" admonishing them to heed Washington's example in their own lives. One of the general's old comrades-in-arms, Henry Lee, asked Wash's permission to publish it, exclaiming, "The sentiments which it breathes do honor to your heart. I ardently pray a similar spirit may pervade the rising generation."

For Custis and Lee at least, that prayer would be answered.

CHAPTER THREE

A WORLD
IN BALANCE

*O*ne day in early November 1808, Washington Custis's coach appeared on the long winding drive leading up the hillside to his unfinished showplace. Along the way and in the distance, as far as Wash could see, were thick stands of virgin oak, maple, and chestnut, the leaves past their peak that late in the season, but still magnificent. Their half-bare branches clung to a scattering of bright yellow, red, orange, and brown leaves; the rest formed a mosaic of color on the ground. Holly berries were turning from hard and green to plump and red; bittersweets peeked out crimson from their yellow husks; pumpkins and acorn squash ripened in the kitchen garden. Robed in its autumn best, Arlington awaited the arrival of it newest lady, one-month-old Mary Anna Randolph Custis.

The nine years since General Washington's death had transformed Wash Custis, underachieving ward of America's greatest hero, into G. W. P. Custis, country squire and self-styled guardian of the Washington leagacy.

For two years after the General's death, Wash had remained at Mount Vernon, where his grandmother, like her late husband, kept a regular routine. Seven days a week she was up before dawn to see to the affairs of the household; then after breakfast she returned to her room for an hour of Bible reading and prayer. The rest of the day she spent supervising the sewing, mending, and other housework, writing letters, and, as one visitor reported, "incessantly knitting."

Washington was buried on the estate, and his crypt became a shrine for the many people who revered his memory. Though seventy years of age, Martha continued entertaining, extending her refined but unassuming hospitality to the many visitors who stopped to pay their respects. Her heart warmed by their sincere affection for the general, she welcomed them all, whether statesman or humble stranger.

In the spring of 1802, Martha took to her sickbed with what she felt certain was her final illness. On May 22, dressed in a white gown selected for the occasion long before, she gathered her family around her bed for final farewells. Moments later Martha Dandridge Custis Washington died peacefully.

Mrs. Washington and the general had been two of the foundation stones of Washington Custis's life. Now he had lost them both, and he soon would lose another. Mount Vernon had been his home since he was six months old, but after Martha's death the estate passed to Washington's nephew Bushrod Washington. Wash tried to buy it from him, but Bushrod had no interest in selling.

Wash inherited family property passed down from his grandmother's first marriage, including the old iron chest in which her £30,000 inheritance had once been stored, furniture, silver, paintings, books, and one-fourth of the wine in the cellar at Mount Vernon. Nevertheless, he longed for historical personal property that had belonged to Washington.

In July 1802 and January 1803, Wash spent recklessly at estate auctions to buy artifacts associated with the general and Mount Vernon. He bought Washington's coach, his campaign tent, the Hessian and British flags presented to him by Congress for his victory at Yorktown, a huge portico lantern from Mount Vernon, the bed the general had died in, and the imported harpsichord he had given Nelly Custis as a wedding present. He also acquired commemorative china given to Washington by the Society of the Cincinnati, a hereditary society of Revolutionary War officers. The whole lot cost $4,545, a debt that would take Wash years to pay off.

Wash may not have had thousands of dollars in ready cash, but he was a very wealthy young man. He had reached legal age only three weeks before Mrs. Washington's death, and in addition to his grandmother's personal effects, he stood to inherit large tracts of land. The 4,000-acre White House plantation was now his, as was other scattered Custis property, including 6,000 acres on the Eastern Shore near the old Arlington estate and Romancock (later called Romancoke), a plantation of over 3,500 acres on the Pamunkey River near the White House. General Washington left him a 1,200-acre tract on Four Mile Run and a lot in the Federal City (by now renamed Washington City).

Wash also inherited some of the old Alexander property that Jack Custis had bought in such a hurry in order to acquire land near Mount Vernon before inflation rendered his cash worthless. His mother and her second husband, Dr. David Stuart, had been living on the Robert Alexander tract, which Jack had bought so recklessly on credit. Because of the inflationary conditions at the time the contract was written, the actual amount of debt was in question; Dr. Stuart persuaded Alexander to take the land back in exchange for a payment representing rent for the time the Custis family had lived there. The Stuarts then moved to Hope Park, an estate west of Alexandria.

That left Wash with the old Gerard Alexander tract of 1,100 acres, including the majestic wooded hillside across the river from Washington City, where the first part of the Capitol and the recently completed President's House commanded the scene with classical elegance, though the roads in front of them were mud pits as often as not. Jack had bought this section outright and it passed to Washington Custis after his mother relinquished her dower rights to the property in exchange for $1,750 a year in silver for life.

Of all the estates, the White House was the best developed and most profitable, producing commercial quantities of tobacco, wheat, corn, livestock, and fish. But Wash didn't intend to live there. He hired James Anderson, formerly the farm manager at Mount Vernon, to run the White House and Romancoke. He himself moved to the Alexander tract.

There was an old four-room brick house on the tract dating from about 1725, solid but run-down from years of neglect. Sometime in the summer of 1802, Wash settled into the house and filled most of the rooms literally to the rafters with his precious Washington memorabilia. He proudly christened the estate Mount Washington and immediately began planning to turn it into a showplace worthy of the name, with a magnificent building on the hillside above the Potomac.

In addition to being his residence, the place would be the first living mausoleum in America, containing the tombs of George and Martha Washington. Congress planned to honor Washington by laying him to rest in a crypt beneath the Capitol dome. Mrs. Washington had given her permission on the condition that she be buried there beside him. The government had agreed, but for now the two still lay entombed at Mount Vernon. Wash hoped to convince the Congress and Washington's heirs to transfer the remains to Mount Washington, where the public could pay them proper homage in suitably grand surroundings.

To design the new centerpiece of his estate, Wash hired a celebrated young Englishman named George Hadfield. A distinguished student at the Royal Academy of Arts in London, Hadfield had studied in Italy for three years before coming to America to take over construction of the Capitol. Though his artistic credentials were impeccable, Hadfield had failed to manage the opportunistic and sometimes deceitful contractors on the project, and he was eventually dismissed. Wash, however, was impressed by Hadfield's classical designs and characteristically unconcerned with his lack of budgetary skill.

Both the prominent site of the house and its noble intended purpose called for a stately and monumental plan. Hadfield delivered, producing drawings for a central portico two stories high and sixty feet across supported by massive Doric columns, flanked by symmetrical one-story wings extending forty feet on each side. The style was plain, almost severe, in the style of the Temple of Theseus at Athens; but its presence high on the wooded hillside would dominate the view from the Capitol, three miles distant across the Potomac—or from anywhere else in Washington City for that matter.

Ornamentation in the design was limited both inside and out. Not only was this austerity in keeping with the simple tastes of Washington, but it also helped hold down costs. Besides, none of it would contribute to the visual impression Wash considered so important. He willingly sacrificed details in the name of a grand design. The steps up to the looming portico would be made of wood, since they were invisible to all but visitors. Instead of being made of stone—nothing suitable was available locally and shipping it in was expensive—the house would be of brick covered in stucco, which could then be painted to look like marble.

Even with these economies, Wash could not afford to build Mount Washington at that time. This presented a dilemma. Rain leaks and rats were destroying the precious Mt. Vernon artifacts stored in the old Alexander house. So Wash decided to proceed with the wings of the house and build the central section later. That way he could safeguard his treasures and have a new place to live without spending too far beyond his means. He and Hadfield settled on building the north wing (facing the house, the right-hand wing) first, followed immediately by the south wing, leaving a sixty-foot gap where the main part of the house would eventually go.

Framing timbers and flooring were cut and milled on the property, most likely by slaves, who also might have made the bricks. By the spring of 1804, the two wings were finished. The north section was a single large room, designed as a banqueting hall. In the basement were the kitchen and laundry. The south section had two rooms, a large parlor and a small office and study. The wine cellar was under the parlor. Admiring visitors thought that the wings, fragments though they were, reflected their owner's "superior taste and elegance."

By the time these first portions of Mount Washington were finished, Wash was engaged. His bride-to-be was sixteen-year-old Mary Lee Fitzhugh, daughter of William and Anne Randolph Fitzhugh. Through the Randolphs on her mother's side, "Molly," as Mary was called, was related to some distinguished figures, including President Thomas Jefferson, Supreme Court Chief Justice John Marshall, war hero Light-Horse Harry Lee, and members of the British nobility. The Fitzhugh and Washington families had been well acquainted, and Wash had known Mary as a friend long before she kindled his romantic interest.

The Fitzhughs had lived at Chatham, famous for its private racetrack, thoroughbred stables, and gracious hospitality. Situated on the main road between Williamsburg and Alexandria, Chatham was a convenient place for travelers to stop—too convenient. To ease the time and money he spent entertaining, William Fitzhugh was building another house more off the beaten path at Ravensworth, a 22,000-acre plantation in Fairfax County that had been in the family for four generations. Though less elaborate in some respects than Chatham, the house at Ravensworth was large and elegant, with white columns supporting a double porch that ran almost entirely across the front.

The Fitzhughs also owned a townhouse in Alexandria, and it was there that Wash courted Molly Fitzhugh. The girl was intelligent and attractive, with kind eyes and a firm chin. Her solid, practical approach to life was a suitable foil for Wash's flighty exuberance. On July 7, 1804, Washington Custis and Molly Fitzhugh were married at the bride's home in Alexandria.

After the wedding, the couple moved into Mount Washington among the vast collection of Washington relics. Wash had the north banquet hall divided into three rooms. The large fireplace on the long back wall of the original room looked comically out of proportion in its new smaller surroundings, but the result was much more livable space. One of the new rooms became the bedroom; another, the family sitting room. Across the empty central gap, the large room in the west wing became the parlor where the new Mrs. Custis entertained; the small room remained Mr. Custis's office and study. Stacked up everywhere were the Mount Vernon mementos.

In keeping with the reserved classical style of the exterior, the rooms were plainly decorated. One modest flourish Wash allowed himself was "Pompeian red" wallpaper in the west parlor. Otherwise the walls were painted light gray, light green, or another unassuming color, and carving and plasterwork were kept to a modest minimum.

For many who visited the house then and later, the most striking decoration was the view. Looking east from the front of the house, an unforgettable vista unfolded at their feet. Down the hill, over a fine stand of trees and across the river, they could see Washington City bustling below them. Officially designated the capital of the United States in 1800, it was gradually taking shape according to the grand designs of French architect and planner Pierre l'Enfant. The centerpiece of the city was the Capitol, which, Wash could point out, was designed (at least in part) by the same architect who designed his house. At the time, both buildings also consisted only of wings, with big gaps in the middle where the monumental main sections would one day be—whenever the respective builders could afford to build them.

Within a few months of Molly's arrival, Wash decided to change the name of the estate. A great many places had been christened in honor of the first president since his death, including a Mount Washington estate not far away where Wash's sister Eliza lived. Casting about for a suitable alternative, he remembered the old Custis plantation on the Eastern Shore of Virginia—Arlington. The name was elegant and refined, embraced family traditions, and was more of a novelty near a city that was named after Washington and filled with places and things also named after him. In a letter written December 11, 1804, Wash referred to his home for the first time as Arlington.

Between the spring of 1805 and the autumn of 1809, Wash and Molly had four children, but only one of them would survive. The first was born on May 15, 1805, and died the same day. The second, born a year to the day later, was named Martha Elizabeth Ann Custis; she died March 10, 1807. The fourth child and only son, Edward Hill Custis, was born October 14, 1809, and died five days after his first birthday. Only the third child lived beyond infancy.

Mary's first two children were born in the Alexandria townhouse where she and Wash had been married. Their surviving sister would be delivered in the more serene environment of a stately country home. In the fall of 1808, Molly Custis traveled to Annefield, the home of Fitzhugh relatives in Clarke County, and there, at that ivy-covered, white-columned mansion in the company of loving relations and attentive servants, Mary Anna Randolph Custis entered the world on October 1. A month later, riding up the drive in a blaze of autumn color, Wash and Molly took Mary home to Arlington, where she was entrusted to the care of Old Nurse, the faithful, beloved slave who had also cared for Little Washington Custis at Mount Vernon.

Mary's nursery was the northernmost of the three rooms in the north wing. One window looked north in the direction of the forest; the other looked out front to the east, down onto Washington City. There was a fireplace on the common wall between her room and the family sitting room; the huge brick cooking fireplace in the low-ceilinged kitchen directly beneath helped keep the nursery floor warm during long winter evenings. Molly furnished the nursery with a small bed, a dresser, toys, and doll furniture.

True to class and custom, Mary and her mother went on frequent visits to Ravensworth or other family plantations, and friends and relatives often came to Arlington. Roads were primitive, and to make the most of the time and trouble it took to get there, visits sometimes lasted several weeks.

Routine visits were exciting enough, with friends and cousins constantly coming and going in a cacophony of horses, carriages, trunks, children, and servants. But Mary's home was also a place where there always seemed to be some great occasion worth celebrating when visitors could enjoy Wash's lavish hospitality. Christmas, Independence Day, and Washington's Birthday were especially lively, with even more people, more food, and invariably a satisfying oration from the host on a topic suitable to the occasion. Wash— short, balding, and already somewhat portly—put his all into these presentations, passionately delivering his flowery phrases with high emotion and sweeping gestures.

One especially grand tradition during Mary's early childhood was the sheep-shearing contest Wash held on his birthday every year. The first, on his twenty-fourth birthday in 1805, had set the standard, and it seemed that each new one was bigger and more elaborate than the last. Arlington was always more of a showplace than a working plantation, and most of Wash's income came from other property. But he was convinced that raising sheep could be profitable. Sheep dotting the landscape also enhanced the idyllic atmosphere of his hill above the Potomac.

With customary enthusiasm, Wash placed notices in local newspapers offering $40 for the "finest ram lamb" and inviting exhibitors and spectators alike to Arlington Spring for a day of livestock showing, judging, eating, and merrymaking. The spring was near the old Alexander house, close to the Potomac shore where one of the two Indian settlements on the property had been.

The fifth shearing, the first after little Mary's birth, was held April 30, 1809, and more than three hundred guests attended. Wash awarded prizes in several categories, including one for the best woolen cloth, and made an impassioned speech in favor of economic independence from England. The celebration had evolved into something of a political rally as well as an agricultural fair, and Wash took advantage of the large crowd to promote his agenda of self-reliance and a strong central government.

As he did every year, Wash set up tables on the grounds and treated all the guests to a lavish dinner with wine—though he claimed that no one got drunk because they "drank only American wines…no wise inimical to the brain." He also pitched Washington's war tent, festooned it with decorations, and furnished it inside with historical artifacts, including a Charles Willson Peale portrait of Washington from Mount Vernon.

One guest wrote that although the sheep and wool on display were "fine specimens," they were no match for Wash's hospitality:

They cannot do justice to the pleasure and the rational joy of the ample refreshments provided by the patriotic founder of the institution. Above one hundred dined with the hospitable gentleman at an elegant table, and the plentiful provision gave rise to toasts and feelings I will not now attempt to describe. In short, we all unite in our admiration of the amiable and yet truly dignified deportment of Mr. Custis, which I never saw excelled on any similar occasion.

Along with routine visits, Wash's grand festivities meant that Mary, an only child except for the brief year her younger brother was alive, was seldom alone. It was also typical for young children to play with the children of slaves, and Mary had friends among the fifty-seven slaves her father had inherited with the Arlington property.

Like both General Washington and Thomas Jefferson, Washington Custis found the idea of slavery distasteful. One of his college professors had been a staunch abolitionist, and Wash had absorbed his lectures on the subject with keen interest.

Wash and Molly both considered slavery "a curse upon their section by the folly of their ancestors," but they accepted it as an economic necessity and as part of the traditional Southern way of life. Even though slave labor was essential for running the Custis plantations, Wash considered it wasteful. It would be more efficient, he suspected, to hire freedmen for the work and not have to pay for slave housing, food, medicine, and clothing.

Wash could admit that owning another human being was wrong and that slavery was an inefficient system of labor, but he could not envision what slaves would do with themselves if they had their freedom. They had no skills, no education, no property. Would they run wild in the streets and seek revenge on their former owners? Riot and overthrow the government? Where could they go? How would they support themselves? What would be the consequences for the plantation economy? These were questions Wash and his peers asked themselves again and again.

One thing Wash was sure of was that their slaves, or "our people," as they were often called, should be able to read. In Virginia and several other slaveholding states, it was illegal to teach slaves to read. Flaunting this prohibition, Molly, with her husband's approval, taught the slaves herself.

Even before she was old enough to attend school herself, little Mary watched attentively as her mother held class for a group of black children—and perhaps some older slaves, as well—teaching them the alphabet and simple sentences, helping them learn to write, and reading to them from the big leather-bound Custis family Bible or one of Wash's other books.

Molly also taught them about Christianity. Every Sunday morning, promptly at ten o'clock, the coach called at the Arlington portico to take the Custis family to church in Alexandria. Sunday afternoons, Mary and her father took a walk while her mother conducted a Sunday school class for the slaves. Molly considered the slaves worthy of God's love and believed it was the duty of Christian masters to bring the message of the Bible to them. Though she could not see how or when it would happen, Molly—and later Mary—felt sure that one day the slaves would be free. When that day came, they wanted to have done their duty by having prepared them for independence.

Mary's mother was a quiet figure with regular habits, pious and unassuming. Molly believed in an inscrutable but just and kindly God. He had chosen to bless her with a magnificent estate and a gracious daughter; at the same time He had called her three other children to Himself while they were still in the cradle. She was willing to submit to God's will even when it was beyond her understanding or when His judgment seemed harsh.

Molly's own property was considerable. When her father died in 1809, she had become a wealthy woman in her own right, inheriting £2,000 (when £60 a year was a living wage), sixteen slaves, and 800 acres of land. Still she was prudent in her expenses and adept at managing her affairs with little or no cash in the till.

Molly ran her household with order and efficiency, appreciating quality and refined taste but never drawn to ostentation. As a hostess, she was generous and hospitable, though not extravagant. She kept her house much as her husband's grandmother had kept Mount Vernon: neat and elegant with no overt displays of wealth, notwithstanding the fact that the Mount Vernon silver and furniture were used regularly when guests were present. After all, they expected it, and Mrs. Custis considered it an honor to oblige.

Seven days a week, Mary's morning began with family devotions, which her mother conducted from her Bible and prayer book after breakfast. All visitors were invited to take part. Then Mary worked at her lessons or followed her mother around the house and garden, checking on vegetables, flowers, and herbs, instructing the house servants in their various duties, visiting with whatever company might be present, and seeing to all the details of a large household.

There was no talk of sending Mary away to school. Boys went off to school, but girls were customarily educated by their parents or by tutors who lived in the household for a period of months or years. When she was old enough, Mary's bedroom also became her classroom, and her mother added a blackboard and reading charts to its furnishings.

Still, Mary's education ranged far beyond the walls of her nursery. Downstairs in the kitchen she watched George Clark, the head cook and another old, trusted slave from Mount Vernon, presiding at the yawing brick fireplace over roasting Virginia ham, cornbread, rice pudding, gingerbread, and other delicacies. At her mother's side she began to learn sewing, knitting, darning, and embroidery. Mary loved gardening, and she mimicked the movements of servants working in the flowerbeds, tending the hedges, borders, ground cover, and a rainbow palette of flowers—roses, tulips, daffodils, lilies, and hyacinths.

Mary's earliest memories were of the stories her father told with such drama and inspiration about George Washington and the great battles of the Revolution, which he recounted with gusto in his "full, rich, and melodious" voice for the visitors who came to pay homage to the general. Strangers at the door asking to see the Mount Vernon artifacts were an everyday event. Invariably, Wash would stop whatever he was doing to show visitors around and let them see and touch a piece of history. People who were particularly persuasive, or who Wash felt sincerely shared his all-encompassing love and respect for the first president, might leave clutching a Washington signature as a souvenir of their tour.

Mary lived surrounded by these mementos of another time. The items were as familiar to her as the clothes in her dresser or the dolls on her floor—Washington's carriage, his sword, his uniform, his china from the Society of the Cincinnati, his campaign tent, his papers, his porch lantern, his candlesticks—much of it stacked up in the parlor of the west wing.

Mary's father was delighted to bask in General Washington's reflected light. He lived happily as the keeper of the flame, content to continue his role in perpetuating the general's memory and promoting his Federalist views against the rising tide of Jeffersonian democracy.

Martha Washington had also believed that Jefferson's policies threatened American strength and stability. Jefferson had been governor of Virginia and Washington's secretary of state, but his idea of democracy—leading toward a weak federal government and more powerful states—was horrifying to old-line Federalists, who thought that America had to keep the states clearly subordinate to federal control to remain strong and free. Wash's grandmother had said that, next to the loss of her husband, Jefferson's condolence call following the general's death was "the most painful occurrence" of her life.

Like his grandmother, Wash opposed the type of democracy Jefferson and his followers described, fearing that it would put power into uneducated, inept, and corruptible hands. As the only surviving male heir in the family line, he expected to carry on the Federalist politics of his famous adoptive grandfather.

Such political issues were far from the world of Mary Custis, a dark-eyed brunette with fair skin who was invariably described as a lively, happy little girl. A more idyllic world would have been hard to imagine. She spent her early years at Arlington in luxury and serenity, surrounded by servants, adored by her parents, watched over by Old Nurse, traveling to and fro visiting friends and relations, playing in the gardens, hearing her father's stories of Washington and Mount Vernon again and again, and taking comfort in the rhythm of the seasons: summer and winter, planting and harvest, sunshine and snow, repeating themselves with a reassuring finality that proclaimed a world in balance perfectly and forever.

CHAPTER FOUR

CHARMS AND GRACES

*I*n the spring of 1812, when Mary, by now nicknamed "Molly" like her mother, was three, Washington Custis hosted what would be the last of the Arlington sheep-shearing festivals. Though the preparations were the most elaborate ever, attendance was off by two-thirds. One reason was that livestock farmers and mill operators preferred merino wool, and tens of thousands of merino sheep were being imported from Spain every year. Another reason was that, for the second time in a generation, the threat of war with Great Britain was in the air.

Wash doggedly promoted his Arlington Improved breed of sheep because he, like other planters, believed America should be more self-sufficient in textiles in order to loose the last ties between themselves and "our veteran enemies," the English. It was also a matter of necessity. In response to the British habit of waylaying American ships on the high seas, America had established an embargo on British imports. This was disastrous for American shipowners, but it caused the value of sheep and woolen goods to skyrocket as merchants looked to domestic suppliers. In the scramble, the price of breeding stock was bid up dramatically, and industrialists built and opened woolen mills as fast as they could.

Mr. Custis continued to publicize his Arlington Improved breed and endowed the Arlington Institution to develop a domestic woolen industry.

He designed a new uniform for American soldiers—made from American wool, of course—that was a dramatic departure from showy European military dress and far ahead of its time: dark gray coat and trousers, high deerskin moccasins, calfskin cap, and a hunting knife hanging from a black leather belt. He sent President Jefferson a coat of "Arlington cloth" to show how soft, fine, and durable it was.

Custis also set out to raise money to build a textile complex, Washington Mills, at Arlington. Like most planters, he had plentiful real estate holdings but never much cash in the bank. He thought that the federal government should provide low interest loans to build up the textile industry. The Arlington Improved sheep, the Institute, the national uniform, the mill—all were projects of Wash's fertile mind and received the benefit of his unflagging enthusiasm and oratorical skill. Yet they all came to nothing.

Tensions between British and American shipping continued to escalate. The British ratcheted up the practice of impressment—boarding American ships at sea, claiming that certain crew members were British subjects, and forcing them to join the British navy on the spot. There were reports as well that the British were supplying Canadian Indians with rifles and helping them attack settlements on the frontier.

Less than two months after Wash's sheep-shearing festival of 1812, the United States declared war on Great Britain. Many Federalists opposed the move. The country was woefully ill prepared to battle the British fleet, which had six hundred ships compared to America's sixteen. Long term, there was also the threat of Napoleon, then at war with England. If, in carrying on a two-front war, Great Britain were defeated, there would be nothing to stop Napoleon from invading the United States.

Custis questioned the wisdom of war against such a powerful foe and, even more intensely, the motives of those who promoted it. Though in the political minority, his fervor never waned, and his dedication to what he considered Washington's ideals of democracy were as strong as ever.

Financial stability was always a problem for Wash. War taxes made it worse, and his missteps in developing his sheep herds only added to his trouble. Desperate for liquid resources, he sold off lots on his Four Mile Run property, cut timber, hired out some of his slaves, and even sold some of them. Wash was a relatively generous and benevolent owner who recoiled at the thought of selling a slave, which usually meant separating him from his family and not knowing how his new master would treat him. Nevertheless, like his peers, he sold them when economics required it.

Mary knew little if anything about all this. Her world remained one of doting parents, attentive servants, welcome visitors, and trips by carriage to surrounding plantations. Her days followed a safe and predictable routine.

Breakfast, prayer, and lessons came in orderly succession every morning. As at Mount Vernon and most other plantations of the day, dinner was a big meal served in the middle of the afternoon, with ham, chicken, turkey, mutton, or wild game; fresh vegetables; breads; and for dessert, the puddings, cakes, and tarts that were a hallmark of the Southern love for sweets.

Afterward, Mary might spend the rest of the time before candle-lighting with her mother learning to sew, or playing with her young friends. After tea in the evening, there was often some impromptu entertainment—her father reading aloud or playing his violin, or a houseguest playing the harpsichord from Mount Vernon—then evening prayers and off to bed.

In the summer of 1814, as the war with Great Britain continued, five-year-old Mary, who had lived all her young life surrounded by the trappings of American history, had a front-row seat for one of America's most humiliating events. On August 24, partly in retaliation for Americans burning the Canadian Parliament building at York (later Toronto), British troops invaded Washington City and set fire to the Capitol, the President's House, and other public buildings.

Mr. Custis, refused a commission on the grounds that he had an arthritic hand, joined the military as a common soldier and was manning a gun on the Bladensburg Road when the British attacked. Disorganized and confused, the Americans were quickly outmaneuvered. After firing one last shot—the last to be fired by the Americans—Wash and the rest of his gun crew fell back from their positions. As the British advanced, he stopped by the President's House to make sure the Gilbert Stuart portrait of Washington had been taken away for safekeeping. Then he went home to Arlington.

Custis rode up the long gravel drive to the still-unfinished mansion in a fierce summer storm. When he arrived, he, Molly, and little Mary watched through rain-streaked windows as Washington City burned. It was a sad time, particularly for one who had watched the cornerstone being laid for the biggest building in the scene, now fueling the biggest fire. Only the heavy rain kept the city from being burned to the ground.

Viewing the destruction, the Custis family would scarcely have believed that by Christmas the war would be over and the British gone. And in any event, life at the mansion went on very much as usual.

In October, just after her seventh birthday, Mary carried out her duties as mistress of Arlington for the first time. One afternoon, Thomas Bayley, a Virginia congressman and family friend, and Federalist leader Timothy Pickering stopped at Arlington for a visit. Neither of her parents was immediately available to greet them, so Mary did the honors, escorting them to the south wing. Her mother returned shortly, and Mary reported that "Mr. Bayley and a very old man" were in the parlor.

Pickering wrote to his own daughter, "The next morning I saw the little girl and took her on my knee, and at parting (after breakfast) called her attention to the 'very old man,' and telling her I wished her to remember him, gave her some impressive kisses."

By December, after years of fighting Napoleon, the British were tired of war. Even the duke of Wellington, the great hero who defeated the French emperor at the Battle of Waterloo, advised against continuing the fight against Americans. And so on Christmas Eve, 1814, at Ghent, Belgium, an American contingency signed a peace treaty ending the hostilities and reestablishing all territorial borders at their prewar locations.

With the war over, George Washington Custis turned his energy and interest to other pursuits. In 1817, he was instrumental in founding the American Colonization Society, whose goal was to free slaves and return them to Africa. The Society purchased a large tract of land on the west coast of Africa and made plans to return thousands of slaves there, even though by that time most were American-born. As in so many of Custis's interests, the project was launched with great fanfare but was ultimately unsuccessful, though about 6,000 slaves were eventually resettled in Africa.

War had played havoc with Wash's financial affairs, and peace proved to be almost as costly. The price of basic supplies increased enormously during the war: Salt alone went up eightfold, from fifty cents to four dollars a bushel. During the conflict, Wash could not ship his wool overseas, or his far more valuable wheat. The one bright financial spot had been the domestic market for grain and wool. But when the war was over and importation of English goods resumed, the bottom fell out of the agricultural markets. Corn that had sold for nine dollars a barrel now brought three or four. Top breeding sheep once valued at $1,000 a head were now "sold to the butcher for a trifle." Mr. Custis found himself writing to merchants to explain that his credit would have to be extended because he did not have ready money even for household notions.

Although Mary had no idea that her father sometimes maintained her luxurious surroundings by the barest of margins, she sometimes helped her mother earn pin money by selling flowers from the gardens at Arlington at the Washington Market. Molly and Mary made wreaths to sell there as well, and both donated generously of their proceeds to the Colonization Society, even after Wash lost interest in it.

In the same year that her father got involved in the Colonization Society, Mary was surprised to see carpenters and bricklayers start to work in the big paved space that separated one part of her house from the other. She liked to play there, and she chased chickens across the smooth sixty-foot expanse. Despite his financially precarious position, Wash had decided to finish the great central portion of Arlington House. About this time he sent an IOU instead of payment to his long-suffering apothecary in Alexandria, "not being able to command cash at this time from the heavy expense of my building."

Like the wings completed fourteen years earlier, the middle portion was built of brick, its floors and millwork were finished with lumber from the Arlington forest, and its exterior was covered with stucco made from hydraulic cement, a material produced by burning fossil shells through a process invented by David Mead Randolph, the husband of one of Molly's cousins. The cement surface was then painted with rectangular shapes and freehand streaks to make it look like cut stone from a distance.

The most notable feature of this central block was a row of six enormous columns across the front porch supporting the portico, plus one more column flanking each side. The columns were twenty-three feet tall and nearly five feet in diameter at the base. Doric in style, they were unfluted and completely unadorned, which made them seem even more massive.

Some observers associated the look with President Jefferson's classical style. Others pointed out that Jefferson's taste invariably ran to delicate, elegantly decorated Roman lines, while these were unflinchingly Greek and plain. It would be hard to imagine Wash doing anything because he thought it would please Jefferson. It was far more likely that he would challenge Jefferson's Roman taste with a bold Greek architectural statement that would command his attention from anywhere in Washington City.

Downstairs in the new section, a long hall extended from the entrance to the back door. On the right was a space separated by three arches into a parlor in the front and a family dining room in back. On the left was the largest room in the house, still unfinished on the inside, which Custis planned to complete as an elegant ballroom. In the meantime it was piled high with Mount Vernon artifacts. Upstairs were four spacious bedrooms and dressing rooms.

When the house was completed, there was no provision for General Washington and his wife to be entombed there as originally planned. Washington had left money in his will to build a tomb for the two of them at Mount Vernon, and his nephew and heir, Bushrod, took that to mean the general had wanted to remain there.

Washington's body may have been absent, but his spirit was as strong as ever at Arlington. George Washington Custis owned by far the largest and most important collection of Washington family artifacts. Now that he also had such an eye-catching landmark in which to display them, the number of visitors who came to look at them steadily increased.

Wash displayed the Washington silver in the dining room in the new central section, which little Mary called "the middle house." His grandmother's tea table was in the parlor, and upstairs was the bed in which Washington had died. On display were flags, statues, paintings, and the beloved war tent. Wash called the collection his Washington Treasury. Also in the house were magnificent paintings from the Parke side of the family by Sir Godfrey Kneller and Anthony Van Dyck, including portraits of Colonel Daniel Parke and his tempestuous daughter Frances.

By this time Miss Mary had heard the stories of her father's life at Mount Vernon over and over. Visitors to the Washington collection always sought out "the child of Mount Vernon" to recount his years in the presidential household. Like Washington, Custis had an air of old-world manners and courtliness about him. Comfortable in any surrounding, he was able to put everyone at ease. One visitor found him caulking a boat and was surprised when he readily put the work aside to engage in conversation.

Custis never tired of telling the tales of hunting deer on the old Mount Vernon estate, of Lafayette's visit, of the cornerstone ceremony at the Capitol, of young George Washington Lafayette, of the great dignitaries and heroes that sat at *this* table lighted by *these* candelabra and toasted this great experiment in freedom called America. Though not related by blood to the first president, Mary was immersed from her earliest days in the traditions, patriotism, and pride that the memory of Washington nurtured in her family.

As Mary began the transition from girl to young lady, she revealed characteristics that confirmed her to be very much her father's daughter. Her conversation and the quickness with which she learned revealed a keen intellect. She had a gift for languages, and before her student years were over, she was reading French, Greek, and Latin. Arithmetic, which her father had so struggled with in college, held little interest for her.

In her study of history, Mary examined the consequences of what the Federalists considered Jefferson's "French style" democracy. Writing in her school notebook, she described the tragic aftermath of the attack on the Bastille by "an army of 40,000 desperadoes," adding that, within days, "Not a noble passion nor a generous sentiment was allowed to display itself in France…but of the conquerors." The defeated ruling class "was rendered subservient to fear." Lafayette himself had eventually been imprisoned. There was a lesson for America here: Democracy could only be entrusted to leaders with the honor, courage, vision, and education to safeguard it.

Some of Mary's lessons taught two subjects at once. A writing exercise on "Style Perspicuity and Precision" included helpful historical reminders such as "Galileo *invented* the telescope" and "Harvey *discovered* the circulation of the blood." Mary also studied essays on "Beauty and other Pleasures of Taste," "Sublimity in Writing," and other subjects designed to sharpen her understanding and appreciation of the arts.

One February morning in 1823, Mary wrote in her notebook:

Taste may be defined as the power of receiving pleasure from the beauties of nature and of art. None are devoid of this faculty. Nothing that belongs to human nature is more universal than the relish of beauty of one kind or another, of what is orderly, proportioned, grand, harmonious, new, and sprightly.…

Like her father, Mary had a taste for art and a natural talent as a painter. Self-taught, Mr. Custis painted large-scale allegorical scenes with General Washington as the central figure. His work was patriotic and heartfelt but suffered from a lack of basic skill in rendering proportion and perspective. Wooden-looking soldiers tended to be the same size as their wooden-looking mounts, and the palette gravitated toward somber grays, browns, and rusts. For all their primitive appearance, Wash displayed them proudly at various political and patriotic events where he was invited to speak.

As a schoolgirl, Mary loved painting. At fifteen she was expertly filling in the black-and-white drawings on the front or her history notebook with watercolors. Her ability soon far surpassed her father's, though her pictures were never exhibited publicly. She painted for her own pleasure and sometimes painted pictures as gifts for special friends. Her pastoral and seaside canvases were styled after the northern Italian or Flemish school, with shading, human figures, landscape features, composition, and perspective that were the equal of much of what hung on the walls of fine homes and museums in America and abroad.

Along with many of her father's personality characteristics, Mary had inherited his sharp nose and chin. She was never described as beautiful, and she never affected the aura of the delicate Southern belle. Nonetheless, she captivated those around her. Her charm, wit, manners, thoughtfulness, and vivacity made her a popular guest, and she was constantly surrounded by friends and admirers. By one account, her cheerful spirit and fun-loving personality "combined to make her a toast in any social gathering in which she might be. She enjoyed society and was as popular in Washington as in Virginia."

Mary enjoyed being in the company of friends, and like most young ladies, she was interested in what others were doing and in the latest fashions and gossip. One letter to a cousin offers a glimpse of Mary's busy and contented life during her teenage years.

Maria's wedding took place on the anniversary of your own April 4th. There were about 90 persons & the bride walked with much dignity through the midst of them with her attendants...whose entrance was beyond description. The evening passed away merrily & the next night we beheld C. Mancomb led to the altar. She looked beautiful in her bridal veil.... [The attendants] all wore worked bobbinet dresses over satin. They were very gay....

We went to a beautiful supper at Mrs. Rush's & every thing in elegant style & Mrs. Rush herself so charming.... Catherine Mason will go to Mexico in the winter & Maria Cooper is to live at Old Point.

I expect to go to the Eastern Shore in a few days, if nothing happens to prevent; the girls are so charming & so very anxious to have me with them that I cannot resist the opportunity....

The Miss Carters have gone down to Shirley on their way to Philadelphia. Their brother Charles Henry is said to be much smitten with Elizabeth Taloe & Mr. Shirley Carter with Miss Ella Wickham. I suppose you have heard of the duel between Mr. Shirley Carter & Mr. Wickham in which Mr. C. would not fire at the brother of his love.

The Miss Carters have not been so much admired as was expected, except by the foreigners. I am afraid they are rather *heartless*; at least I did not *love* them. On a better acquaintance though I admired their accomplishments.

We have been trying to persuade Aunt Lewis to come and stay with us...but she seems to think her first journey must be to Cincinnati. I hope indeed she will go; the change of air and scene will be so beneficial to her & then to see you & her darling grandson will be ecstasy....

Mother sends a great deal of love & many kisses to your babe...

Farewell & believe me,
Your devoted cousin & friend,
Mary Custis

One day Mary was sitting with her mother in the Supreme Court, listening to a case involving a confiscated slave ship. A visitor to Washington City, momentarily distracted by her "placid and winning face," judged her to be about sixteen. He later wrote:

She was richly but plainly attired, as was her mother, and there was a modest and reserved dignity about both of them that significantly bespoke their rank and bringing up. Miss Custis was described to me by those who knew her best as a young lady of sound and vigorous intellect, in which judgment and discrimination decidedly predominated.

Like Mr. Custis, Mary was interested in whatever subject was at hand and passionate to know as much about it as possible. She was an attentive student of current events and read several newspapers a day. She also shared her father's love of history, and only days after her sixteenth birthday, she once again enjoyed a front-row seat at a signal moment in history—this one as triumphant as the British invasion of the capital had been tragic. At the invitation of President James Monroe, the sixty-seven-year-old Marquis de Lafayette had returned to America for a valedictory tour. With her father's often-told story of Lafayette at Mount Vernon ringing in her ears, Mary was delighted at the prospect of meeting the legendary old gentleman.

On October 12, 1824, in a ceremony that also marked the opening of the Capitol rotunda, the mayor of Washington welcomed Lafayette. Mr. Custis had painted one of his large paintings for the occasion, and as a member of the official welcoming party, he made a speech honoring the general. On his way out, Lafayette passed through the old Washington tent, pitched in the rotunda as a "Pretorium of Valor" and filled, according to the *National Intelligencer,* with "ladies, Revolutionary officers, and other gentlemen." Mary Custis and her mother were surely among that distinguished group.

Three days later, Lafayette spent the day at Arlington. Though his hectic schedule did not permit him to accept his host's invitation to stay overnight, his visit gave Mary the chance to speak with him and to hear from his own lips the stories of the Revolutionary War. Lafayette, in turn, smiled in approval at this energetic young woman who not only read and spoke French, but who also was knowledgeable of current affairs and thoroughly steeped in the history of his own remarkable life.

The next day, Mary went with her family to Washington City to watch her father in the parade honoring the French hero. He rode with Lafayette's son—the two George Washingtons together again—in the coach immediately following the guest of honor. Mary and her mother watched proudly from a reviewing stand.

On October 17, a host of historical threads dear to Mary's father came together for the first and last time. As master of Arlington and self-assigned keeper of the Federalist flame, George Washington Custis welcomed Lafayette to Mount Vernon, where, at Washington's tomb, he presented the Frenchman with a ring containing a lock of Washington's hair. In presenting the gift, he said:

> Last of the generals of the Army of Independence! At this awful and impressive moment, when, forgetting the splendor of a triumph greater than Roman consul ever had, you bend with reverence over the remains of Washington, the child of Mount Vernon presents you with this token, containing the hair of him whom, while living, you loved, and to whose honored grave you now pay the manly and affecting tribute of a patriot's and a soldier's tear.

Overcome with emotion, the stately old general was silent for a moment. Then, pressing the ring to his breast, he said, "The feelings which at this awful moment oppress my heart do not leave the power of utterance. I can only thank you, my dear Custis, for your precious gift and pay a silent homage to the tomb of the greatest and best of men, my paternal friend."

Lafayette returned to Arlington at least twice that winter on his way to or from engagements in the vicinity. One of his trips was to Alexandria for a courtesy call on Ann Carter Lee, a Custis family cousin and the widow of Henry Lee, in honor of her husband's exemplary service during the war. Sometime during the season, Custis presented Lafayette with Washington's umbrella and a cup and saucer from the Washington state china. Standing on the portico, looking out over the parkland to the Capitol and the other buildings of Washington City, the general proclaimed the view the finest in the world. "Cherish these forest trees around your mansion," he advised Mary's mother. "Recollect, my dear, how much easier it is to cut a tree down than to make one grow."

Mary may have overheard her father's conversations with Lafayette concerning slavery. If not, she surely read "Conversations with Lafayette," which her father published beginning in early 1825.

Lafayette thought that slavery was a barbarous institution and that it was on the decline everywhere in the world except the United States, where it was becoming ever more entrenched. In his article, Mr. Custis explained his own plan for "gradual emancipation" of his slaves. He proposed to free them all in sixteen years if they would work one day a week until then to buy themselves and then move to the Colonization Society settlement in Africa. Noteworthy in concept, the plan was ultimately unworkable. Before sixteen years were up, there would be many new slaves born who would not have had the time to earn their freedom. Also, as dear as the idea of freedom was, few slaves were willing to emigrate to get it.

Some months after Lafayette's visit, at the annual meeting of the Colonization Society in January 1826, Custis characterized slavery as "the mightiest serpent that ever infested the world." The American West, he declared, had achieved more with free men in one generation than the South had in two hundred years with slaves. Slavery was a burden and curse visited on Southern landowners by their ancestors. Yet, again, he feared for the fabric of American society if slaves were freed without education, skills, or homes. It was a problem for which he had no ready answer.

Obviously troubled by what Southerners themselves called the "peculiar institution" of slavery, Custis felt helpless to abandon it. The irony was that indulgent treatment of his slaves resulting from this unsteady resolve probably complicated the situation even more; had he worked his slaves more efficiently, he would have been in the financial position to free them sooner.

After her own visit with Lafayette, Mary Custis scarcely had the chance to return to her normal routine before another dramatic episode began unfolding at Arlington—this time with her at the center.

The spring of her sixteenth year found Mary fond as always of weddings, travel, and the latest news about the amorous attachments of her friends. She was the girl the crowd gathered around at parties: a wit, a painter, and yet at the same time a thoughtful supporter of the Colonization Society. Mary Custis was still hardly more than a child, but already, to friends and strangers alike, she fairly radiated the charms and graces of a woman worthy of her patrician and patriotic lineage, charms and graces that were becoming evident to every eligible bachelor in the District of Columbia and others besides.

Early in 1825, during one of the social gatherings that were so much a part of Custis family life, Mary was introduced to Sam Houston, a handsome, dashing army veteran beginning his second term as a member of the House of Representatives from Tennessee. He had been elected state attorney general at twenty-six and was a close friend and political protégé of Tennessee's governor, Andrew Jackson, hero of the Battle of New Orleans. Mr. Custis admired Jackson—hailing him as "the second Washington," he later gave him Washington's telescope—and was pleased with what he knew of Houston's policy views by virtue of his association with "Old Hickory."

As Houston made clear in letters to his friends, he was looking for a wife. He was thirty-two, successful, well connected, and ambitious. He was ready for a helpmate and saw plenty of prospects among the young ladies from prominent families in and around the capital. Before long his gaze fell on Miss Mary Custis: intelligent, quick in conversation, well bred, rich, and, that spring, blossoming into a young woman.

Congressman Houston crossed the Potomac to pay his respects to Miss Custis a number of times. He dined with the family, talking politics with Mr. Custis and paying special attention to Mary. He wrote her poetry and courted her resolutely. Nevertheless, he was twice her age and an outsider in a world where land, tradition, and family connections were of paramount importance. More importantly, Mary's heart was unmoved.

According to one traditional account, when Mary had attended the parade honoring the Marquis de Lafayette, her eyes had not been entirely on the general, her father, or the festivities at hand. Instead, they had strayed to a lifelong friend serving as one of the parade marshals—Robert Edward Lee.

CHAPTER FIVE

LIEUTENANT LEE

ne late autumn day, two figures moved across the sweeping lawn separating Arlington House from the riverbank. Slaves often worked there, pruning, planting, and turning new soil, refining the view of the capital from the portico. But this would have been an unexpected sight to anyone happening by: a boy and girl in their middle teens, fashionably dressed, their cheeks rosy with cold and exertion against their fair complexions, planting trees together.

Mary Custis enjoyed gardening as much as her mother always had. She lovingly tended the flowerbeds of her mother's rose arbor on the south lawn, its paths as familiar to her as her own room. Now she was doing something even more meaningful. She was planting trees that would last long after she and her children, her grandchildren, and her great-grandchildren had watched the sunrise filter through them.

It was fun, besides, especially with her friend and distant cousin Robert Lee to help her. It was something they could do together.

Robert was from a branch of a distinguished Virginia family that had fallen on hard times. Two of his relations were Francis Lightfoot Lee and Richard Henry Lee—the only brothers to sign the Declaration of Independence. Robert's father, Henry Lee, had distinguished himself early in life under General George Washington during the Revolutionary War, where he earned the nickname Light-Horse Harry Lee because of his successful cavalry raids on the British.

Henry Lee was one of Washington's favorites, and the general supported him when he ran for Congress from Virginia in 1799. Lee won the seat. When Washington died weeks later, Lee was chosen to deliver the funeral oration, and though the words were actually read by Supreme Court Justice John Marshall, he wrote the famous description of the first president as one who was "first in war, first in peace, and first in the hearts of his countrymen."

By the time Robert was born, however, his father's fortunes were in a steep decline from which they would never recover. Henry Lee's first wife was his cousin Matilda Lee, whose family owned the stately Stratford Plantation in Westmoreland County between the Potomac and Rappahannock Rivers. Matilda died in 1790. Three years later, while serving as Governor of Virginia, Lee married Ann Carter, seventeen years his junior, at her father's magnificent Shirley Plantation on the James River. After his term ended, the family moved from the governor's official residence back to Stratford. Robert Edward Lee was born there on January 19, 1807.

At the time of Matilda's death, Stratford consisted of 4,000 acres. Ten years later it was reduced by half, squandered by Henry's financial mismanagement and reckless speculation. According to tax records, by 1802 only 236 acres were left. In the spring of 1809 the former war hero and statesman was sentenced to debtor's prison.

Henry was released the following year. In the hope of generating some income, he concentrated on writing his memoirs, while his wife looked for a new place to live. Henry and Matilda's son and heir, also named Henry, had reached legal age and stood to inherit what was left of Stratford. This meant that Ann Carter Lee and her children—Carter, Anne, Smith, Robert, and Mildred—had to leave. The family relocated to a modest townhouse in Alexandria, where they lived for a year before moving in with their cousin and benefactor, Mary's uncle William Fitzhugh.

The great plantation families were connected in all sorts of indecipherable ways, as one writer observed, "like a tangle of fishhooks." People married their cousins because often "there was nobody else to marry." By one count the landed aristocracy consisted of about only three hundred families, and in the two hundred years or more since the days of the colonial land grants, these families had intertwined their branches to the point where Mary Custis had cousins by the dozens and was somehow related to almost everyone she knew.

Mary's Uncle William's great-grandmother, an earlier Ann Lee, was the granddaughter of Richard Lee, who had immigrated to Virginia from Shropshire, England, before 1638 and established the Lee line in America. His descendants included Mary's playmate, Robert. So Mary Custis and Robert Lee were related. There were also ties through the Carter and Randolph families, both among the oldest and wealthiest in Virginia.

Robert may have visited Arlington as early as 1810, just after his family moved to Alexandria. He was certainly well acquainted with Mr. and Mrs. Custis and their daughter when his family moved into William Fitzhugh's townhouse in 1811. By the time the heroic central section of the Arlington mansion was underway, Robert Lee was a frequent visitor there.

Robert was five when his father was nearly killed by the same rabble that murdered Lee's friend and fellow war veteran General James Lingan in a riot that took place in the opening weeks of the War of 1812.

When the *Federal Republican,* a pro-Federalist newspaper published in Baltimore, came out in opposition to President Madison's declaration of war, a mob destroyed its press and tore down the building. Within days a group of citizens led by Henry and supported by Lingan set up a new press. When a mob attacked again at the new location, Lee, Lingan, and others were escorted to jail, to remain in protective custody until the crowd cooled off. Instead of dispersing, the mob broke into the jailhouse and beat Lingan to death. Lee was beaten senseless, knifed repeatedly, and left for dead in a pile of bodies. To see if he was still alive, someone dripped hot candle wax in his eyes. Another attacker tried to cut off his nose with a penknife.

Finally doctors were allowed to come in and carry off the dead, including Lee. But somehow the former governor, dissipated and overweight at fifty-six, had survived the assault. Eleven days afterward his doctor reported, "He cannot yet converse or take any other substance except liquids, and of these very little." Still, there were some hopeful signs. "He is restored to the use of his mental powers and is able to make himself understood by uttering a word or two at a time."

By all accounts, the greatest speech of the many hundreds Washington Custis made in his lifetime was the one he had made in the aftermath of that senseless tragedy. Enraged Federalists planned an impressive public funeral for Lingan. Francis Scott Key, a prominent Georgetown attorney who would soon become famous for writing "The Star Spangled Banner," was scheduled to present the funeral oration, but then declined. When George Washington Custis agreed to speak instead, an administration paper sneered at the choice of "that ridiculous creature Custis…the standing laughing-stock of the whole district."

To accommodate the huge crowd, the funeral was moved from St. John's Church in Georgetown to a grove on the edge of town. Above the hastily built speaker's stand, Custis had Washington's war tent draped on the branches of a huge oak. After praising Lingan and condemning those responsible for his murder, he spoke to the honor of the old general's sacrifice. "When the right of opinion, the liberty of speech, and the liberty of the press are prostrated at the feet of lawless power, the citadel of freedom must soon surrender." These rights, he concluded, were the only sure means for protecting America's legacy, and brave men must never shirk from defending them.

"Attend me, friends, to a Federalist's house in 1812," he cried, standing beneath those iconic sheets of worn and faded canvas, his voice hoarse with emotion, his fist pounding on the railing. "Near the cradle of my sleeping child stands the musket and bayonet; near the pillow of my…wife the sharpened sabre. And why? Because I will enjoy freedom of speech, and the liberty of the press—those sacred privileges I inhaled with my first breath, and will only lose with my last!"

Deeply moved, his audience responded with profound silence, according to news accounts, "only interrupted by their sighs and tears."

Henry Lee never fully recovered. His nose was permanently disfigured, and he suffered from the effects of the beating for the rest of his life. In 1813 he sailed to Barbados to escape his creditors, leaving Ann and their five children to fend for themselves. Wisely, Ann's father had rewritten his will to provide a trust for her that her husband could never invade. Lee boldly claimed that he would return restored to health and financially secure.

Robert was just six when Henry sailed down the Potomac on his way to the Caribbean, and he scarcely knew his father. He grew up in Alexandria and at William Fitzhugh's Ravensworth estate under the watchful eye of his mother, who, weak and plagued by respiratory problems, accepted her difficult life without complaint. After his sister Anne married, Robert and his younger sister, Mildred, cared for their mother. On days when she was unable to walk, Robert carried her up and down stairs and in and out of her coach.

Henry Lee died in 1818. For five years he had drifted from one place to another in the West Indies, his body continuing to deteriorate and his dreams of financial success unrealized. Perhaps sensing that his end was near, he sailed for home; but he was taken ill and stopped on the way at the plantation of his old friend and former commander, General Nathaniel Greene, on Cumberland Island off the coast of Georgia. Greene had died more than thirty years earlier, but his family graciously welcomed this sick and world-weary visitor in his honor. Lee died there on March 25 and was buried nearby.

After their father's death, the Lee children spent much of their time at Ravensworth, where Mary and her mother often visited them. Mrs. Custis liked the Lees and admired the dignity they maintained in the face of their strained financial circumstances. Mary liked the Lee children too, and her special favorite was Robert, the youngest of the boys and only a year older than herself. They played together at Ravensworth and saw each other often at Arlington.

Ann Carter Lee's small trust allowed for nothing like the opulent life other members of the family led at Shirley Plantation and elsewhere. Though her lineage was a proud one, Ann could see there would be only a modest inheritance to leave her children. Her oldest son, Carter, had enrolled at Harvard, but her financial straits made it impossible even to consider sending her two other sons there.

A military career was a promising avenue for a bright but landless young Virginia aristocrat, and Smith eventually joined the navy. Robert was intelligent, studious, and responsible. He excelled at mathematics, and the Corps of Engineers seemed an ideal place for him. Early in 1824 William Fitzhugh wrote Secretary of War John C. Calhoun to request an appointment for Robert at the United States Military Academy at West Point, New York. Founded by the Corps of Engineers in 1802, the Academy by this time was the most prestigious military duty station in the country.

Competition for admission to the Academy was keen, and more than twenty-five applications from Virginia were rejected that year. But Calhoun received a number of letters on Robert's account, including one signed by seven members of Congress, all lifting up his qualifications and sterling disposition. Calhoun made the appointment in the spring of 1824, but because of the crush of applications that year, he delayed Robert's admission until July 1825.

True to form, Robert spent the latter part of those sixteen intervening months preparing for the academic rigors of West Point with a schoolmaster who lived nearby. The teacher later described his earnest student as "a most exemplary pupil in every respect. He was never behind time in his studies; never failed in a single recitation; was perfectly observant of the rules and regulations of the institution; was gentlemanly, unobtrusive, and respectful in all his deportment to teacher and his fellow students."

On Independence Day, 1825, just before Robert entered West Point, Mary's father hosted a picnic at Arlington Spring. It was cast somewhat in the mold of the old sheep-shearing festivals, which had faded from the scene more than a decade before. But this time there was no pretense of formality. The whole affair was just for fun. Responding to a public notice Mr. Custis put in the newspaper, hundreds of guests arrived by land and water to feast at long tables set up on the lawn. The venerable Washington tent was a popular draw, and there was also music and dancing. Children and dogs ran everywhere, babies prattled and crawled about, and young people flirted under the watchful eyes of their mothers.

Some had taken to calling their host "the inevitable Custis" because whenever there was a patriotic celebration in the city, it was inevitable that he would be there to speak. That beautiful Independence Day, he did not disappoint. Accompanied by the sound of water lapping at the Potomac shore and the whistle of the wind in the majestic trees of Arlington Forest, Mary's father delivered a rousing declaration on the inevitability of freedom.

He spoke warmly of General Lafayette, then still on his American tour, and of the struggle for freedom going on at the time in Bolivia and Ireland. Freedom, he insisted in his rich, resonant voice, was universal and unstoppable. "The mark of liberty is beyond all human ken.... What barrier can resist its great force? What alliance of power can long impede its progress?"

The Arlington Spring picnic became an annual event. But even such a generous celebration left Custis feeling that he could do more to share the hospitality of Arlington and the memory of Washington with others. In time, he opened Arlington Spring as a public picnic ground, available to all comers without invitation. He built a dock on the river and a large dance pavilion for public use, as well as other outbuildings. Eventually he bought a little steam ferryboat, christened it the *G. W. P. Custis,* and made it available to carry merrymakers back and forth from Washington City across the Potomac.

When she was not on one of the extended visits to her relatives that she and her mother so enjoyed, Mary Custis reveled in the festivities at Arlington Spring. She was as much at home dancing under the picnic pavilion as she was conversing in the most important drawing rooms in the district.

Like her mother, Mary was circumspect and sincerely pious, but these traits did not keep her from occasionally checking her position on the social ladder and sometimes having a high opinion of herself.

A letter from one of her Stuart cousins, written the first week of 1827, inadvertently painted a telling picture of Mary's privileged circle and her interests, which straddled the worlds of girlish chatter and national politics:

> You have really, Mary, acquired a considerable deal of *vanity* since the last visit—to think that you were the most brilliant lapis at Mrs. Adams' house [possibly the White House] is no inconsiderable compliment to pay one's self—but I have long since known that unless we hold ourselves in high estimation...others will not think so much of us—therefore vanity is pardonable I hope....
>
> Soon Mr. Adams [President John Quincy Adams] must follow his father & quit the Presidential chair at the expiration of his 4 years—are you politician enough to care who is & who is not—I am obliged to fly sometimes to the affairs of *state* for *amusement*— this will amuse you I'm sure....

During the summer of 1827, Mary went for a visit to Kinloch, the estate of her distant cousin Edward Carter Turner in Fauquier County, Virginia. Turner was also related to the Lee family, and it was to Kinloch that Cadet Robert Lee came that same summer as a rising second classman (junior) at West Point. It was his first leave in two years. Because cadets were allowed only one four-week leave during their four years at the Academy, it was telling that Robert chose to spend part of his at Kinloch in the company of Mary Custis.

It would also be no surprise to learn that Mary had planned her visit to coincide with one by her cousin and onetime playfellow. His military experience had completed his transformation from an attractive boy to a handsome man. Robert was twenty, with chiseled features and dark hair, his impeccable manners further polished and enhanced by army discipline. Even casual observers remarked at the elegant figure he cut on horseback. The ladies flocked to him, including Mary.

It was the first time Mary had seen him in his cadet uniform: elegant gray coat with sparkling buttons and gold braid over crisp white duck trousers, with the whole topped by a seven-inch-high black leather hat with a pompon.

It was also the first time Mary knew she was in love with Robert and that she wanted to be his wife.

Robert graduated second in the class of 1829, without having received a single demerit in four years. His homecoming, however, was saddened by the fact that he returned to his mother's house in Georgetown just in time to be with her when she died of tuberculosis. He stayed at nearby Arlington while his mother's estate was settled and then visited again afterward while awaiting orders for his first duty assignment.

In October, Second Lieutenant Robert E. Lee, U.S. Army Corps of Engineers, was ordered to Cockspur Island, a desolate marsh at the mouth of the Savannah River where a fort was being built.

When Robert left for Georgia, taking his mother's old coachman Nat with him, Mary felt a swirl of emotions. She was sad to see him go after what seemed like so short a visit but delighted and encouraged at the way their relationship had deepened over the summer. She shared his sorrow over his mother's death, yet at the same time, she knew that Mrs. Lee's passing brought an end to Robert's years of worry over her health and finances.

Mary's parents gave Robert permission to write her. Both his request and their granting of it were encouraging, even thrilling signs that the bonds between them would not weaken with distance, but grow stronger in spite of the separation. By summer's end, Mary knew that, no matter how far Robert's duties took him from Arlington, their love would endure.

At the end of the summer there was also a subtle but important shift in Mary's relationship with her parents. Her mother had always been her natural ally, teacher, spiritual guide, example, and companion. But that summer, if not before, Robert Lee became the center of her life and thoughts. He was her soul mate and confidant, and Mrs. Custis moved into a secondary role. The time had come when the one who held first place in her heart was not one of her family, but the man she was now sure she would marry someday.

Mary's mother read her letters, including the ones from Robert. It was a sign of the special place he held in the family that Mrs. Custis agreed not to read them when she learned that it made Robert uncomfortable. Returning to Arlington from a few days at Ravensworth in mid-September, Mary found a letter waiting for her from her lieutenant. She happily wrote him that her mother "promises not to require a sight of your letters, though I told her I could not imagine anything you had to say that she might not see, yet I know it is sometimes unpleasant, so you are perfectly at liberty to say what you please, trusting in your discretion to say only what is right."

The two still made their respective rounds in society, Mary in Washington and Alexandria, and Robert at the homes of friends and fellow officers in Savannah when he could get away from his duties for a day or two. As always, Mary was a center of attention at social gatherings, and Robert quickly caught the attention of Savannah's eligible young ladies. Through the winter and spring they lived in their separate worlds, but their commitment to each other never wavered.

After nearly a year of work in Georgia, Robert returned to Arlington in the summer of 1830. Construction work on Cockspur Island ran from fall through spring but stopped for several months in the long, stifling days of summer. The heat, humidity, mosquitoes, and sand flies of the marshy coast made working impossible then, giving Lieutenant Lee a break from his responsibilities. After a visit to his brother Carter, who was practicing law in New York, Robert lost no time heading to the cool forests and sweeping lawns of Arlington to see his dear "Miss Molly."

Mary counted the days until her handsome soldier's return. From the time he arrived from New York by steamer—more filled out and manly looking than ever, the wiriness of youth gone, shoulders square, almost six feet tall, naturally graceful, always at ease—the two were together nearly every waking hour. Mary caught Robert up on the latest news of Arlington and the family. They walked in the gardens and along the river. They visited neighboring plantations. They spent their evenings in the sitting room discussing current events or listening to Mary's father play his violin

Sometimes Mr. Custis or Robert read aloud. They all enjoyed the great adventure stories of Sir Walter Scott, whose Waverly novels were among the most popular of the time. One day, Mary sat listening as Robert read, her mind wandering from the tale of knights and crusaders, her eyes transfixed by the profile of the young man she loved: his eyes shining, his concentration focused upon the page.

Mrs. Custis interrupted Mary's thoughts by suggesting that, since Robert had been reading a while, he might like some refreshment. Eager to comply, Mary got up and walked through the triple archway separating the sitting room from the family dining room to see what she might fix for him. As she stooped over the Mount Vernon sideboard to cut a piece of fruitcake, she felt Robert's arm slip around her waist. Both startled and pleased, she whirled to face him. Their eyes met.

"Molly, will you be my wife?"

Her decision had been made long ago, so the answer took only seconds to form on her lips. "Yes, Robert. Yes."

Mary's mother gave the couple her blessing right away, but her father would not be rushed into a decision. Like his daughter, he had long anticipated the question, but now that it was actually before him, he hesitated. Mary was confident that it was only a matter of his getting used to the idea and that he would come around soon enough.

Custis had known Robert's father well. He knew of his distinguished service early in life as well as the tragic later years. Though the Lee family circumstances were modest according to the standards of the Virginia aristocracy, Robert and his brothers had inherited 20,000 acres of land (plus a bill for back taxes) and proceeds from the sale of 30 slaves from their mother's estate.

Custis also knew the sad tale of Robert's half brother, Henry Lee, who had inherited Stratford Plantation. Henry was forced to sell the property to pay debts and had admitted to an adulterous relationship with his young sister-in-law, who was also his legal ward. Derisively known as "Black-Horse Harry Lee," he had escaped his creditors by moving to Europe, where he lived in exile with his morphine-addicted wife.

If anything, these blots on the family record seemed to make Robert all the more determined to live an honorable and upright life. He was absolutely honest, morally unassailable, financially responsible, and obviously dedicated to Mary. He would make a fine and worthy husband.

Still, it took Custis some time to think the matter through. It may have been the idea of his little Mary marrying a soldier and living so far from home. Or it might have been the natural hesitation any father would have about letting his only child marry anyone under any circumstances. He also questioned whether Robert would eventually be willing to resign his commission and settle at Arlington to help manage the estate, with an eye to taking it over one day.

When Robert left for Georgia in October, carrying a special memento (probably a miniature) from Mary as a keepsake, Mr. Custis had not yet given his blessing. There was little doubt, though, that the decision would come soon. Anyone who knew Robert and Mary could tell that it was only a matter of time before they would be husband and wife.

BORN AGAIN

*A*s if becoming engaged were not enough, Mary experienced another profoundly joyful and life-changing event in the summer of 1830. The faith that she had embraced as a child overflowed in an expression of newfound zeal and commitment. It was an experience she would cherish for the rest of her life.

Mary believed all that her mother had taught her about Christianity, and like Mrs. Custis, she lived it. Nevertheless, on Sunday, July 4, 1830, something miraculous happened that brought her faith to a new and profoundly deeper level. It was the evening of the traditional Independence Day celebration at Arlington Spring—perhaps within days of her betrothal to Robert. That day a new light shone on Mary and led her to a fresh expression of her holy place in God's creation. It would be weeks before she stopped to figure out exactly what had brought her religious commitment to this climax; for the moment she was content just to revel in it.

That Sunday night, Mary began a prayer journal. In it she poured out her heart in repentance and thanksgiving with a transparency and frankness unmatched in any letter she wrote. Her pen flew over the page in an effort to keep up with the flood of emotions. No one would ever read this. She was writing only to her Lord, so she wrote with abandon, the widely spaced words and atypical scratch-outs bearing silent testament to the high emotion of the moment:

> O my Father, let me thank Thee for Thy mercies to me, that Thou hast drawn me to Thee by the cords of love—What shall I render to the Lord for all His goodness? I would say my vows in His courts this day. I would dedicate my life to Him. I would live with a single eye to His service—yet—O my Saviour, Thou who hast borne our human nature knowest how weak we are, how utterly unable to do any thing of ourselves. Thou wilt pity me & support me.
>
> O my Father in Heaven, enable me daily to offer up fervent supplications to that throne of mercy from which none ever went empty away—enable me to feel that what Thou hast promised Thou wilt surely perform, for Lord in whom shall we trust, if not in Thee. Keep me from spiritual pride, selfishness, indolence. Make my heart soft to receive Thy holy word & never suffer it to turn again to the world. Oh I dread that snare, but if Thou uphold me I shall be safe.
>
> Make me humble, my Saviour. Make me to abhor and hate myself on account of sin and above all make me love Thee more & more. I trust Thee though Thou slay me.

Four days later, Mary felt composed enough about her feelings to confide in her mother. That night she wrote about their discussion and about the experience of falling ever deeper into the loving arms of God.

> This morning it rained & as I could not take my usual walk I had a most comfortable time reading my Bible & praying to my God & went on my way rejoicing—but after breakfast I communicated to my dear Mother the state of my feelings. She wept & thanked God for this great blessing—Oh, then I was so overwhelmed with a sense of my unworthiness that my heart felt as if it would burst. I prayed to my Saviour for pardon. If I did not trust in Him I must faint, for I have years of worldly thoughts & indifference to contend with, yet I wish to thank Him whenever I feel the burden of my sins & my base ingratitude.

When I examine my heart & my motives, they are so weak, so sinful. Selfishness pervades even my prayers for I pray that I may feel more comfortable & not always from love to my Creator—May He who has begun this good work in me…finish it when I am able to believe that He will do this. I am happy for if I know my own heart there is nothing I so much desire as the assurance that nothing in the world could ever wean me from His love, but my views are sometimes so dire & my faith so weak that I am assailed with doubts & fears. Oh my God, strengthen & sustain me.

Even before her own spiritual reawakening, Mary had fretted that Robert's faith was superficial and incomplete. Like her own mother, Robert's mother had been firmly grounded in the Bible and had taught it to her children. Robert had learned his catechism before he could read and had grown up attending church. But he had never been confirmed, and from the time Mary had begun to think of him as her husband, she had worried about the depth and sincerity of his Christian faith.

Although she had broached the subject repeatedly, Mary had no idea whether or not her words fell on fertile ground. The previous September, when Robert was visiting at Eastern View, a plantation in Fauquier County, she had written him:

You will pardon my thoughtlessness which has occasioned you so many blushes & believe me when I assure you that there is nothing I have so much at heart as your *true* interests & for these my petitions are daily offered to my Heavenly Father & from whose love & mercy I hope for every blessing—I cannot say all I would on this subject for I might weary you & I know how I *once* felt. I only beg you to consider it & not to banish it from your heart.

Interwoven with pieces of news, Mary's concern for spiritual matters always seemed to bubble to the surface in her letters to him:

I have gained 3 pounds & ought to be as happy as possible, could I feel as thankful as I ought for all the blessings which are daily lavished on my head, but we are so accustomed to them that we do not feel them until they are taken away & then we murmur & repine…. I wish for you very often…[and] unwillingly bid you adieu. That *God* may protect & bless you & above all things may turn your heart to Him is my unceasing prayer for you. Then I should have nothing more to wish for on earth….

Mary continued mulling over the matter of Robert's religious commitment. He had never indicated a personal relationship with Christ like the one she now treasured. From her new spiritually enlightened perspective, she saw a man with all the trappings of Christianity—prayer, humility, recognition of sin, faith, participation in church liturgy—without any assurance that he held Christ in his heart as she did. How could she reach him with the message of her Savior? She prayed faithfully for the salvation of her husband-to-be, asking God that, in His time, Robert would come to know, as she had, "the peace that passeth all understanding."

Having loved Robert so sincerely for so long, Mary now secretly questioned whether she should marry him, whether she would be compromising her own standard of faithfulness to do so, and whether she was being called to sacrifice their relationship. Her entry for July 10 revealed the turmoil in her heart:

I feel no desires now for the vain pleasures of the world. I feel as if I could give them up from love to my God. But could I give up my attachment to him who I love? I thought I [could] do even that, if my Heavenly Father had required it, but our hearts are so deceitful that I doubt my sincerity. I did *not feel* that He required that sacrifice. Oh God search my heart…if I am deceived by Satan open Thou my eyes…. Oh draw him also to Thee that we may with one heart & one mind live to the glory of our Redeemer. May he never draw my soul from Thee.

Oh my Father, guide & direct Thy poor feeble child in all her steps for without Thee her footsteps must fail. Enable her to confess Thee before men not with spiritual pride but in lowliness of mind & deep self-abasement for the sins of her past life & an humble dependence upon the death of her Saviour whereby alone she can hope for pardon.

In the privacy of her prayer journal, Mary dedicated her life to Christian service, continued her unblinking self-examination, and rejoiced at the ever-increasing sense of comfort she found in prayer and thanksgiving:

July 12:
11 o'clock
Blessed be God for His amazing mercies. Now all is calmness, hope & peace. When I am perfected in love then I shall rejoice— but I would not exchange the hope I have now in my Saviour for all that the world could give. I now solemnly dedicate myself & all that I have or may possess to His service—an unworthy offering for His immeasurable love, but it is all I have. Oh gentle Saviour who receivest the faintest cries for mercy, receive this gift polluted as it is; wash it in Thy blood & let not all the powers of Satan ever tempt me to break this vow which has been heard & witnessed by angels in Heaven & God upon His throne.

July 14:
Peace, peace that the world knows not of. I was reading the Commandments & felt that I had certainly broken them all except one & yet the pardon of Jesus is free & sweet. He is faithful who promised. He will support me when flesh & heart fail for His word is truth. Oh, I have had dark, dark seasons from want of faith. Then the Comforter has come, my compassionate Redeemer, & has raised me to joy & confidence. These mercies seem so unmerited I scarcely comprehend them as yet—I feel a new being, a new spirit within me & yet I know not how it happened. Truly the wind bloweth where it listeth & we hear the sound thereof but know not whence it cometh or whither.

A short time later, Mary looked back over the incredible events of the past month and found what she considered to be the precipitating cause of her spiritual awakening—her aunt's reaction to the death of her uncle William Fitzhugh. At first, Mary had felt no more than "transient sorrow." More than anything, she had worried that having to wear mourning dress would "prevent my entering gay society during the winter."

Mary's Aunt Maria was despondent, and Mrs. Custis admonished her daughter not to disregard "the awful Judgments" of God. In her journal entry for July 22, Mary quoted her mother's words: "If this blow does not turn your thoughts to Heaven, what will do it?"

The view of [my aunt's] utter wretchedness impressed me with the vanity of earthly things, and one night I prayed fervently that God would comfort her. I do not recollect whether I prayed for myself— I returned home still thirsting after the world & its honours.

We went to Ravensworth where I had spent my happiest hours—there all was desolation and woe—there first I prayed to my God to change my heart & make me His true & faithful servant until my life's end. I was led on by His blessed spirit from day to day more & more to desire His favour, to see my base ingratitude & unworthiness to Him who so loved us as to give His only son to die for us, to see my utter helplessness, to cast all my hopes upon my Saviour, to feel a willingness to give up all I had formerly delighted in for His sake & afterwards through His grace not to desire them, to feel my heart melted with love to God though sometimes it was hard enough.

Above all I was enabled to pray without ceasing & though sometimes my prayers were cold, dead & selfish, yet I always felt some comfort from the promise that they would be heard, if not answered immediately. I did not despair. Though ready to faint, some sweet promise would come into my thoughts & keep me up.

Her prayer-inspired introspection continued:

August 2:
When I look back 5 weeks ago when I first prayed that I might be enabled to persevere in prayer, has not that prayer been answered? Could I have persevered without the grace of God when I found but little pleasure in it & indeed when it was a burthen? Oh my soul, look to the promises of God & faint not, even though thou gropest in darkness, for thou mayest attain a view of Him who is radiant in glory & who even now is watching over you with a Father's love.

Through the new lens of faith, every occasion took on a new perspective.

October 1st 1830, my birthday
This day, oh with what different feelings do I hail it. Instead of viewing with sorrow the season of my youth passing away, I rejoice that I am so much nearer to my home—my heavenly home, my mansion of rest where I shall have no struggles & conflicts to apprehend, but an eternity too short to utter all the praise of Him who has called me from darkness to light, who has led me safely thus far & given me a good hope through grace that He will never, no never, forsake, who made all his goodness to pass before me & melted this stubbourn heart, yet dear Lord Thou knowest how vain & foolish & prone to wander from Thee. Wilt Thou purify it & refine it ever by fire. If Thou seest fit wilt thou draw it closer to Thee & suffer not the snares of this alluring world ever to draw me aside. Wilt Thou make me more diligent in the use of Thy appointed means. Wilt Thou enable me to prove my faith by my works that when Thou makest up Thy jewels Thou mayest say well done good & faithful servant. I have already erred, already sinned, but I trust it is forgiven.

On October 5, the first Sunday after her birthday, Mary was confirmed in the Episcopal Church at Christ Church in Alexandria.

I have communed today for the first time. I expected it would be a rejoicing time, but I was bowed down with a spirit of infirmity, a sense of unworthiness & ingratitude & did not enjoy it as I expected.... I knew I was a sinner. I had felt the Saviour's love & therefore went to His feast. I know He died for me. I know that I desire to live entirely to Him & to renounce the world & die to sin. I knew His table was spread for sinners, for those who desired His favour. Oh my Father, wilt Thou bless this ordinance to the refreshing & quickening of this dull soul! I know I was born again. That feeble as I am, I am called by grace to follow in my Saviour's footsteps, & I went hoping to receive the pardon of all my sins through His blood & to be renewed to a closer walk with God.

Robert most likely stayed at Arlington through Mary's birthday and confirmation. Before mid-October he left for Baltimore to visit his sister; from there he would head back to the construction site near Savannah for another building season. Between the first account of her spiritual awakening and the time of Robert's departure, Mary confided to her journal all the tension and anxiety she felt at being shown her sins and at her uncertainty over Robert's soul.

As her journal entries made clear, Mary's uppermost thoughts were of her salvation and her concern for Robert's soul. It was a topic of deep discussion between them: effusive, emotional Mary doing her best to plumb the spiritual depths of her reserved, rational army engineer. Robert had nothing to hide; he just could not then give Mary the inner peace she craved—could not assure her he had been "born again." After Robert left, Mary became more relaxed. The distance helped, no doubt, and she brought her worry under control.

Perhaps she was learning what it meant to "cast your anxieties upon Him," for even when she became gravely ill the following month—so ill that she thought she might not recover—she expressed no fear or worry. On Sunday, November 21, she wrote:

> Still upheld from day to day by the free mercy & love of my Redeemer. I think my confidence in this love & faithfulness is more firm & I have had less anxiety for the last few weeks & blessed be His name. When laid in a bed of sickness I thought I may now die, this may be my last sickness. My heart could say sincerely, Lord, if it be Thy will, take Thy child to dwell with Thee, for it is far better to depart & be with Thee than to remain here. I have many blessings & ties to make life desirable—I have often thought that the love & goodness of God has been so great & astonishing to me, that He designed me for an early tomb. For certainly it is a great mercy to His children when He makes the period of their probation short—that He may be glorified in my life & death is my earnest prayer.

By the new year, Mary had recovered, and on Sunday, January 9, 1831, she reflected back on the six months since her engagement. As she wrote upstairs in her room, Mary could gaze out the windows flanking the fireplace on the south wall and see her beloved rose garden, bare this time of year, its brick walkways swept clean, its sturdy ground cover still lush in spite of the cold. Beyond the garden, where the ground began a long, gentle slope away from the house, was the edge of a forest of huge oaks and chestnuts, their empty gray branches moving back and forth gently in the breeze. It was a view she loved even more than the one out front of the river and the city.

She reached for the sheaf of papers that made up her journal, took a seat in front of the cheerful fire, turned to the end of the last entry, and started to write. Words poured from her pen by the hundreds. Dusk faded to candle-lighting time and then to darkness, and still she wrote, scarcely able to move the pen across the page fast enough.

I feel entirely divested of anxiety for myself & a cheerful confidence in the wisdom & love of that dear Father who has been so merciful, so kind during all my ungrateful life & for the last six months has done great things for me. His holy angels have rejoiced that a sinner has been brought to repentance, that the wandering sheep has been found.... I want to be more earnest to obtain the quickening influences of His sacred ordinances. I want to be more humbled for my sins, to love with warmer affections Him who has engaged to save me from their condemnation....

I lay a wretched slave pleased with my chains and fond of my captivity, fatally deluded & undone 'til love—Almighty love—rescued me. Blessed effects of unmerited grace! I shall stand forever an illustrious instance of boundless mercy....

Never was there a more obstinate heart than mine & never such unconquerable love as Thine. How gloriously has it triumphed over my rebellious faculties! How freely it has cancelled all my guilt! Let me here begin my eternal song & ascribe salvation & honour, dominion & majesty to Him that sits on the Throne & to the Lamb forever, who has loved me & ransomed me with His blood.

Many miles and days beyond the forest outside Mary's window, Robert had resumed his duties in Savannah. There had been some talk about the possibility that he would leave the army, but it looked now as if he was happy in military service and ready to stay indefinitely. Although it was almost impossible for Mary to imagine living anywhere but Arlington, their wedding was set for sometime in the spring, and great changes were on the horizon. Drawing strength from her faith, Mary felt calm and prepared.

More than anything, Mary had an assurance of her salvation in Christ far more profound that what she had known a year ago, and it had completely transformed her view of the world. It still excited her to think of the changes her conversion had brought in every part of her life.

That did not mean that Mary felt any better about her worthiness before God. In fact, she felt worse, and she regularly rehearsed a newfound sense of remorse at her own vanity and worldliness. Those traits were not going away. Like any young lady, she still enjoyed compliments and flattery. But now she was on guard against them, aware of their threat to her spiritual purity. With Christ's help, she would triumph.

Mary had dealt, at least for the present, with her lingering doubt about Robert's faith and was comfortable with the thought of leaving her lifelong home. Whatever lay ahead, wherever she was to live, she and Robert would be together, and the Lord would be with them. Whatever the world threw at her, Mary would face the world as Mrs. Robert E. Lee with confidence and serenity.

CHAPTER SEVEN

TWO ROOMS AND
A DIRT FLOOR

ary and Robert's wedding was set for Thursday, June 30. Arlington was consumed with preparations for the event, and Mary asked Robert not to come until the day of the ceremony. She had all she could manage without the bridegroom underfoot.

As was the custom (and because there was nowhere else to stay), family and guests crowded into the mansion in the days before the wedding. Mrs. Custis had to scramble for extra candlesticks and blankets; she borrowed cots for some visitors, and others slept three to a bed. Far from inconvenient, the arrangements only added to the excitement and gaiety of the occasion.

Mrs. Custis also supervised the friends and servants who were at work on Mary's trousseau. She herself was an excellent seamstress, and several of the house slaves were as good or better. Along with friends, she and Mary set to needle and thread to produce exquisite pieces with stitches so fine that they were almost invisible: magnificently embroidered yokes and sleeves for chemises and nightgowns, petticoats with their seven yards of fabric painstakingly hand-tucked from hem to waist, and sheer linen nightcaps.

Determined to make Mary's wedding one of the great social events of the season and send his only child off in grand style, her father lived up to his reputation for gracious hospitality. No guest who arrived at Arlington that week would have had any idea that its master was in financial straits. Earlier in the month he had sent a promissory note to a merchant in Alexandria explaining, "As rich a man as I am *in property,* I cannot do more for you at the moment." In a letter to his creditors at the Bank of the United States, he described himself as a "poor farmer" who could not manage his short-term obligations. A little later he would be unable to pay a note for $65, saying "I am very short of cash at this time." All told, Mary's father began the summer $12,000 in debt.

Two Sundays before her wedding date, Mary asked God's blessing on her marriage:

> O Lord, suffer me not to be drawn aside from Thee in the new situa-
> tion I am about to enter on, but with a single eye may I now live to
> Thy service & by a blameless life & conversation endeavour to shew
> forth Thy praises. It seems my heart is too much engrossed with this
> approaching bridal. Oh Thou who of old didst honour a marriage
> feast with thy glorious presence, wilt Thou deign to be present on
> this occasion & comfort the heart of Thy servant with the sweet
> influences of Thy spirit & sense of Thy favour & forgiveness.

Her heart was calmed; four days before the ceremony she could write, "Now there is perfect peace."

When the wedding day arrived, at first it looked as if the groom might not be able to attend his own nuptials. A month earlier, Lieutenant Lee had been reassigned to Old Point Comfort, Virginia, where Fort Monroe was under construction. The change was good news for Mary and her family because it meant that the newlyweds would be closer to Arlington. But it also meant that Robert was assured of leave only at the last minute.

Robert had ordered new white trousers from New York for the occasion, and on the afternoon of the thirtieth he arrived by steamer in time to refresh himself and change into his summer uniform. His best man, his brother Smith, was already at the house, as was the rest of the wedding party. His other groomsmen were his cousin Thomas Turner of Kinloch, then in the navy; his West Point classmate John Kennedy; and three other junior officers, James Chambers, Richard Tilghman, and James Prentiss.

Mary's six bridesmaids were lifelong friends, and most were also relatives: Marietta Turner, Thomas's sister; Catherine Mason of Analostan Plantation; cousin Britannia Peter of Tudor Place, whose mother was Mr. Custis's sister Martha; Mary Goldsborough, a cousin through Mrs. Custis and her sister-in-law, Mary's Aunt Maria of Ravensworth; Julia Calvert, a cousin by way of Mary's paternal grandmother, Eleanor Calvert; and Angela Lewis of the family of Lawrence Lewis, General Washington's nephew and the husband of Mr. Custis's sister Eleanor, Mary's Aunt Nelly.

Toward the end of the day it began to rain, and by nightfall a summer shower was cascading down in sheets. The minister, the Reverend Reuel Keith, head of the Virginia Theological Seminary in Alexandria and former rector of Christ Church, arrived on horseback soaked to the skin. He was hustled upstairs to change, but there was little that he could change into. The groom was in uniform, so the groomsmen probably were too, and the visitors would have brought few extra clothes with them.

That left the father of the bride as the only source of dry civilian dress clothes. He was short and portly, while Reverend Keith was tall and thin. The planter's clothes hung around the preacher's middle, and Keith's long, bony arms and legs extended out comically from the short sleeves and trousers. Fortunately his vestments had been securely packed and were still dry, and for the most part they covered up his borrowed finery. It was only after the ceremony that the secret of his improvised costume got out.

Even on an ordinary day, Arlington was stately and elegant. On Mary's wedding night it was also beautifully decorated and ablaze with light. Last minute arrivals joined those already crowded into the parlor to the right of the great entrance hall. The three arches separating this room from the family dining room were hung with garlands from the estate and illuminated by everything from borrowed candlesticks to the Mount Vernon porch light in the hall and the Washington candelabra on the table. From the center arch, Mary would be able to see the sideboard where she had been standing cutting cake when Robert proposed to her. It seemed impossible that a whole year had passed since then.

Mary walked down the stairs and into the hall with her father. The butler signaled Aunt Nelly at the piano, and when she began to play, Robert and Smith came in from the door to the north wing and took their places beneath the center arch. The bridesmaids and groomsmen formed a double row leading into the room, and Mary walked in between them on her father's arm to her place beside Robert. He looked more handsome than ever. He had grown luxuriant sidewhiskers that came nearly to his jaw, lending an aura of maturity and experience to the fine face that many a young woman had hoped to capture for herself one day.

Mary Custis was at her most appealing: elegant, aristocratic, and tasteful without ostentation. Perhaps she was not a beauty in the conventional sense, but on her wedding day she was the beautiful bride every girl in the room dreamed of being: radiant, poised, surrounded by loving family and friends, filled to bursting with joy and anticipation.

Her hand trembled in Robert's as he held it during the ceremony. Reverend Keith read the Episcopal service, Lee recalled later, "as if he had been reading my death warrant." Then in a brief moment it was over. Mary Anna Randolph Custis was Mrs. Robert Edward Lee.

"My cousin, always a modest and affectionate girl, was never lovelier," Marietta Turner later wrote of that night. "Though mid-summer rain denied the company the enjoyment of the gardens, which commanded an unparalleled view of the Potomac and the city of Washington, the evening was one long to be remembered," thanks in part to "the elegance and simplicity of the bride's parents presiding over the feast and the happiness of the grinning servants."

The merrymaking began at once, and as was the custom then, the newlyweds and most of the houseguests stayed for several days after the wedding. The hours were filled with sparkling conversation, horseback rides, and walks in the woods, through the rose garden, and along the riverbank.

In the evenings after supper, slave musicians were summoned to the parlor, where they struck up Virginia reels on the banjo and fiddle. Couples danced late into the night, and the gentlemen refreshed themselves from one of Mr. Custis's favorite Mount Vernon artifacts, the ship punch bowl that French naval officers had given George Washington after the Revolutionary War. It was a large china bowl with a painting of a ship on the inside, the hull even with the bottom and the mast extending up the side all the way to the brim. Arlington guests were welcome to drink down as far as the base of the mast; that much punch gone signaled the end of the evening.

The days of celebration had just concluded when the July 6 edition of the *Alexandria Gazette* carried a brief notice:

MARRIED. At Arlington House, by the Rev. Dr. KEITH, Lieut.
ROBERT LEE, of the U. States Corps of Engineers, to Miss MARY
A. R. CUSTIS, only daughter of G. W. P. CUSTIS, Esq.

After the last wedding guests left, Mary and Robert went with her
mother for a visit to Ravensworth. There the two ladies fell sick with what
Robert described as "an attack of the fever and ague." They both recovered,
but even though Mary's symptoms disappeared, Robert thought she looked
pale and drawn. This attack and her illness the previous November were
early signs that Mary's health might not be as robust as it should be.

When the women were well enough to leave Ravensworth, Mary,
Robert, and Mrs. Custis continued on a round of visits to other kin.
Lieutenant and Mrs. Lee spent time at Woodlawn and at Kinloch before
returning to Arlington, where they made preparations to set up housekeeping at Fort Monroe.

As she prepared to move to Old Point Comfort, Mary stole a hurried
moment to make an entry in her journal:

What can I say for this week but that in the circumstances with
which I am surrounded my poor vain foolish heart has been too
much drawn aside from Thee. Oh my Father in Heaven, to whom
I owe all both for time & eternity, oh listen to the voice of Thy
child & when Thou hearest, pity & forgive.

During her engagement, Mary's journal had been her inseparable con-
fidante. Now she made this last entry on the threshold of a whirlwind of
change, and it would be a year and a day before she again picked up the
neat little stack of pages.

Arlington was strangely quiet after the excitement of the wedding
week faded and it finally took hold that Mary was gone. "I will not attempt
to tell you how I felt at your departure," Mrs. Custis wrote in one of her
first letters to Fort Monroe. "I hasten to turn from my own loss to a contemplation of your happiness." She was worried that Mary might be "too
little affected" by her departure from Arlington but assured her daughter
that "on my part, I promise to try to be as happy without you as I can."
She gently chided the newlyweds for sleeping too late to get a letter to the

government steamboat that traveled up and down the Potomac with mail and supplies. Every day she waited impatiently for the servant to bring the mailbag from Washington, and on days when there was no letter from Fort Monroe, she shook it upside down just to make sure nothing had been left inside by mistake.

The adjustments Mary was called on to make so abruptly were enormous. Compared with Arlington, Old Point Comfort was another world. Mary had traded life in a famous mansion on a magnificent estate for two dirt-floored rooms in the quarters of Lieutenant Lee's friend and commanding officer, Captain Andrew Talcott. The building, designated as Quarters No. 17 but known informally as "The Tuileries," was also home to Talcott's sister and brother-and-law and their two daughters.

Mary had been the only child of a distinguished family, with parents who were loving and indulgent—perhaps overly so. Now she was an army wife, the keeper of her own household, cut off for the first time from the attention and support of her mother and father. Surrounded and waited on all her life by obedient slaves grateful for the least attention they received, she had seldom wanted for even the smallest comfort. Now she had only one household servant, Cassie, whom her mother had sent along with the newlyweds.

Mary was a woman after her father's own heart—intellectual, patriotic, artistic, well read, articulate, and admirable, but not keen on order and organization. Now she was married to an engineer who had spent four years at West Point without a single misstep and who was already noteworthy for his punctuality and attention to detail. Though her father was chronically short of cash, Mary had always had the best of everything; now she would make do on a lieutenant's pay.

Mary had little natural interest in housekeeping and hardly knew where to begin, because servants had always done it at Arlington. But Mrs. Custis had given Robert fair warning and hoped for the best. Six weeks after their marriage, she had written to Mary, "I hope Robert will…tell me how you improve in order, now he has you all to himself. I shall be disappointed in my daughter if she does not profit by examples united to precept."

Mary dutifully began establishing her new home. She arranged her two rooms with a few simple furnishings from Arlington and the things Robert already had on hand. Her mother wanted to send more household goods, but Mary insisted that she was all right. Besides, there was no room for anything else, though she did accept an oilcloth and a few decorations.

Before long, Mr. Custis arranged to send produce from Romancoke and the White House by steamboat. If they were short on furniture, Lieutenant and Mrs. Lee soon enjoyed an abundance of ham, bacon, molasses, vegetables, flour, fish (one of Mary's favorite foods), and other bounty from the Custis properties. Mary's father did not send money; he could not even afford to replace his old worn-out Mount Vernon carriage—still in use—that the coachman insisted was beyond repair.

Mary had been at Fort Monroe less than a month when, before dawn on August 22, Nat Turner led a slave revolt in Southampton County, less than a hundred miles away. Within twenty-four hours he and his followers killed at least fifty-five white people and then disappeared into the countryside, where they evaded capture for more than two months. Local militia troops contained the violence, though rumors of massacres and fugitive sightings continued until Turner's capture on October 30.

Partly as a result of the uprising, the garrison at Fort Monroe was considerably reinforced with artillery troops. While this gave Mary more officers' wives with whom to cultivate friendships, it caused some friction between the artillery and engineering commands. The commander of the fort, Colonel Abram Eustis, issued an order stating:

> No negroes or persons of color of either sex, other than the servants
> of officers, and those employed in the Hospital and Quarter Masters
> Dept. are to be harboured or tolerated within the walls of the Fort.

Lieutenant Lee protested the order to the commander and to his superior in Washington. It was completely impractical for two reasons. First, the engineering work crews were black, and they had to go into the fort for drinking water and mortar. Second, draftsmen and others not "employed in the Hospital and Quarter Masters Dept." owned slaves who had to enter the fort on errands or in the performance of other routine duties. Nevertheless, the colonel's order stood.

There was a Sunday school at the fort, but the soldiers seemed to think it "quite a condescendation" to send their children there, and so it was poorly attended. Mary thought it a "great omission" that there were no seats for blacks. If the powers that be refused to accept slaves' need for religious instruction, Mary was willing to argue that it would at least keep them out of mischief part of the day, "if that was the only light in which they would view it here." Since Cassie was not allowed in the chapel at the fort, Mary conducted Sunday school for her at home.

Mary did her best to cultivate friendships with families she thought were pious and grounded in Scripture, but it seemed to her that there were few of them. Most of the ladies seemed "not to be *exerting* of themselves" in religious matters, though Mary admitted that their expressions of Christian piety and charity could be "of that unobtrusive kind" which only the recipients ever knew.

"I still feel the consolations, the soothing influences of religion," Mary wrote her mother from Fort Monroe in September, "still feel [I] am anxious & desire to do something to show forth my gratitude to the...Saviour who has done all for me, but it is hard to find what I can do." Mary also continued to fret about her husband's faith. Her mother was a tower of religious inspiration, but Mary feared for Robert's soul and prayed fervently that he would hear and respond to God's call and direct his life wherever his Savior led him.

Whatever sickness Mary had had at Ravensworth just after her wedding lingered into the summer. On August 10, her mother wrote from Ravensworth that she was still worried Mary was not fully restored to health. Though in fact scarcely recovered from illness herself, Mary sat up two nights straight with a sick neighbor.

Captain Talcott and Lieutenant Lee were away most of the day, and Mary read a great deal during her hours alone—she read her Bible daily, often supplemented by collections of sermons her mother sent. She and a neighbor began reading a biography of Martin Luther together, but the neighbor was so busy with her children that she soon gave up the effort, leaving Mary to continue on her own.

By the end of the summer, Mary felt a little more at home. She enjoyed visiting with Captain Talcott's young nieces, Rebecca and Catherine Hale, and helped them befriend a white cat that showed up at the house. She and the other ladies went saltwater bathing, taking the children and servants with them. "I walk every morning before breakfast on this beautiful beach & inhale the sea breezes which are said to bring health along with them," she wrote her mother. "I have got through very little work except mending up some of Robert's old clothes—a coat of his I have darned & new lined the sleeve. You ought to see how nicely it is done."

But memories of home were never far beneath the surface. "What would I give for one stroll on the hills at Arlington this bright day," she confided. "The only objection I have to this place [is that] it is so public that you can never go out alone except to the bath." She was grateful for "a husband always ready to go with me when his duties will permit. I must give him a little just commendation sometimes."

Mary had never spent Christmas away from Arlington, and she was delighted at the news that she and Robert would travel there for the holidays, with stops along the way to visit other relatives. Roads were primitive and railroads just starting to be built, so travelers went by boat whenever they could. The Lees took a steamer up the James River to Shirley, seat of the Carter family, where Robert's parents had been married. After several days, they went on to Baltimore to visit Robert's sister Anne Marshall and her family.

When at last they docked at the river landing near Arlington Spring, Mary's homecoming was all that she could have hoped for. The mansion was lavishly decorated for Christmas, and her parents and the servants welcomed her with smiles and tears. The Lees spent about a month at Arlington before Robert returned to duty at the fort. Even then, as much as Mary and her mother had written each other in the five months since she left home, there was still so much news to catch up on that their time together seemed only an instant.

Mary learned that the old Mount Vernon coach had finally fallen apart for good and been left at Annefield as a playhouse for the children. An Episcopal bishop used the carriage seat for a sofa in his study. Later, Mr. Custis granted permission to break up the carriage for souvenirs, which produced a tremendous amount of money for charity when walking sticks, picture frames, and snuffboxes were made from the wood and sold. Two-thirds of a single wheel brought in $140.

Mary heard too of her father's latest theatrical projects. He was as exuberant a playwright as he was a painter, and his plays generally received as little critical acclaim as his pictures. *Montgomerie, or The Orphan of a Wreck,* an adventure set in the Scottish Highlands, *Pocahontas,* an idealized account of the Indian maiden and Captain John Smith, and other works were all passionately patriotic, mediocre in quality, and uniformly unsuccessful on the stage, though *Pocahontas* enjoyed some modest measure of acclaim when it premiered in Philadelphia, thanks in part to its stupendous sets.

Mr. Custis was also planning to publish the memoirs of the Marquis de Lafayette, and he had convinced the old soldier to turn over all his papers. The only condition was that Custis come to France and get them in person. Custis had no money to make the trip, and despite an impassioned plea to his banker underscoring "the importance of my voyage across the Atlantic to secure these precious mementos, from accident, if not oblivion," his credit was too much overextended already, and the bank denied him the loan.

The week after Christmas, Mary and Robert were invited to the wedding of Eliza Mackay, a friend of Robert's in Savannah. The invitation arrived too late for them to make the trip, but Robert wrote a note in his friendly, teasing way, insisting that upon hearing of her wedding plans, "I have been in tears ever since at the thought of losing you. Oh, me!"

The tone of Mary's postscript to her husband's note was more serious and revealed both the disconnected, unsettled feeling all the recent changes had brought about in her life and her constant reliance on faith:

> [I] wish that your pathway in life may be as bright as our beneficent Creator and Father sees best for you.... I am now a wanderer on the face of the earth and know not where we are going next....
> I suppose you remain in Savannah near your mother? What happiness! I am with mine now—the past and future disregarded.

As much as she loved Robert and wanted to be with him, Mary missed her mother. Their Christmas reunion made her realize how much she had longed for home and how she would miss it when the holidays were over and she returned to her two rooms in the Talcott house.

When Robert left for Fort Monroe in January, 1832, Mary stayed on at Arlington. She was not ready to leave the luxury, privacy, and spaciousness of her old surroundings so soon. Her life in the military was her future, and she accepted that. But that season she was a willing captive to the vestiges of her old sheltered, carefree life.

The winter was a cold one, and Mary further delayed her return to Fort Monroe because of ice on the river. When spring came and the ice melted,

Mary still lingered as the flower gardens awakened and blossoms filled the warm air with their fragrances. Here there were no household chores, no cramped quarters, and no want unmet, however small.

Furthermore, she was pregnant. She had conceived a child during the Christmas holidays, and the anticipation of its arrival made her want all the more to stay home, surrounded by loving friends, generous parents, and doting servants.

On February 22, 1832, the centennial of Washington's birth, Mary was dangerously ill again. She wrote wearily in her journal:

How sad & depressed with bodily indisposition on which my mind continually dwells. Oh that I were more spiritual & could bow beneath Thy chastening rod & say "it is the Lord, let Him do with me what seemeth to Him good" that I could profit by His all-wise dispensations. Gracious God bestow upon me Thy grace that I may not dishonour the sacred name I fear.

A week later the crisis had passed, and Mary could reflect on her feelings with a sense of perspective:

When I review all my last & dangerous illness I am more convinced that it was a special visitation from my Heavenly Father for my eternal good in answer to one of my first sincere prayers after my conversion. "Lord," I then prayed, "let me *suffer any thing* rather than have my heart turned away from Thee." Be still my murmuring heart & know that it is the Lord. Set thy affections on things above & not on this poor perishing earth. Be thankful that thou hast still so many mercies around thee. Remember that whom the Lord loveth He chasteneth & scourgeth every son whom He receiveth. Waste not thy hours in languor & idleness but look to Him who can heal the diseases of the mind & body & who doth not willingly grieve or afflict the children of men.

Uninformed of the danger Mary had been in, Robert wrote her joking about how he flirted with the ladies in her absence. He wondered too whether his previous letters asking when she would return to the fort had reached her, or whether they had been misdirected, "parading about the 'ten miles square' [the District of Columbia] in search of a house that any one might see with half an eye...."

"Hasten down," he teased, "if you do not want to see me turned out a beau again." For all the lightheartedness, there was a justifiable edge of concern and irritation. Robert insisted that they should look ahead, wean themselves from Mary's parents' generosity, and make an independent life of their own:

> You seem to think, Molly, you would prefer living as we are, but are you right in this? We ought not to give others the trouble of providing for us always, and besides I can see how we might incommode & be a restraint upon them.... I know your dear Mother will be for giving you *every* thing she has, but must recollect *one* thing, & that is, that they have been accustomed to comforts all their life, which now they could not dispense with. And that we, in the commencement, ought to contract our wishes to their smallest compass, & enlarge them as opportunity offers.

They should, in other words, live within their means. Robert knew the consequences of failing to do so: His mother and siblings had survived on relatively little. But Mary was used to having whatever she wanted, and Mr. Custis was not the type to forego any sort of luxury merely because he could not afford it.

Robert changed his tune somewhat after Mary wrote that she was expecting. "Take care of yourself," he wrote back. "Don't ride on horseback, or go into crowds, or hurry about the house." She should stay home from church. "Suppose the carriage was to break down, what would you do then?" At the same time, however, he renewed his campaign to get his wife back. The shores of the Potomac were not a healthy place in the summer, he warned. She would be better off at Point Comfort, nearer the ocean, and ought to come back by the first of June.

Thanks to a combination of the months of relaxation she had enjoyed, the end of her sickness, the desire to see her husband, and a pang of guilt for so long an absence, Mary agreed and started packing to leave. Six months pregnant, she sailed for Fort Monroe.

In the meantime, Captain Talcott's brother-in-law had died, and his sister and her children had moved out. On April 11, Talcott married Harriet Randolph Hackley, one of Mary's cousins. The captain and Lieutenant Lee agreed to redivide the quarters they shared to give the Lees more room and both families more privacy. The Lees took the upstairs at The Tuileries, and the Talcotts lived downstairs.

Mary's mother accompanied her to her new quarters, bringing some more furniture for the Lees and two more slaves. Then she returned to Arlington, expecting to come back to the fort when Mary's baby was due.

Mary was disappointed when her mother had an attack of chills and fever and had to delay her visit. As the delivery day drew closer, Mrs. Custis worried about the rumors of cholera in the area. It would have been ironic if, in an attempt to get to a healthier climate, Mary had ended up in a worse one. There was no outbreak at the fort, though the citizens of Norfolk took the precaution of fumigating their sheets every day over fires of burning tar.

Mary felt a responsibility for visiting newcomers to the fort, but with the baby coming, her time was limited and she was "much occupied at home." In mid-August, she thought the baby was about two months away and was concerned about getting all its clothes finished in time. So she began sewing more in the evenings after supper, while Robert read aloud to keep her company. Despite all the distractions of preparing for the upcoming event, Mary thought she had made great strides in learning to keep house. She wrote her mother that Aunt Eleanor "ought to be down here to see what a fine housekeeper I am."

Mary developed a large appetite and a craving for currant jelly from Arlington. Her father resolved to send that and more, but by the time it arrived, her craving had disappeared. On September 16, 1832, Mary Custis Lee delivered a healthy son. With Robert's enthusiastic consent, she named him George Washington Custis Lee.

Robert was beside himself. In his typically jovial style, he wrote to his brother Carter, "I have got me an heir to my estates! Aye, a boy! To cherish the memory of his *father* & walk in the light of his renown!"

According to her husband, Mary was amazed and enraptured by the new arrival and pointed out his features and seemingly endless lists of his accomplishments every day. Before the end of the month, Mrs. Custis finally arrived to help, teach, and encourage Mary in her new role. By all accounts, it was a normal birth and Mary recovered quickly. Four days after the delivery, she was out riding with Robert, delighting in the feel of freshness in the earth and trees after her days of confinement.

As Christmas 1832 approached, Mary and the baby traveled to Arlington. Again Lieutenant Lee was left alone at his post, but when bad weather put an end to construction work for a while, he followed his wife and son. Christmas Day found them all together at the mansion, Yule log blazing on the hearth, and Washington's punch bowl filled to the top of its mast. Mr. Custis played old war tunes on his violin, the sideboard groaned with the best and most elaborate dishes the estate could produce, and little Custis Lee slept quietly before the fire. It was a time of thanksgiving, joy, and contentment.

CHAPTER EIGHT

A TEST OF FAITH

*D*uring the next year at Fort Monroe, Mary settled more comfortably into her role as a military wife and the mother of an active little boy. After Christmas 1832 she spent less time at Arlington than she had the year before, no doubt because she felt so much better than she had during her pregnancy. But there was also a sense that this year, instead of leaving her lifelong home for a strange and unfamiliar new place, she was going from one household to another.

Between her first Christmas as a bride and her first as a mother, Mary Lee had begun—tentatively, though with growing confidence—to establish a home of her own at Old Point Comfort. True, the Lee's quarters were furnished with Arlington tables and cabinets, and its larder was filled with cheese, apples, herring, and bacon from the Custis estates. At least one Arlington slave helped with the housework. And yet Fort Monroe was where her first child had been born and where her husband hoped to advance his career. Those modest rooms in The Tuileries were her very own domain.

Mary was an attentive parent, and little George Washington Custis Lee became the center of her world. Robert and Mary decided to call him Custis, but Mary referred to him by a whole catalogue of pet names—Bouse, Boo, Booty, Bunny, Bun, and Dunket. She took parenting seriously and acknowledged that she was not as strict with her son as she should be. When Custis woke up in the night, it was Robert who could get him to stop crying and go back to sleep. Though he obeyed his father "most implicitly," he took every advantage of his mother's indecision and hesitation in applying discipline.

Mary was candid about her shortcomings. She wrote her mother that Custis was "a very good natured fellow" whose development was at risk because of her inability to discipline him as she knew she should:

> If his energies can only be well directed, they may be the means of much usefulness. But I already shrink from the responsibility. It requires so much firmness & consistency to train up a child in the right way & I know that I am so remiss in the government of my servants & so often neglect to correct them when they do wrong. I must endeavor with God's assistance to be more faithful.

Mary's feelings of responsibility ran deep. In her first journal entry following Custis's birth, she again admitted her weakness and prayed fervently for God's help. She had faith that whatever she lacked as a mother, God would supply:

> Truly I have found Thee all sufficient & had I done my part all would have been well—had I kept close to Thee as when first Thy divine image was impressed on my soul all would have been well, & now that I am a mother, that my responsibilities are doubled, O Lord, bestow on me a double portion of Thy grace that I may train up this young spirit to glory & immortality. To Thee have I dedicated the precious boon Thou hast bestowed upon me—wilt Thou early take possession of his young heart & fill it with a holy ambition to love & serve Thee. This is all I desire for myself & all with whom I have concern. Hear my prayer Father for Thy dear love's sake. Amen.

Mary took pleasure in the simple, everyday activities of a boisterous one-year-old. Custis enjoyed riding a wooden goat someone at the fort had given him and swimming at the beach. He learned to push open the door to a stairway, so Mary had to keep a chair in front of it. After he began making wordlike sounds, Mary proudly wrote her mother that when she asked him if he had anything to say in a letter to his grandmother, he clearly replied, "loodle, loodle."

The routine at the Lee quarters was as quiet as could be expected with a toddler in the house. During the day when Robert was on duty, Mary read, painted, sewed, looked after the baby, and, in her somewhat intermittent way, supervised the servants and saw to the cooking and cleaning. Robert lightheartedly criticized her lack of industriousness, confiding to a friend his opinion that "Mrs. L. is somewhat addicted to laziness and forgetfulness in her housekeeping," but that "she does her best, or in her mother's words, 'The Spirit is willing but the flesh is weak.'"

Mary also kept up with the local fashion leader, the wife of Benjamin Huger, another of the officers at the fort. Though she dressed modestly and conservatively, Mary had an artist's eye for fashion. Returning from a trip, Mrs. Huger brought Mary clothes she had ordered: "a very nice silk dress & a cape, & gave me the very welcome information that all stiffening was quite out of fashion, so I shall be quite *à la mode* myself."

Mrs. Huger set the style that spring with an elaborate new sunbonnet. Since Mary could not go to Norfolk to get the fabric to make one herself, she asked her mother to bring the material the next time she came to visit, and she took the time to describe very precisely what she wanted:

> It takes 2 yds. of the muslin, which is pretty wide; but of gingham, which is narrower, it would take 2-1/2 yds. I should like either yellow, purple, or pink. You know that it does not require *very fine* muslin. If you do not see any you think would answer…get me a piece of colored french chintz or some plain pink cambric, not too deep but a pretty shade.…

In the same letter, Mary asked her mother to "bring down a Latin dictionary, as I brought a Greek one by mistake." She had inherited her father's love of reading, and even as a wife and mother she made time to study the classics on her own.

At night when Robert was home, Mary sat by the fire sewing while he read to her. She was grateful that he was content to spend the evening with her, even though many of the other officers met for card parties most nights. His reading always concluded with a chapter from the Bible, followed by prayers. Both their families had the tradition of reading from Scripture before bed, and it was a practice Lieutenant and Mrs. Lee established early in their marriage and continued faithfully from then on.

Nevertheless, Mary continued to worry about Robert's spiritual commitment, and she still felt that when the conversation turned to bedrock truths of faith, her husband's attention wandered. He read the Bible regularly and always spoke and acted as a Christian man should. Yet something was missing. In a letter to her mother, Mary admitted, "I cannot but feel that he still wants the one thing needful without which all the rest may prove valueless."

Mary saw to other people's Christian education as well. Because black children were not allowed in the chapel at the fort, Mary taught them the Bible in her home. Her own slaves never seemed able to finish their work in time to attend, so she gave them their lessons on Saturday. She also donated money toward the cost of catechism books for other slaves at the garrison.

Mary was at ease attending the seemingly endless round of receptions and social functions at the fort, but she chafed at their shallowness. "We have been quite satiated with tea drinking lately," she wrote her mother, "almost every evening an invitation somewhere. Except that we generally get some nice cake and fruit, they would be rather stupid. I suppose it is my fault, but there are not many persons here very interesting." She did become acquainted with Captain Talcott's beautiful new wife, Harriet, and visited regularly with Mrs. Huger and other ladies at the fort. Still, she struggled to build deep, significant friendships with women who for the most part were not on the same intellectual level.

In the summer of 1833, a visit from President Andrew Jackson interrupted Mary's predictable routine. The fort went into a frenzy of activity to welcome the commander-in-chief in grand style. Old Hickory inspected the engineering work in progress on the fortifications and conferred with the officers so often that Robert was away from home far more than usual. One day Mary and little Bouse had the opportunity to call on the president.

The old war hero—two decades past his triumph at the Battle of New Orleans—held Bouse in his arms "for some time," Mary wrote a few days later. "Bouse looked at him with a fixed gaze, put his hand over his nose but did not pull it hard, & put his fingers in his eyes. The old man gave him Rachel's picture to play with, which delighted him much." Then the president, himself a childless widower, gave the boy a half-dollar, instructing Mary to put a hole in it so he could wear it around his neck. Jackson "said he was a fine boy and a good boy," Mary reported, "and that I must take off his shoes & let him run around barefoot."

Flattered as she was with Jackson's attentions to young George Washington Custis, Mary was still glad when he and his entourage left so "we shall have a little quiet & Robert will have a little time to be at home."

In mid-November, Mary and Bouse went to Arlington for the holiday season. Mary expected Robert to follow as soon as his duties permitted, but by the first week in December it was clear he would not be at Arlington for Christmas. He hoped to make it by New Year's, but even that pleasure was denied him—not so much by the construction work as by further political squabbling between the Corps of Engineers, who were designing the installation at Old Point Comfort, and the Artillery, who would man it later.

It was the first Christmas of their married life that Mary and Robert had spent apart. Mary was willing to accept occasional separations from her husband as the price of keeping close to her parents, and Robert seemed to enjoy some time alone. During the previous summer when Mary, her mother, and Bouse had gone on an extended visit, Lee had written his friend Captain Talcott, "Mrs. Custis & Mary have gone up to Shirley, which is as much to say that I am as happy as a clam in high water."

Christmas at Arlington was as grand and festive as always. Mary watched and listened eagerly as her father dramatically recounted his most recent exploits. He had abandoned his sheep-raising operation; grain and tobacco were trading well; the fisheries were profitable. He had developed a new wooden-soled shoe for the slaves that cost half the price of a leather shoe but lasted just as long. His play *The Rail Road* had delighted audiences in Philadelphia, and there were other dramatic productions in the works. He had painted a large allegorical canvas for the centennial of Washington's birth the year before and was now getting back to work on his memoir of the first president's life and times.

The dining table, heavy with President Washington's silver and dishes, was covered with the bounty of Arlington, Romancoke, and the White

House. Whether holding forth around the table or in the sitting room with one of his endless collection of stories, Mr. Custis presided with jovial good humor and old-fashioned courtliness. He talked theater and politics, played the violin, laughed at the antics of Bouse running through the house, and lavished his hospitality on everyone who came to see Mary and the baby.

Finally, nearly a month after Christmas, Robert arrived, and for a few precious days, Mary had her husband, her baby, and her parents all together again under one roof. Those were days of true and complete contentment, when everyone she loved most in the world was with her and the familiar ease and luxury of Arlington pushed aside the daily trials of housekeeping and military life.

Lee had to return to duty the first week in February. The Potomac was too icy for the steamboats, so Mary and Bouse remained behind while Robert traveled overland by horseback, as he wrote a friend, "up to my ears in mud and alone."

In the summer of 1834, responsibility for finishing the work at Fort Monroe was handed off to the Artillery, and Lieutenant Lee received an assignment as assistant to General Charles Gratiot, chief of engineers, in Washington. After five years in the army, Lee was still a second lieutenant. Though he preferred supervising projects in the field to pushing paper at a desk, there was a good chance that being in Washington would help advance his career.

Mary was ecstatic at the thought of moving to the capital, literally within sight of Arlington. She supervised packing up the household at Point Comfort, and by the time Robert reported to his new duty station in November, his family was already back at the Custis mansion. They would stay there until Lee could secure a place to live in Washington.

As it turned out, Robert could find nothing suitable for his wife and son that he could afford. He also knew that his duties would demand work at odd hours, making it impossible for him to live across the river at his father-in-law's estate. So he rented a room in Ulrick's Boarding House, where several young officers lived. He had his lunch there every day and slept there when he got off duty too late to travel to Arlington for the night. Though it was a long ride to take after a full day of army paperwork, Lee made the four-mile trip as often as he could.

Mary felt Robert becoming gradually more comfortable in her family home. Mrs. Custis reserved one of the upstairs bedrooms for the lieutenant's friends who came for dinner and decided to stay the night. "Those who can sleep three to a bed will find 'comfortable accommodations,'" Lee promised them with wry humor.

Arlington was also the setting of a lavish wedding party for Robert's brother Smith in February 1835. During the reception, when Mary was out of the room, her sister-in-law playfully introduced Robert to a group of young single ladies as her "younger brother." "Sweet, innocent things," Lee wrote his friend Talcott, "they concluded I was single and I have not had such soft looks and tender pressure of the hand for many years."

After only a few months in Washington, a restless Lieutenant Lee requested reassignment. General Gratiot consented and attached Lee to an expedition that was to survey the boundary between Ohio and Michigan. Mary Lee was seven months pregnant when her husband left by Potomac steamer for New York, where he would pick up his surveying instruments and then head west. Probably they both expected the lieutenant to be back home before their second child was born. But there was a delay in getting the surveying equipment, followed by other snags along the way. Soon it was obvious that Robert would be away when the baby came.

As the delivery day approached, Mrs. Custis had some of the house servants rearrange a dressing room off Mary's upstairs bedroom. Though small, it had a window looking south over the rear drive to the fields and forests beyond. Trunks and clothing were cleared away, and the room was whitewashed and disinfected from ceiling to floor with lime and then furnished simply with a small bed, a chair or two, and a washstand. There, on July 12, 1835, Mary gave birth to a daughter. She named her Mary Custis Lee, confident that the new arrival would in time be the third Mary to reign at Arlington House.

At first Mary recovered well, and it seemed that she would regain her health after this second birth as quickly as she had after the first. Just as she had after her confinement with Bouse, she soon returned to walking, riding, and the daily routine. Within a short time, however, she caught a cold. It passed quickly, but then she caught a more serious one, and it sent her back to her sickbed.

The date of Robert's return had been pushed back time and again, and he was still away. Mary wrote to him, imploring him to come home even if it meant leaving his work out west unfinished. She felt that under the circumstances, his friend Captain Talcott, the leader of the expedition, and their commander back in Washington, General Gratiot, would excuse him from whatever remained to be done in order to attend to the needs of his family. She did not, however, even hint that she was ill.

Mary's letter reached Robert in Detroit. He felt duty bound to remain where he was and to put his responsibility ahead of family matters. By return mail he scolded his wife for making what seemed a selfish and completely unreasonable request.

> Why do you urge my *immediate* return & tempt one in the strongest manner, to endeavor to get excused from the performance of a duty imposed on me by my profession for the pure gratification of my private feelings? Do you not think that those feelings are enough of themselves to contend with, without other aggravations; and that I rather require to be strengthened & encouraged to the *full* performance of what I am called to execute, rather than excited to a dereliction, which even our affection could not palliate, or our judgment excuse?

Mary grew sicker, developed a fever, lost her appetite, and was soon unable to nurse her baby. She fed her cow's milk from a bottle whenever she was able, but more and more she had to entrust the infant's care to her mother, faithful Old Nurse, and Bouse's nurse, Kitty. Mr. and Mrs. Custis had their daughter moved to Ravensworth, hoping the cooler, dryer air would help her recover faster than she could in the muggy summer heat of Washington.

Nothing seemed to help. Mary developed a soreness and stiffness in her legs, which doctors diagnosed as "rheumatic diathesis"—early signs of rheumatism. Her inner thighs also swelled with painful abscesses that may have been the result of infection during childbirth. By October 1, she was completely bedfast. It was her twenty-seventh birthday; very possibly she would not live to see her twenty-eighth.

During the first week of October, after an absence of five months, Robert returned to Washington. Arriving at Arlington expecting to meet his new daughter, he was surprised to find only his father-in-law at home.

Alarmed when he learned about Mary's illness, he quickly rode the ten miles to Ravensworth, where he found his wife pale, emaciated, listless, and in constant pain.

Appalled by her condition, Robert immediately brought her back to Arlington, where he thought better medical care would be available. To reduce her discomfort during the move, Mary was transported in the bed from Ravensworth, which was loaded in a wagon for the trip and then carried gingerly by slaves up the stairs to her bedroom. There she was lifted out and placed on crisp, fresh sheets in her own bed.

Just as on the day Mary had come home to Arlington as an infant, the trees on the estate were approaching their autumn peak. The last roses of the year were being gathered and the bushes trimmed and banked for the winter, the grain harvest was in progress, and the tobacco was already cut and stored. But Mary was too ill to notice or appreciate any of this.

Robert and his father-in-law summoned the family doctor and called in another for consultation. The doctors prescribed fomentation (the application of warm ointments) and cupping, a method of bleeding patients to remove what medical science of the day considered contaminated or "bad blood" responsible for the illness. A cut was made in an arm or leg and then covered with a glass cup that had been heated. The heat formed a vacuum that rapidly drew out the blood and filled the cup. Mary was also bled with leeches.

Whether because of or in spite of these treatments, on the morning of October 7, Lee could tell Talcott that Mary was "decidedly better." "God grant that it may be the commencement of her recovery," he wrote. A week or so later, Mary could still not get out of bed, though by then she was carrying on conversations and had some of her faculties about her. Then her improvement slowed, and her condition leveled off. The fever left; the soreness and pain remained.

Mary was relieved of the most acute pain when the abscesses on her thighs were lanced—the one on the right leg on October 19, followed by the left two weeks or so later—but she continued a helpless invalid into the fall. Finally by mid-November she could sit up in bed, and she began to eat more than the chicken broth and barley gruel she had lived on since the summer.

Robert and the rest of the family began to feel some assurance that Mary would eventually recover. She was still ghastly thin, but her appetite returned with a vengeance, and she began eating ravenously—a welcome sign that the danger was past. Writing to Talcott on November 18, Lee joyfully reported, "May [one of his nicknames for Mary] gets better every day.... Her appetite is famous and the partridges, buckwheat muffins & etc. disappear at breakfast as fast as the pheasants, chickens & etc. at dinner."

A prolific correspondent by nature, Mary took up her pen after a long absence to try to describe something of what she had endured and how she felt. In a letter to Harriett Talcott on November 21, her handwriting reflected a frequent shifting of position as she sat propped up in her bed, sitting first one way and then another trying to get comfortable. When she finished, she folded the sheet, sealed it with wax, and left it for Robert to address for her.

I have been too sick to answer your kind letter before, my dear Harriet, & it is only for the last week that I have been able to sit up at all, in consequence of being relieved from the most exquisite pain by the discharge of the tumor in my side. Since then I have recovered rapidly & have an immense appetite, though I have not yet gained strength sufficient to *stand*. You may suppose after a confinement to my bed almost of 4 months I am much reduced & I fear it will be some time before I shall be able to walk. Yet I desire to be thankful that I am this far restored to a state of comparative ease & enjoyment....

Mary also brought Harriet up to date on the new arrival. Even though she had not been able to nurse her daughter, the baby, soon nicknamed "Mee," was pink, plump, and happy at four months old.

My little Mary Custis has become very engaging & promises to be a beauty. She is a clear brunette with brown hair, very fine large black eyes, a *perfect* little mouth & *respectable* nose & is perfectly fat & healthy with no other nurse than her bottle and cow's milk. She is too remarkably good, never cries, & sleeps well at night. Indeed I have no trouble with her...

A sign of Mary's improving health was her interest in the dress Harriet had sent her from Philadelphia. "I have seen nothing so pretty this fall," she wrote, "but you should have got a belt to match it." She doubted she could find one in the fashion backwoods of Washington.

Harriet had also sent a silver comb, but Mary had little use for it. After the worst was over and she began sitting up, Mary discovered that her hair was a hopeless tangle. Neither trimmed nor arranged for four months, her thick, long, brown tresses had become a mass of knots on the pillow. This was one problem she could solve quickly and definitively. Calling for scissors and a mirror, she cut her hair off on the spot. His wit at the ready as always, Lee observed, "[Mary's hair] is now coming out so rapidly that when I left today she talked of having it shaved off, and I expect on my return to find her bald."

Whether she had threatened to do so in jest or out of frustration, Mary did not shave her head. She was, however, still unwell when Christmas came, and the season that was usually so joyful at Arlington was a little more subdued. Mr. Custis went about his traditional merrymaking, and carriages full of visitors came and went; but if Mary participated at all in the festivities, it was from a pallet on the sofa in the parlor or the sitting room.

Her near-fatal illness and slow recovery put Mary in a reflective mood in the first months of 1836. On January 8, for the first time in twenty-seven months, she wrote in her prayer journal to ask God's blessing on herself, her children, and—without naming them—her husband and father, for whose salvation she still feared:

Oh my soul, what account can be given of Thee during this long period? How cold, how insensible is my heart! Why has Almighty Love chastened me sore & raised me from the brink of the grave, to be again engrossed by the gratification of this poor perishing body? Thou who hast sustained me in the hour of anguish, Thou who hast restored me to health, friends, & placed another cherub in my bosom, Thou whose name is Love, forsake me not now. Warm this lifeless heart that it may pour its affections into Thee....

And the children which Thou hast given me I would consecrate to Thee. I only ask for them Thy grace, Thy divine Love shed abroad in their young hearts ere the world with its alluring vanities has taken possession of them. Enable me to be faithful in training them up for Thee.

Oh my Father in Heaven, lend an ear to my petitions for those most dear to me. Sad is my heart where they seem more & more indifferent to the things which concern their eternal peace. Why dost Thou withhold from me this blessing?...

Grant in the name & for the sake of Thy Son Jesus Christ the babe whom I have dedicated to Thee, O God. Preserve her from the temptations of a world that knows Thee not.

As winter ran its course and spring buds began appearing in her rose garden, Mary continued her slow recovery. Her hair grew out, she gained weight, and eventually she was strong enough to spend her days downstairs with the family and take short walks in the garden or across the lawn. Still, she felt weak and not inclined to do much. Burdened already by her own inadequacy, she feared that after her illness she might never have the energy to correct her shortcomings, no matter how desperately she wanted to.

In early 1836, Mary unburdened her troubled heart in a series of journal entries:

February 14th, Sunday
This sacred day—Oh how much of it has been wasted in lassitude & indolence! O my Father in Heaven, arouse me from this torpid state as regards things spiritual & temporal! Why am I so careless in mind & body when I have so much to be thankful for? Why am I so inert when there is so much for me to do?

O my Father, forgive what is past & give me grace to do better in time to come. Let not the late alarming visitation of thy Providence be lost upon me.

March 3
This winter has passed like a dream & oh how many misspent hours languishing for a return of health, & vainly regretting the attractions lost—perhaps never to return. Lord, I would bow beneath Thy chastening hand. I would arouse myself & shake off this spiritual sloth. I would thirst & hunger after righteousness instead of those attractions which would bind me again to the world.... Change my song of mourning into gratitude & praise for Thine unnumbered mercies....

Take my little ones & that loved one of my soul under Thy fatherly care. Let me not dishonour Thy cause in their eyes. I fear I have shewn but few of the Christian graces in my last trial. Though feeling myself upheld by Thy mercy, how impatient, cold & careless have I been, wishing that it had been with me as in times past, when the voice of gladness was in my mouth & the rose of health on my cheek....

Thou Great Physician of souls, heal the diseases of mind & body. Enable me patiently in Thy appointed means to wait and expect an answer to my prayers.

As the honeysuckle and yellow jasmine came into bloom, Mary's spirits lifted somewhat, especially at the sight of little Mee drawing Lieutenant Lee closer to his family.

Enraptured by his daughter, Robert declared her the brightest flower on the estate. "Oh she is a rare one," he insisted, "and if only she were sixteen, I would wish myself a *cannibal* that I might eat her up. As it is, I have given all the young ladies a holiday and hurry home to her every day."

He also gamely addressed the mysteries of teething, childhood diseases, and discipline. When Custis had the whooping cough, Robert recorded the boy's plucky spirit in a letter to his brother Carter. "The *Boo* has the whooping cough, God bless him, but he does not mind—whoops, falls down (not tolerably), gets up, and whoops again...." He also ventured the opinion that Mary and her parents were too lenient with Custis, which left him—in whatever time he had at home—to keep his firstborn in line.

In June, just as Mary seemed poised to return to full health, she suffered a serious setback. Pain and swelling in her ears were followed by fever and headache. Once again she was confined to bed, this time with the mumps. Her illness was further complicated by stiffness in her neck, probably due to inflammation of the brain and spinal column. Already weakened by months of illness, she seemed headed for another long period of infirmity. She was in agonizing pain, and seeing her suffer was agonizing for Robert as well.

At last the crisis passed. After the mumps had run their course, Robert decided that Mary should escape the summer heat and take the cure at one of the mineral springs that were so popular at the time. He packed up his wife and children, along with four slaves to serve as maids and nurses, and took them to Warrenton Springs in the foothills of the Blue Ridge Mountains about forty miles from Arlington.

Two generations earlier, Richard Henry Lee, Robert's famous first cousin twice removed, had settled the land around Warrenton. The springs contained chemicals that were supposed to alleviate symptoms of arthritis, rheumatism, and other infirmities, and a modest resort had grown up around them. Visitors drank the water and also bathed in pools of it.

While the restorative powers of the water were the springs' main attraction, a close second was their function as social centers. Families of the Virginia aristocracy came to Warrenton Springs and similar places expecting to spend weeks with other families like themselves. They met friends and cousins there, made new acquaintances, and generally continued the endless round of visiting that was an essential part of plantation life and Southern hospitality.

Unless they were infirm or indisposed, guests took their meals together in a large dining hall, where the food was served at a leisurely pace that invited conversation. After meals and at other times during the day, groups of guests gathered on the veranda of the dining hall for more visiting: women gossiping as they watched their children running and playing on the lawn, men smoking cigars and talking of crops, finances, and politics. People went walking or riding along the roadways or hiking through the woods as their interests led them. And of course there were the mineral baths, which the men took in one building and the women and children in another. Between the hotel staff and the slaves they brought with them, vacationers could look forward to a season free of distraction and unwanted responsibility.

The change of scenery, mountain air, spring water, and the company of family and friends all combined to strengthen Mary's constitution, boost her spirits, and improve her health somewhat. She no longer wrote the anguished entries that had filled her prayer journal in the winter and spring.

When the family returned to Arlington at the end of the summer, Robert resumed his commute from the estate to Engineers headquarters in Washington. A number of the Lees' friends, including Captain Talcott, had left military service for civilian jobs that paid much better, and Mary knew that Robert was wondering whether he should resign his commission and help her father manage his estates.

But Robert was hesitant to strike out on his own at a time when Mary's health was so unpredictable. Even after the restful summer at Warrenton, she was weak, listless, and disinclined to take on any responsibility. She was nervous, almost frantic, in crowds; and although she remained physically inactive, she had what Robert observed as "a restless anxiety, which renders her unhappy and dissatisfied." So Robert stayed in the Corps of Engineers, and on September 21, after seven years in the army, he was finally promoted to first lieutenant.

Not long after she and the children were settled back at Arlington, Mary discovered that she was expecting again—child number three would be along before Mee's second birthday. About the same time, Robert, ever on the lookout for opportunities to get out from behind a desk and advance his career, accepted an assignment in St. Louis. Hearing the news, Mary anticipated being without her husband yet again when another little Lee joined the family.

CHAPTER NINE

OUT WEST

*T*he Mississippi River was changing its course at St. Louis, threatening to devastate the economy of the whole region by winding away from the city docks and leaving them landlocked. Lee's work at Point Comfort had involved design and placement of riprap, rock embankments that protected shorelines from erosion and channeled tides and currents. Riprap, along with dredging and dikes, seemed to be the best solution for keeping the Mississippi in its banks at St. Louis, and because of his experience, Lee was chosen to supervise the job.

When Robert's orders came through in April, Mary resigned herself to the fact that he would be gone again when their next child came along. However, his departure was delayed. Mary's dressing room was freshly scrubbed down once more for her "lying in," and on May 30, 1837, another son was born. With Robert's approval, Mary named him William Henry Fitzhugh Lee, after her late uncle, William Henry Fitzhugh of Ravensworth.

About two weeks later, Robert left for St. Louis, traveling overland through Baltimore to Philadelphia and then on the Pennsylvania Canal to Pittsburgh, where he boarded a river steamer for the voyage down the Ohio to the Mississippi and his destination. His companion and assistant was a second lieutenant only a year out of West Point, Montgomery C. Meigs, a

Georgia native who had grown up in Pennsylvania. The two reached St. Louis in early August and began their work trying to harness the "Father of Waters."

Hoping for another round of modest improvement in Mary's health, Robert encouraged her to "be off to the Spring the *first week* in August, not to return till October." She took his advice to travel, though she spent the time visiting friends and family at their homes instead of at the springs. She and the three children—Boo, five years old; Mee, just turned two; and newborn William, nicknamed "Rooney"—traveled to Chantilly in Fairfax County, built by the great-granddaughter of Richard Henry Lee. They also visited Kinloch, home of Thomas Turner, an old family friend and Lee's former guardian, and of course Ravensworth, where Mary was surrounded by the attentions of her Fitzhugh relations and where her mother often joined her.

The children were all hale and growing, and Mary felt healthier than she had in many months. Although she now had enough energy to discipline, she was more indulgent than she should have been with the children, especially Boo. Her father was little help, seeing in the boy as he did the heir of Arlington who could do no wrong. The Fitzhughs were inclined to spoil him too.

Writing from St. Louis, Robert said that he hoped their return from Ravensworth to Arlington in October would make it easier to tighten the discipline a little, or as he described it, put them "under proper restraint." The oldest, in particular, could be a handful if Mary allowed it. "Our dear little Boo seems to have among his friends a reputation of being hard to manage, a distinction not at all desirable, as it indicates self-will and obstinacy.... I pray God to watch over and direct our efforts in guarding our dear son, that we may bring him up 'in the way he should go.'"

On his last extended trip away from home, when Mee was born, Robert had criticized Mary for urging him to come home to her before his work was finished. This time, with three children in the family, Mary sensed a change in Robert's attitude. He had always been a faithful correspondent and had taken care to ask after her, the children, and the rest of the extended household. But now he seemed to long for them in a deeper and more heartfelt way. When he got to St. Louis, he wrote, "Now that the anxiety and excitement of the journey are over, my thoughts return more forcibly and longingly to all at dear Arlington." And later, "I am very anxious, my dear Mary, to get back to see you all…. I dream of you and the dear little children nearly every night." His family seems to have come a long way in his affections from the "aggravations" he had felt after Mary implored him to leave Detroit two years earlier.

When Mary was away from Arlington, Robert wrote to her at Ravensworth and elsewhere. If the letter came to one place and she had already left for another, a trusted slave was dispatched to deliver it. She relished word of her husband's adventures in the biggest city on America's western frontier. With an engineer's mind for detail, Robert was a keen observer, and he described his adventures as vividly as he could.

"Tell Mr. Boo I see plenty of Indians paddling their canoes along the river," he wrote September 10 from his campsite on the shore of the Des Moines River, "dressed in all their finery and blankets, and some not dressed at all…. Tell him I can find no ponies, though I see quantities of squirrels, partridges, hares, prairie hens & etc. as I pass along the banks and shores."

When Mary was at home, she usually had company, and she and her parents continued living up to the Custis reputation as gracious hosts. A letter from one of her Lewis cousins listed other visitors who came to Arlington during just three days of her own extended stay:

> We have Sister Esther and her three boys, Mrs. Fitzhugh, Miss Meade, her little niece and myself. On Monday Mr. Pettigrew dined and spent the evening, and Mrs. Palmer came after dinner. Yesterday Mr. Turner and Mr. Barlow Mason dined here, [and] Mr. Carter who married my cousin Miss Calvert also. Today the Mason family will call and probably dine.

In December, cold weather and river ice brought Robert's work to a halt, allowing him to return to Arlington for Christmas. He made part of the trip by way of the new Baltimore & Ohio Railroad, its wooden coaches pulled some of the time by steam locomotives and the rest by horses.

During the holidays, Robert told Mary and her parents he had decided that being separated as a family for so long was not right and that she and the children should go back to St. Louis with him when he returned in the spring. Thinking of Boo, Mee, and Rooney, he wrote to a friend, "Life is too short for them and their mother to be in one place, and I in another." While it would take her farther from Arlington than she had ever been, the move meant that Mary could keep her husband and children together. Lee was sure he could find decent and affordable lodging for them all in such a big city.

As spring brought the gardens of Arlington into fragrant bloom, Mary, her mother, and the servants began packing up everything the family would need for an extended stay out west. Rather than shipping any of the valuable Mount Vernon antiques, Robert decided to buy furniture for them on the way and have it sent to St. Louis.

While Mary was preparing for the move, a young artist came to Arlington and asked permission to sketch the view of Washington from the portico. Proud and generous as always, Mr. Custis readily agreed. No doubt he was delighted with the commentary on the lithograph of the drawing that went on sale some time later:

> Those who have visited Arlington have never failed to admire the beauty, variety, and magnificence of the prospect that opens before them. We have seen nothing in the United States to surpass it. The Capitol, the President's House, the broad and winding Potomac, the entire City, with the glorious ampitheatre of the hills beyond, are before the eye of a spectator as on a map.

When the time came for the Lee family's departure, Mary and Robert had an unexpected decision to make. Mee was too sick to travel, but Robert could delay his return to work only so long before he would have to leave the whole lot of them behind. They decided to take the two boys with them and leave Mee at Arlington with her grandparents. Once they were separated, Mee and Rooney cried for each other at night. Boo took the whole matter in stride; after all, he was the oldest.

With Kitty along to help mind the two boys, the Lees took the train to Baltimore to visit Robert's older sister, Anne, and her husband. Both the children got sick there, and the stop in Baltimore stretched to ten days. During this unexpected lull, Mary and Robert decided to sit for portraits by William E. West. Lee planned to send the paintings back to Arlington to give the Custises "something to look at" while the family was away.

West was an American portraitist who had recently returned from Europe. Although his work was a success, he could not support himself there financially. It was Mary's idea to have West paint Robert's portrait, but the painter convinced them that she should sit as well. Mary had her heart set on having Robert in his dress uniform, and she wrote asking her mother to send it to Baltimore by rail right away—and to come herself for a visit if she could. "You must pack up directly & come here on Monday," she urged, "& then you will have a week to stay with us. It will only cost you $5.00, as they will not charge you for 'Mammy.' Robert will meet you at the cars...."

West went ahead and started Lee's portrait, and then when the lieutenant's uniform arrived a few days later, he painted in the high-collared jacket and large gold epaulettes. Mary at first wanted her own portrait painted by Thomas Sully, an Englishman working in Philadelphia who had achieved notoriety that year for his magnificent full-length, life-size portrait of Queen Victoria. As a young man he had studied with George Washington's renowned portraitist, Gilbert Stuart, and was considered the most gifted portrait painter of the day. Mary changed her mind, however, and so West painted both their portraits in oil, the two canvases complementing each other: Robert in three-quarter left profile; Mary in three-quarter right.

At thirty-one, Robert was handsome and elegant in his uniform, his face framed by luxuriant black sidewhiskers that extended to his jawline and down over the high collar of his white shirt. Mary, who would turn thirty in October, radiated refinement in a pale yellow silk dress, the neckline trimmed in white lace, the lower part draped by a velvet shawl of emerald green. She wore no jewelry of any kind.

The painting was a marked improvement over Mary's only previous portrait, which she had sat for the year she was married. That picture showed a bland, nearly expressionless face and featured the bizarre distraction of a large parrot perched on Mary's hand—painted there, according to family tradition, because the portraitist could not paint hands.

In West's portrait, Mary's dark eyes met the viewer's straightforwardly; her thick, dark hair was arranged in fashionable side curls and parted in the middle, with just a wisp out of place above one eye to keep the whole effect from appearing too severe. The picture showed a patrician nose, a flawless, graceful neck, high cheekbones, and a square, almost masculine jaw. But for all its stateliness, Mary's likeness also revealed a tension around the mouth and a slope to the shoulders that subtly hinted at her long months of illness and the chronic fatigue she continued to battle off and on.

While the Lees were in Baltimore, Mary attended lectures, did some shopping, and tried to keep the children occupied by singing songs, reciting poems, and reading to them. Kitty was something of a disappointment as a nurse. The slave was very "kind" and "obliging" to Rooney, Mary said, but "she does not seem to be remarkably smart." Mary missed Mee and faithfully asked about her in letters to her mother: "Tell her her Mamma sends her a thousand kisses & has been looking all about town for a pair of garters for her."

At last the family moved on to Philadelphia, where Mary walked in awe through the huge city market, which she visited one rainy morning before breakfast. "I never saw wooden ware kept in such beautiful order," she reported to her mother. "The tubs of milk & butter were as white as snow & the butchers & butchers' boys, of which I suppose there were more than 50 in the market, had all long linen shirts most beautifully white put over their clothes."

At 6 A.M. the following day the family left by train for Harrisburg. Arriving that afternoon at three, they boarded a canal boat for the two- or three-day trip to Pittsburgh, where there was a week's wait for the westbound steamboat. Pittsburgh was a busy metropolis that settlers and pioneers passed through by the thousands on their way to the frontier. Blast furnaces had already been operating there for a generation, and glass factories and cotton mills were well established and growing rapidly. In another thirty years, half the steel and a third of the glass produced in the United States would come from this one city alone.

Dependent on countless coal fires belching black smoke into the sky, steel refining and glass blowing were dirty businesses. The scenery contrasted miserably with the rolling green hills of Virginia, and the Lees despised it. Writing to Mary's parents, Robert described the surroundings as "the darkest, bleakest place I have ever put foot in. Even the snow, milk, and everything intended by nature to be white, not excepting the rosy cheeks of the pretty girls, partake of its dingy nature...."

The boat came at last, and the family boarded—with Kitty riding herd on little Rooney—for the voyage west. The next major port, Cincinnati, was far more attractive than Pittsburgh, and Mary and Robert went ashore to buy household furniture, arranging to have it packed and shipped on a later boat.

Thirteen hours downriver, Louisville offered another short respite from the journey, allowing Mary time to attend a wedding and make a round of visitations. When a steamboat docked in town overnight, passengers who could afford it sometimes went ashore, and the Lees may well have traded the confinement of their cabins for a hotel.

Their vessel was crowded, and people always seemed to be scurrying about willy-nilly. The close quarters and commotion on board were a strain on Mary's nerves; to escape her situation, her husband noticed, she spent a lot of time napping.

Napping may have been the best recourse, if the scenery along the Mississippi was as depressing as Charles Dickens described it in his *American Notes* after taking the same route four years later:

What words shall describe the Mississippi, great father of rivers, who (praise be to Heaven!) has no young children like him? An enormous ditch, sometimes two or three miles wide, running liquid mud, six miles an hour.... The banks low, the trees dwarfish, the marshes swarming with frogs, the wretched cabins few and far apart, their inmates hollow-cheeked and pale, the weather very hot, mosquitoes penetrating into every crack and crevice of the boat, mud and slime on everything....

The Lees landed at St. Louis on May 1. The city was becoming a major transportation hub and was more like two cities in one—the original French settlement with its narrow, crooked streets, and the newer outlying blocks with wide streets, right-angle intersections, and river vistas. A town of 1,000 at the beginning of the century, St. Louis had a population of 15,000 by the time the Lee family saw it in 1838. By 1845, there would be 40,000 residents there.

Immediately upon their arrival, the Lees received two pieces of bad news. First, the boat carrying their new furniture from Cincinnati had exploded and sunk with the loss of all cargo. Second, the quarters Lee thought he had rented were not available. The family would have to make do with temporary quarters until the lieutenant could make other arrangements. Finally on June 1, they moved into part of a fine house at the corner of Main and Vine Streets.

After the weeks of travel, the loss of her furniture, and a month in temporary quarters, Mary was relieved to be settled with the children in their part of the house, which was freshly painted and had a view of the Mississippi. The rooms were small compared with what she was used to, but because they had only a little furniture, it was just as well.

The house belonged to William Clark, a fellow Virginia native, former territorial governor of Missouri, and one of the leaders of the famed Lewis and Clark expedition to the Pacific Ocean. Clark did not live in the house, but the Lees shared it with Dr. William Beaumont, a distinguished army surgeon, who lived there with his wife and three children. Boo immediately made friends with Israel Beaumont, who was nine. Lucretia was eleven and Sarah was sixteen. In typical fashion, Lieutenant Lee began an innocent, teasing flirtation with Sarah.

Though probably not as active around the house as she—or Robert— would have wished, Mary had ambitious plans. She started teaching Boo to read and write, did some painting, resumed her habit of following political issues and current events (her mother sent her the Washington newspapers), and read poetry voraciously: Coleridge, Shelley, Wordsworth, "some French books," and "other little things." She also took up riding, which she always enjoyed at Arlington when she was healthy enough, and wrote her mother asking her to send her riding clothes.

Mary also began to write a book of her own on the life of Washington. Along with other characteristics, she had inherited her father's admiration for his famous guardian. But whereas Mr. Custis had worked on his "Recollections" year after year without ever seeming any closer to finishing them, Mary resolved that her book would be a full, complete, and worthy monument to both Washington and her father. She set up a study in one of the closets where she could write in peace and keep her notes and research materials as safe from tiny hands as possible.

Mary soon found a church, "a large congregation," though, as she informed her mother, "much in need of a good minister" since the one they had was resigning because of poor health. The Episcopal Church had a significant presence in Washington, Virginia, and American politics, but with its French heritage, St. Louis was predominately Catholic, and the Cathedral of St. Francis Xavier was one of the largest and most impressive buildings in town. The number of Episcopalians was growing, however, and they were building a new church that Mary predicted would "be spacious & handsome & filled to overflowing, notwithstanding the Unitarian is considered the fashionable church" in the city.

"The Unitarian clergyman…is quite the fashion & is said to preach very handsomely," Mary admitted to her mother. Fashionable it may have been, but the theology of Unitarianism puzzled Mary. "Capt. Hitchcock…lives here & is a Unitarian so I hear much more of it than I ever did before & am more astonished that any one who professes to believe in the Bible can hold doctrines so contrary to it."

During the summer, Mary endured the heat, nursed her boys through the usual childhood crises, and staved off the threat of summertime diseases—whooping cough, scarlet fever, measles—and an infestation of rats "so numerous that they come up two pair of stairs & make such a noise you would think robbers had got into the house."

Rooney, suffering already because he was cutting teeth, got "quite sick" on the Fourth of July, kept awake by all the commotion and fireworks and afflicted by "diarrhea, vomiting & fever." Being the new boy on the block, the thirteen-month-old had his share of run-ins with the neighborhood. "The children here tease him," his mother admitted, "and he screams at them most powerfully, tho' he rarely cries."

Through letters from her mother, Mary kept up with Mee's activities, and, in her replies, tried to keep the little one from being too sad at being left behind: "Mee must keep up her spirits & think of me out here almost devoured alive with moschetaes [mosquitoes], for they are as thick as a swarm of bees every evening."

At the same time, Mary confessed mother-to-mother that she wished she had some of the slave children with her to keep Rooney busy when Kitty was doing the washing and could not mind him, "for I find it rather tiresome to nurse all day such an unsettled brat, tho' his Father has come to the conclusion that there is not such another child in all Missouri & that he would not exchange him for the whole state."

Mary's youngest was, in fact, turning into "the most mischievous & cunning little fellow you ever saw.... Excuse this very stupid & unconnected letter, for Rooney is playing around me pulling my pens, paper & ink & is now trying to throw his Papa's hat out the window." Regarding little Custis, Mary was considering enrolling him in school in the fall to see if it would "stimulate" him, but she feared the influence other children might have on his behavior.

As much as she had to occupy her time, Mary's thoughts were never far from the green hills and grand columns of Arlington. She even dreamed about being separated from her home: that "the carriage road wound along on the outside of the vegetable garden & that Father & myself were riding & when we got near the corner there was an immense gully or chasm into which Daniel [the Arlington coachman] drove headlong & while we were scrambling out the windows I awoke."

Ever the planter's daughter, Mary took careful notice of the rich Mississippi bottomland, the soil that Robert had once told her could be "cultivated with the foot." It was some of the most productive farmland anywhere in the world.

"I went out to Capt. Shreeve's to breakfast not long since & there was the most splendid cornfield I ever saw," she wrote her mother in August. "The stalks stood as close as possible & he said it would produce from 60 to 80 bushels the acre; but all the soil here is like a rich alluvial deposit." No matter how productive it was, in Mary's mind and heart no land could compare to Arlington. "Yet rich as it is," she concluded, "I would rather a thousand times live in Old Virginia."

On August 7, 1838, Lee was promoted to captain after less than two years as a first lieutenant. This was a doubly welcome advance, coming as fast as it did after his six long years as a second lieutenant and in a time of peace, when promotions were relatively rare. Still it was a mixed blessing: Robert was more torn than ever between his duty to his country and his responsibilities to Mary and the children.

In the past, duty had always come first, but in a letter written on the day of his promotion, Lee mused, "I do not know whether I ought to rejoice or not...as in all my schemes of happiness I look forward to returning to some quiet corner among the hills of Virginia where I can indulge my natural propensities without interruption, and I suppose the more comfortably I am fixed in the Army, the less likely I shall be to leave it."

Late in the summer Mary fell ill again, "rather low & weak," as she described it, though not as seriously as before. Her condition may have been related to her earlier sickness, or it may simply have been because she was pregnant again. She wanted to return to Arlington for Christmas and await the birth, but by the time Lee stopped his work for the winter and could escort her home, the river was too icy for boats to run. Traveling overland in her condition was impossible, so she, Robert, and the boys spent Christmas in St. Louis with the Beaumont family.

It was the first Christmas Mary had spent anywhere else. Instead of her accustomed view down the sloping lawn of Arlington to the Potomac, she saw the Mississippi—empty of traffic because of the ice—and the bustle of St. Louis. Instead of sharing Christmas with her parents and extended family in the spacious rooms of Arlington, she spent it with only her husband and two of her children in a house they shared with five other people and visiting army officers. Letters from her parents recounting all the Christmas festivities at home only made Mary miss "Old Virginia" all the more.

CHAPTER TEN

HOME AND AWAY AGAIN

*A*s soon as warm weather came, Captain Lee began planning the trip back east. For him the challenge was to get Mary home in time for the birth of their fourth child while still carrying out his engineering responsibilities with the level of attention his sense of duty demanded.

By the time she left St. Louis for home on May 1, 1839, Mary was nearly eight months pregnant. The family traveled by steamboat as far as Wheeling, Virginia, then overland by stagecoach the rest of the way. Though it was a remarkably fast trip—only eleven days—the journey was a trial for her. The boys, sensing their mother's discomfort, were fussy and troublesome the whole way. Even with Kitty along to help, Mary was exhausted by the time they reached Arlington.

After only a couple of weeks, Captain Lee returned to his post, leaving his family again in the care of Mary's parents. Though he was called away by his duties, Mary could sense that his love for his family had grown and strengthened as they welcomed more children into their lives. She treasured tender letters like the one Robert mailed from Louisville on his way back to St. Louis, even though it contained one of his frequent admonitions about her discipline:

You do not know how much I have missed you and the children, my dear Mary. To be alone in a crowd is very solitary. In the woods I feel sympathy with the trees and birds, in whose company I take delight, but experience no pleasure in a strange crowd.

I hope you are well and will continue so, and therefore must again urge you to be very prudent and careful of those dear children. If I could only get a squeeze at that little fellow [Rooney] turning up his sweet mouth to "keese baba!" You must not let them run wild in my absence and will have to exercise firm authority over all of them. This will not require severity or even strictness, but constant attention and an unwavering course. Mildness and forbearance, tempered by firmness and judgment, will strengthen their affection for you, while it will maintain your control over them.

In a now-familiar routine, Mrs. Custis and the servants scrubbed down the small dressing room off the south side of Mary's bedroom, and on June 18, 1839, the Lees' fourth child and second daughter was born. Mary named her Anne Carter Lee after Robert's brave and forbearing mother.

Mary was concerned for the baby, who was born with a red birthmark on the right side of her face. She hoped the mark would fade, but it showed no signs of doing so. Robert joked that it was caused by "some *whim wham* of that *Mama*"—referring to the wives' tale that nervous or frightened women gave birth to abnormal children—and nicknamed her "Little Raspberry." Still, he was concerned about how the disfigurement would affect his new daughter's future. He wrote Mary, "We must endeavor to assist her to veil if not eradicate it by the purity and brightness of her mind."

Mary suffered no complications this time. Nevertheless, Robert urged her to spend some time at Kinloch, forty-five miles west of Arlington, where the air was cooler and, they all hoped, more healthful for everyone. Five weeks after the baby's birth, Mary packed up her family for the visit. Mrs. Custis traveled with them, as did maids, nurses, a coachman, and a footman. The master of Kinloch, Mary's cousin Edward Carter Turner, noted the beginning of their visit in his diary: "At night Mrs. Custis & Mrs. Lee (her daughter) with a squad of children, negroes, horses, and dogs arrived."

After a peaceful summer, Mary and her children returned to Arlington. She had started schooling Boo at home before they left St. Louis and now decided it was time to resume his studies and to start Mee as well. With her mother's help, Mary taught her two oldest children in the old playroom on the north end of the house, where she herself had studied as a child. Kitty and the other servants took care of Rooney and Little Raspberry (soon called "Annie" by the family) while the older ones tended to their studies.

Mary and the children fell into a regular routine, comfortable and soothing in its regularity, much like that of Mary's childhood and even Mr. Custis's early days at Mount Vernon. Mrs. Custis invariably rose early (as Martha Washington had always done), and Mary and the three oldest children soon followed. Little Custis—who was gradually losing his childish nickname Boo—along with Mee and Rooney went outside to play under the watchful eye of one of the servants until breakfast. When mealtime came, they joined their mother and grandparents at the table; afterward they adjourned to the parlor for family prayers led by their grandmother.

After the brief devotional service, Custis and Mee followed their mother to the classroom. Rooney was turned over to his grandmother or one of the servants, and another servant took care of baby Annie in her cradle upstairs, in the parlor, or out in the garden. Mrs. Custis was often out there too. The garden was her special domain, with its cuttings from Mount Vernon, Shirley, Chatham, and other places dear to her. She knew every plant, and the beautiful, living reminders of treasured places were among her most cherished possessions.

When there was company in the house, which was most of the time, the children's lessons were likely to be shortened to give them time to play with their visitors and allow Mary and her friends to sit in the parlor, on the spacious portico, or in the cool main hall of the house, sewing and exchanging the latest news and gossip.

Everyone eagerly awaited the arrival of the mailbag, hoping for a letter from Robert. When their expectations were rewarded, Mary or her mother would read their letters from him and then read aloud any part written especially to the children.

Dinner was served in the middle of the afternoon. Later, as the day drew toward a close, guests and household slaves joined the family for evening prayers. After that came story time, when Grandpa Custis entertained the children, and anybody else who cared to listen in, with stories of Mount Vernon, General Washington, and the Revolution. After the little ones were all in bed and tea had been served, Custis retired to his study to answer letters or work on his paintings, while Mary sat sewing with her mother, reading, or writing a letter to Robert.

At times, Mary could tell from Robert's letters that, deep down, he was as weary as she was of moving and having the family separated. Mary and the children had left St. Louis thinking they might go back, but the question was still up in the air. On November 3 he wrote to his "dear May" from St. Louis, "This is a terrible kind of life we lead, Molly, unsatisfactory, profitless & irksome." Then as quickly as he revealed the tender center of his feelings, he covered it up again. "I shall leave these unpleasant reflections and get on to more agreeable subjects."

The letter continued on to more mundane matters: Robert inquired about her father and discussed the market for cotton and the strength of bank stocks. Then almost as a postscript, written beside the address and folded under when the letter was sealed, he returned to thoughts of his children so far away. "I have not mentioned those darling children, not because I have not thought of them, for they are never out of my mind, but it makes me melancholy to think how long it will be before I can see them. Kiss them all for me & don't let them forget me."

After a hard journey down the Arkansas and Red Rivers, inspecting engineering projects along the way, Robert returned to Arlington about six weeks later, just in time for Christmas. He came home to a joyful family reunion and his first meeting with six-month-old Annie. Mary reveled in those days. Everyone was together again, and Robert's stay promised to last indefinitely.

A national depression had hit the country in 1837, and congressional appropriations to finish the St. Louis project were in doubt. Even unfinished, Lee's ambitious project had already removed the threat to the city port, so he had no idea exactly when or if his work there would continue. He was content to resume commuting to a desk in Washington for a while, and even that was interrupted when the bridge to the city washed away and ice made ferry travel almost impossible.

With her husband working in the capital, Mary had some rare and longed-for help with the children. Robert relished the time with his little ones, becoming "a horse, dog, ladder, and target for cannon" as he joined in their play. Walking through the woods one day with little Custis, he looked back to see the boy stretching to put his feet exactly in his father's footprints. Later Lee admitted, "It behooves me to walk very straight, when the little fellow is already following in my tracks."

Captain Lee decided that when he returned to St. Louis, he wanted to take the family with him. Mary and her parents tried to convince him to stay close and help manage the Custis estate instead; Robert could have a hand in the farms and still continue his career in Washington. During a period of illness, Mrs. Custis admitted that she regretted the thought of her only child and only grandchildren leaving again when there was such potential at Arlington.

But Robert knew that his father-in-law and the Custis estate were heavily in debt. Mr. Custis was chronically short of cash and always more interested in painting a picture or making a speech than attending to harvesting, fence-mending, and making a profit. The last two years had been particularly bad; the same financial downturn that had restricted the flow of federal funds to the St. Louis engineering project had put the Custis estates in worse financial straits than ever. Some of his creditors had not been paid in the entire two years of the depression.

Ever precise and conservative in financial affairs and with the shadow of his father's failure hanging over him, Robert concluded, "We cannot live where we please." He told his father-in-law, "If we could and you would permit it, we would locate ourselves at Arlington and I would have $20,000 a *year* to put everything in apple-pie order and make us all comfortable." That was about ten times his salary as a captain, and Mr. Custis continued to spend more money than he made. As far as Lee was concerned, running Arlington the way it ought to be run was a pipe dream.

That being the case, Robert felt that he could neither give up his profession nor advance in it without the "experience and study" assignments like the St. Louis project provided. And if he had to accept those assignments, he now thought it "highly *proper* to be as much as possible with my wife and children."

It wasn't until July that Robert learned that Congress would appropriate no more money for the St. Louis project and that he would have to return there to close it down. The boys had enjoyed all the bustle of the river, pretending to be steamboats and whistling and chugging until their father feared they would "burst their boilers." But Mary had dreaded the thought of returning. She shared her feelings with her friend Harriet Talcott: "[St. Louis] is quite a large place and I have found some very fine & agreeable people, but I am getting too old to form new friends and would rather be among those I know and love." At thirty, Mary wanted no more of life west of the Blue Ridge Mountains. What was more, there was yet another little Lee on the way.

At the end of July 1840, Captain Lee left for St. Louis to auction off his equipment and close out his accounts. After six happy months with Mary and the children, the pointlessness of this final visit made him more home-sick than ever. One summer night, feeling especially lonesome, he went out for a ride and happened upon a yard full of little girls attending a party. "I saw a number of little girls all dressed up in their white frocks & pants & their hair plaited & tied up with ribands, running and chasing each other in all directions," he wrote Mary. "I counted 23 nearly the same size.... I do not think the eldest exceeded 7 or 8 years old. It was the prettiest sight I have seen in the West, and perhaps in my life."

Back at Arlington, Mary resumed her routine as hostess, teacher, painter, student, seamstress, and observer of current events. For the first time in many years, her father took an interest in the presidential election, and so Mary followed the events of that election year even more closely than usual.

Washington Custis supported the candidacy of William Henry Harrison, a fellow Virginian who had earned the nickname "Washington of the West" as a general in the War of 1812. He was the candidate of the Whig party, which sought to return to the Federalist ideals of Washington, Alexander Hamilton, and John Adams and steer America away from what they considered the populist government favored by Thomas Jefferson and Andrew Jackson. During his military career, Harrison had distinguished himself in fending off a surprise attack by Indians on Tippecanoe Creek in 1811. Pairing that achievement with the name of his vice presidential running mate—John Tyler, another Virginian—the Whigs came up with the slogan, "Tippecanoe and Tyler, Too."

Mr. Custis campaigned vigorously for the man he thought embodied the beliefs upon which America had been founded. The Democrats, largely on account of the poor economy after the financial panic of 1837, went down to defeat, and Harrison was elected. Elated at the Whig victory, Custis visited the president-elect on March 3, the day before his inauguration, and presented him with a walking stick made from the old Mount Vernon coach.

Though he was away inspecting forts in the Carolinas when the election took place, Captain Lee had finished his assignment in St. Louis and returned home in October. With Harrison's election, he hoped the government might come up with additional funds for canals, roads, and other engineering projects. Through the winter he worked in Washington, waiting for new opportunities.

Mary tried to involve herself in her accustomed routine as much as she could, but pregnancy sapped her meager energy. Occasionally even light work such as sewing was too much for her. Robert, quick though he had been at times to comment on her "lassitude," was deeply concerned for her health and encouraged her to conserve her strength.

The Lees' fifth child and third daughter was born at Arlington on February 27, 1841, only twenty months after Annie. Her parents named her Eleanor Agnes Lee. The captain admitted that he "could have dispensed with" another child "for a year or two more. However, as she was in such haste to greet her Pa-pa, I am now very glad to see her."

Since Annie was still so young and all four upstairs bedrooms were already occupied, Mary's dressing room-turned-delivery room was transformed into a temporary nursery. After a time, Eleanor Agnes (soon known simply as "Agnes") was moved in with Annie, and the two quickly assumed a shared identity as "the girls." Mary and Robert's room was in the southwest corner of the second floor. Toward the front of the house, in the southeast corner, was the boys' room. Across the hall from the boys, sharing their magnificent view of the Potomac, Mee had a room to herself, known as the Lafayette bedroom because the old general had stayed there during his visit in 1824. Behind Mee and across the hall from their parents, Annie and Agnes had the fourth corner bedroom, where they shared the simple four-poster bed in which George Washington had died.

However President Harrison's budget might have affected the Army Engineers and the lives of their wives and children, Captain Lee's prospects for the future changed abruptly when, on April 4, 1841, exactly one month after his inauguration, William Henry Harrison became the first American president to die in office. With the approval of Congress, John Tyler became president. Though officially a Whig, he was what one later historian described as "a Democrat in everything but name" and immediately reversed the policies of his predecessor.

Mary Lee soon realized that the new president's fiscal policy left her husband with few opportunities for the hands-on engineering assignments he felt he had to have to move up through the ranks. One of his options, she learned, was the North Carolina installation he had visited in November; the other was in New York, where new forts were being built at the entrance to the harbor. Neither place promised the engineering challenges of his Mississippi River work, but the New York site was strategically more important and a big project that would take several years to complete. The long-term nature of this work, plus its location in a big Eastern city that made travel back and forth to Arlington relatively easy, swayed the captain in that direction.

So once again Mary and the children bid farewell to their husband and father as Lee left for New York to start work and find a house for his wife and five children. Four installations were under construction there, two on either side of The Narrows at the entrance to New York Harbor. Lee chose one of the two on the Brooklyn side, Fort Hamilton, for his quarters; from there he would travel by boat to Fort Lafayette, on a reef just offshore, and Battery Hudson and Battery Morton on the Staten Island side.

Mary dutifully began preparing to move her household, but when Robert wrote that there was an outbreak of measles at the fort, she waited for it to pass. She was further delayed by news that their quarters were in poor condition and would have to be repaired and painted before they could move in, though, Robert chided, "a nice yankee wife would soon have it in fine order." He wrote that he would have their new home whitewashed and cleaned but promised Mary that she could supervise the furnishings and decorations. "You can get everything you desire in New York," he informed her, "but they show you so many handsome things that it is dangerous to go in the stores."

When the Lees left Fort Monroe at Old Point Comfort, they had brought their furniture to Arlington and put it in storage. Now Mary and her mother went through it to see what they could use in New York. On her mother's advice, Mary picked out several items for the estate carpenters to repair and recover. Mrs. Custis gave her a few things from Arlington and ordered more from a furniture maker in Alexandria. The whole lot was shipped ahead to New York so it would be there when Mary and the children arrived—no doubt in order to keep her out of those "dangerous" New York stores as much as possible.

In the summer of 1841, Mary arrived at New York with her brood, ready to set up housekeeping at Fort Hamilton with her furniture from Virginia. But before she could get settled, her quarters were commandeered for officers of the garrison, and she had to move her family to a rented house off the post.

The idea that a wife and mother would have servants to keep house and raise her children was somewhat foreign to the Lees' new neighbors, and Robert joked to Mary that they appeared "to have some misgivings as to whether you possess all your faculties." But Mary had been surrounded by slaves all her life, and as far as she was concerned, servants were essential for proper management of the household. Besides, she was the mother of five children and in delicate health. Behind all his teasing, her husband surely agreed that Mary needed the servants.

Mary still felt that her husband was displeased with her parenting skills. Robert had spent much of his time as a father parenting by mail, advising, cajoling, and admonishing Mary to be as consistent and firm as he thought he would be if he were there in person. He even wrote his mother-in-law to enlist her help, claiming, "It requires much earnestness to induce her [Mary] to conform to what she is not herself impressed with the necessity of....discipline will be too lax, too inconstant, too yielding." He begged Mrs. Custis "to *make* her do what is right."

The captain played no favorites, however. From St. Louis he had written his in-laws, then keeping Mee, concerned that they were overindulging their granddaughter: "I hope what may now have a different appearance may in time be laid to the door of her *vivacity* of temper and omit an harsher name."

Mary organized her household in Brooklyn and started teaching the oldest two children their lessons at home. Young Custis took his instruction easily; Mee, whose childhood nickname was giving way to "Daughter"—short for daughter Mary to differentiate her from her mother—had a little more trouble at first because she had never lived away from Arlington before, but she soon made the transition.

As another step toward settling in, Mary and Robert moved their church registration from Christ Church in Alexandria to Saint John's at Fort Hamilton. If New York was to be her family's home for the time being, Mary was determined to have a spiritual home there as well.

CHAPTER ELEVEN

NEW YORK YEARS

ew York was the largest urban center in the United States, with a population of over half a million. Brooklyn, where the Lees lived, was relatively pastoral, with "quantities of handsome country seats in all directions," as Captain Lee described it, and a population of 30,000 scattered over twelve square miles. It was a good combination: a quiet neighborhood for the children with the excitement of New York City close by.

Mary loved bathing in the ocean, and though it was considered a bold move for a refined woman, she took her children to the shore from as early in the season to as late in the summer as the weather and water temperature allowed. Wrestling the lot of them into bulky bathing costumes that covered them from wrists to ankles, she relished mornings or afternoons on the beach, although she was careful to protect her skin from the sun. A milky white complexion was a sign of gentility—no lady would think of exposing herself to sunburn and the implication that she had to work out of doors.

While she continued to dress conservatively, Mary still had an eye for fashion and found shopping in New York a fantastic experience. She didn't buy clothes for herself often, but she could not resist a bargain on clothes for the children or members of the Arlington household. After one expedition into the city, she wrote her mother:

This will I think be my last visit to town, for if I go much oftener Robert says I shall have no money left to take me home. There are such bargains to be had & so many beautiful & tempting articles I have ventured as far as I might...some clothes for the girls...a dress for you...a good many handkerchiefs & some aprons for the White House & would have got more but for the want of space to carry them.

Her mother sent seeds and cuttings from the gardens at Arlington—raspberries, tomatoes, honeysuckle—and Mary started them in her garden in Brooklyn, sharing them with other Virginia friends living nearby. The planting season was a little behind Arlington's, but Mary learned to compensate. Under her experienced hands the garden around her house grew lush and fragrant.

Best of all, for the first time in years, Mary had an extended period of good health. From the time she arrived in the spring of 1841 to the winter of 1842, she rode often, visited the beach in good weather, and took walks to enjoy Fort Hamilton's commanding view of ocean traffic in and out of New York Harbor.

One night on their way home from a visit, Mary and Robert witnessed the arrival from Europe of one of the first and most famous passenger steamers afloat. "We heard afar in the stillness of the night the rolling of immense paddles in the water," she wrote her mother. " We stopped on the bank to listen, & presently a gun & then a rocket announced the arrival of the *Great Western*. How the monsters of the deep must have been amazed at the commotion raised on their elements by this great steamer."

Compared with the trek to and from St. Louis, Mary traveled back and forth between New York and Arlington with ease. Sometimes all the children were in Brooklyn with her; other times various combinations of boys and girls lingered behind with their grandparents when Mary returned to Fort Hamilton after a visit. As Christmas approached, the family all gathered at Arlington, with Mary and the children coming early and lingering into the spring. Robert joined them as soon as his construction project stopped for the winter and then worked at the engineering office in Washington until the weather allowed him to resume his project in New York.

The next year, in 1842, Mary and the children went to Arlington for

Christmas as usual, but when Robert returned to New York, Mary stayed behind, too sick to travel. Once more the captain was alone at his duty post while everyone else stayed at his in-laws'. His only companion was a dog named Speck, whose mother, Dart, he had rescued after she had fallen into the harbor from a passing ship. On March 24, 1843, Robert wrote Mary from New York:

> Speck and I sit each side of the hearth every night, I with my book & he napping…. Bless the children, I wish we were fixed down with them somewhere never more to separate…. You must write soon my dear Mary. I hope you are well again & that you will soon return. I feel very forlorn without you & the house is very cold & cheerless.

Mary rejoined her husband in April, hoping her parents could pay them a visit there soon. Mr. and Mrs. Custis made plans for the trip off and on, but they never followed through. George Washington Custis, "the inevitable Custis," one of the most famous estate holders in Virginia, could not afford the fare.

Even though her parents were absent, Mary enjoyed a great deal of company. She renewed her acquaintance with her second cousin Martha Custis Williams—called "Markie"—whose mother, America Pinckney Peter, was Mr. Custis's niece and whose father, Captain William George Williams, owned the elegant Tudor Place plantation in Virginia. A beautiful eighteen-year-old, Markie caught Captain Lee's eye, as all the pretty young ladies did. With Mary's permission, the captain began an innocent, playful correspondence with her as he had with Dr. Beaumont's daughter Sarah, and other young women.

Mary's Aunt Eleanor, widow of General Washington's favorite nephew, Lawrence Lewis, came for a brief stay. Mary went shopping but found nothing for herself—the fashions were "all too dashing" for her taste. Her aunt had better luck shopping for the two grandsons who traveled with her, though Mary suspected the boys had a hand in the selection: "felt hats…trimmed with black velvet & steel bugles—I believe their own choice."

By fall, Mary was back at Arlington to await the birth of her sixth child.

A son was born October 27, 1843, and named Robert Edward Lee Jr. When Captain Lee met his namesake that winter, he noted jovially, "He has a fine long nose like his father, but no whiskers."

In 1844 Captain Lee was appointed to the Board of Visitors at West Point, his alma mater and the proving ground for the army's brightest young officers. He visited the academy, a short distance up the Hudson River from New York, several times in the line of duty, and in June he traveled there to help conduct final examinations. His abilities attracted the attention of Major General Winfield Scott, general-in-chief of the Army.

A bear of a man at six feet five, Scott was a Virginian who had practiced law before beginning his military career with a personal commission from President Thomas Jefferson in 1808. He had distinguished himself as an officer in the War of 1812 and as an Indian fighter; but his greatest diplomatic triumph to date had been as the leader of the federal troops who peacefully defused a threat by South Carolina to secede from the Union in 1832, when the state claimed the right to nullify federal tariffs on cotton exports.

Also in June, President John Tyler visited Fort Hamilton, and Captain and Mrs. Lee attended receptions and inspections in his honor. Mary thought that the welcoming procession was "a rather poor one & there seemed to prevail among the crowd but little enthusiasm, tho' there was a plenty of hurrahing at the Navy Yard where he made a speech." She and other officers' wives were invited to the commandant's house for refreshments, but because of the crowd, many of the guests sat outside under the trees. Afterwards they all went down to the wharf, where "the boats and crews, collected there from all the ships in the harbor, were ready for our reception & we embarked & escorted the President over to Castle Garden [an entertainment pavilion on a small island off the tip of Manhattan], forming quite a pretty regatta."

It was an election year, and Mary was interested to note that there was little mention of antislavery sentiment or abolition. "Colonization is a subject never mentioned in this part of the world," Mary told her mother; "neither do I hear much of the subject of abolition." In fact, she was surprised that there was so little support in New York for the Colonization Society or any other program to benefit slaves or prepare them for freedom. New York had abolished slavery in 1827 and seemed eager to ignore the entire matter.

The big campaign issue in 1844 was the annexation of Texas, which the Whig candidate, Henry Clay, opposed and Democrat James Knox Polk favored. "We were in Brooklyn last week & there was a tall hickory pole planted at every corner"—promoting Polk, whose boundless admiration for Andrew Jackson had earned him the nickname "Young Hickory"—and a "procession more than a mile long, partly civil & partly military, in which were carried three coons & a bust of Henry Clay crowned with dahlias."

By the time Polk was inaugurated in March 1845, Mary's family was separated in a different way than usual. So often during their marriage, Mary and the children had been in one place while Robert was in another. This time, Robert and Mary were together at home while half of the children went off in various directions. After Christmas, Custis, now twelve, went off to boarding school at Fairfax Institute near Arlington; Daughter and Annie stayed with Mary's parents and continued their schooling with a governess. Lee resumed his duties at Fort Hamilton, and Mary spent the spring and summer with him there, along with Rooney, Agnes, and Rob.

Until the older children's schooling was over for the summer, Mary had only three children to watch over instead of six, and she enjoyed taking them for swims, particularly in the cool of the morning. Agnes loved the water; Rob, still an infant, was fearful at first, but came to enjoy it too; Rooney was his usual rambunctious self, running along the shore and splashing in the waves with delight.

Mary also spent time in New York City and on Long Island, including a visit to Morrisania, a community surrounding the elegant home of Gouverneur Morris, who had been a Federalist and staunch supporter of George Washington. To get there, she crossed over to Long Island at Hell Gate, named for the treacherous rapids that constantly threatened commercial shipping at that point on the East River. There were beautiful country mansions in the neighborhood across the way, and the Morris mansion was particularly elegant, though in need of repair. During her visit, Mary secured the promise of some flower seeds and dahlia roots to plant at Arlington.

Mary knew that four former slaves from Arlington were free and living in New York and, wondering about their welfare, made it a point to find them. She was particularly worried about Cassy, the daughter of Old Nurse, the old slave who had first been a "yard girl" at Mount Vernon and then Mr.

Custis's governess when he was a baby. (More than fifty years later, Old Nurse was still serving the household at Arlington.) At first Mary thought of going into New York herself to find Cassy. But Robert could not find the time to go with her, and she hesitated to go unescorted. "You know what a wilderness New York is," she wrote to her parents in the summer of 1845, "and there are many parts of the City into which it is not safe for a lady to go without risk of being insulted."

Mary eventually found Cassy through another former servant, Lily, whose husband, Eddison, was working as a steward on a steamboat. Lily and Eddison were doing well, but Cassy and her husband, Louis, were having a rough time. Cassy said that Louis had been sick since Christmas and that they had sold everything except their clothing to pay rent and doctor's bills. She was working as a laundress to buy food and cover their room rent of four dollars a month.

Mary relayed Mrs. Custis's invitation for them to return to the country around Arlington, where they could live more comfortably and work for wages until their fortunes improved. Cassy took the steamboat to Ft. Hamilton to visit Mary and spent the night there, but in the end she declined Mrs. Custis's offer. She felt she could not leave her husband in New York, and he was too embarrassed to return to Arlington a failure.

"It seems there is a good deal of *pride* in the matter," Mary concluded, though she was determined to help them if they would accept it.

> She says I must tell her Mammy [Old Nurse] she does not wish all the servants to know that they are not in prosperity. I told her that was all nonsense; to tell Louis from me that I thought the best thing he could do would to be to go on at once to the District, that the journey would be of service to him, & that he could lodge as cheaply in Washington as New York till he was well enough to get employment, & that Cassy could stay with her mother till then, where he could see & hear from her, & that they could all probably get passage in a packet to Alex[andria] for about $10, which sum I would send them as soon as I heard they had decided to go…. I gave her a little money & some few things, as many as she could carry back with her.

In the end, the shame of failure was greater than the opportunity to make a fresh start; Cassy and Louis did not return to Arlington.

That summer, as he had for years, Mr. Custis welcomed the public to Arlington Spring for picnics and dancing. More visitors came that year than ever before, thanks in part to the small steamer that made three round trips across the Potomac from Washington City every day—twenty-five cents a ticket, no liquor sold on board, and no free Negroes or unaccompanied children allowed. Occasionally, merrymakers looking for a free trip to the spring would go to the Washington market and find Lawrence, a slave in charge of the booth selling Arlington produce. If he had room, he would carry them across in his rowboat when he returned to the estate.

In her journal, one particularly observant visitor preserved her memory of an idyllic day at Arlington:

As we approached the Arlington landing, a number of small boats are seen drawn upon the shore, the murmur of voices & music is heard; by which we know that one of the many picnics that resort to the Arlington Spring is in progress. Our boat grates upon the shore, & we are soon on land. Not far above the high water mark is the spring, welling out from under the gnarled & exposed roots of a glorious old oak, some of which embrace the basin of the spring with protecting care; others run along the edge of the green bank some three or four feet high on which the tree grows. The shadow-greened, yet sparkling & limpid water, invites to refreshing drink.

While we are lingering at the spring, Mr. Custis comes to give us a friendly welcome. He may always be found at the Spring when there is a picnic going on. He is fond of talking with the young people & with the older ones, particularly those who are familiar with the events of his young manhood, with whom he can give anecdote for anecdote, joke for joke. He plays some good dancing tunes on the violin, with which he occasionally (when much urged) delights his visitors. He more willingly yields to the request for a speech, for he is the "old man eloquent," & has a mind full of memories that stir, & incidents that thrill.

> He…at his own expense has erected a kitchen & dining room
> & a shed under which to dance when it is too damp or sunny to
> make use of the green lawn that lies near.

Custis also often gave the merrymakers free ice and dairy products and escorted groups of picnickers to the house to see some of the Washington artifacts. The young guest enjoyed her walk from the spring to the portico of the mansion:

> Following the road that passes through the dripping tunnel under
> the Chesapeake & Ohio Canal, by the farm garden & several
> houses occupied by slaves, until, crossing the road from
> Georgetown to Alexandria, we come to the gate that enters on the
> grounds around the mansion.…
>
> As we enter the front door which stands wide open, Mrs.
> Custis, who is passing through the hall, pauses to see who is enter-
> ing, then comes to welcome us. The world around is full of beauty
> & joy; but what is there of sweetness & goodness in this loving
> kiss & cheery smile that has more of beauty & joy in it than air &
> sunshine?

The young lady marveled at the precious Mount Vernon relics and, across the main hall from the family and parlor and dining rooms, the enormous, still-unfinished ballroom piled high with memorabilia, including furniture, uniforms, the war tent, and the harpsichord (which had "reached such a stage of dilapidation that we are allowed to do as we will with it, to run at random over its yellow, loose & rattling keys, banging out sounds"). She also enjoyed the bounty of Arlington: dinner and tea that day, and a breakfast of stewed oysters in gravy, corn pone, biscuits, tea or coffee, and dessert the next morning. After both tea and breakfast, Mrs. Custis rang the prayer bell, signaling all within the house—family, visitors, servants—to gather in the parlor. On their knees, members of the group listened as Mrs. Custis prayed aloud.

"One night when the prayers were longer than usual," the visitor later recalled, "we all got up from our knees but Mr. Custis, who was asleep, with Torm [his cat] on his back, also asleep. Our laugh awakened the sleepers."

For once, Mr. Custis could afford the hospitality he lavished on family, friends, and the large crowds at the spring. A dramatic increase in grain prices made 1845 his most profitable year in many. At last he could visit his daughter and make a long-planned pilgrimage to the Revolutionary War battlefields of New England.

Mary had repeatedly invited her father to visit them in New York. When he agreed that summer, she came to Arlington to make the trip with him and to bring Custis, Daughter, and Annie to Fort Hamilton for the season. They arrived in New York in August, and Mayor William F. Havemeyer honored Mr. Custis with a reception and a tour of the city. The old gentlemen had last seen New York as a young boy, when it was the nation's capital and Washington was president. In the intervening fifty-four years, the city had grown more than fifteenfold. The sight of it astonished him.

Mary, Robert, and little Custis also accompanied Mr. Custis to a reception for hundreds of people who remembered the Revolutionary era. The "child of Mount Vernon" entertained the "aged contemporaries of Washington" with rousing anecdotes, which he told "in the most easy and delightful manner imaginable."

Mr. Custis went on alone to Boston, where he was saddened to see the old entrenchments on Bunker Hill obliterated by houses and streets. "In vain, with patriotic pride, is the eye of the American cast around him...seeking to rest on some reminiscence of the past," he wrote. At Lexington he was pleased to find the town relatively unchanged; he also met an eyewitness to the battle there and sat for a long time gleefully conversing with him. He found a door to a blacksmith's shop with British bullet holes in it and "reverently laid his hand upon the mark of the shot, as possibly, on the day of the massacre, it may have passed through a patriot's bosom." After a turn through Concord, "a neat and thriving New England village," he returned to Fort Hamilton, and then went home to Arlington, along with young Custis, who was returning to Fairfax Institute, and Daughter, who was going with him to study with a French tutor.

The Revolution had taught young America something of the cost of freedom, but George Washington Custis feared that the lesson was being lost on a new generation. In an article for the *National Intelligencer* after his journey north, he warned:

It is most true that while in our colleges and public schools of all sorts, the young Americans are literally *crammed* with every thing that relates to other people and countries, they learn nothing touching their own. [The young American] is conversant with the fame of Scipio and Epaminondas, with Carthage and Mantinea, but has yet to learn of Lexington....

By fall, Mary was packing her family to return to Arlington for the holidays. Pregnant with her seventh child, she planned to stay on there until after the baby was born in February and then return to Robert at Fort Hamilton in the spring.

Her plans changed abruptly on November 24, 1845, when for the second time an accident involving the children cast a shadow over the family's happy New York years.

The first had occurred shortly after they arrived. Annie, then three, was at that intensely curious stage when she seemed to poke her nose into everything around her and pick up anything that attracted her interest. Somehow she got hold of a pair of scissors in the house and, before anyone was aware of the danger, pierced her right eyeball. She was blinded in that eye and permanently disfigured. Her childhood birthmark had prompted her father to call her his "Little Raspberry" and to hope her personality would make up for the abnormality. The birthmark may have faded, but the injured eye was a disfigurement she had to live with from then on.

The second accident involved eight-year-old Rooney. Captain Lee was in New York for the day, and Mary was over at a neighbor's house saying good-bye before leaving for Arlington. Rooney, always the most active one in the house, somehow eluded Jim, the servant charged with watching him while both his parents were away. Attracted by activity out in the nearby barn, Rooney went to watch some men pitching hay for the horses. He climbed into the hayloft unseen and found a straw cutter left there. Mimicking what he had seen the big people do, he began cutting straw with the razor sharp tool.

In an instant, he sliced off the tips of two fingers on his left hand: the index finger at the root of the nail; the middle finger at the first joint. Horrified, Jim retrieved the fingertips, sent for Mary, and escorted mother and son to the post infirmary. The doctor was away. Rooney waited more than an hour for him to return and then manfully endured the ordeal of having the two tips sewn back on. Afraid that he might disturb the reattached fingers during the night, Mary and Robert took turns staying up with him, sitting beside his bed as he slept.

The Christmas trip to Arlington was canceled. Custis and Daughter were already there, but Rooney was housebound for weeks, so the rest of the family stayed at Ft. Hamilton.

Despite the doctor's best efforts, Rooney's fingertips did not mend, and he was left with two short fingers, though to a casual observer his hand seemed normal. Nonetheless, his father was distressed by this second accident in his family. On November 30 he wrote an admonishing word to his son Custis:

See how two have been punished for their inattention & disobedience. One with the loss of an eye, another with the amputation of two fingers.... If children could know the misery, the desolating sorrow, with which their acts sometimes overwhelm their parents, they could not have the heart thus cruelly to afflict them.

Though she missed the great parties and rounds of visits that accompanied Christmas at Arlington, Mary had a wonderful Christmas in her own house. It was "a day of great enjoyment to the young ones," she wrote her mother on Christmas Day, 1845. Captain Lee filled the children's stockings, which the children began exploring at an early hour. "The children were awake at 4 o-clock this morning discussing the contents of their stockings & could not be induced to sleep again so that I feel pretty tired tonight"—and understandably so, after a day riding herd on four of her six children while she was seven months pregnant.

My children here are so engrossed with play that I find it almost impossible to get them to attend to anything, tho' I hear them read every day.... This is a very stupid letter but I am very tired.... I am confined almost entirely in the house & in a constant state of watchfulness with Rooney, whose great flow of spirits prevent his being quiet an instant—& all the children together keep such a clamour that I can scarcely get a moment to think or rest.

I have felt sad that we could not all be together, but thankful that our young ones were all well & Rooney well enough to accompany us to Col. Staunton's where we dined.

The ground is covered with snow but not deep & the weather quite mild. I took Annie & Wig [Agnes's nickname] to church, which was beautifully decorated with evergreens. Mr. Gardner gave us a very good sermon & then administered the communion.

Rob is standing by the table & says I must tell Grandma to get him...a carriage & horses...very moderate requests. He is the sweetest little fellow you ever saw & the most incessant chatterbox."

She had a present for Custis—a box of tools Captain Lee had paid $16 for—but it would have to wait until she could get to Arlington to deliver it. She also had a book called the *Christmas Annual* to bring Daughter. Annie and Rob received books as well; from her husband, Mary got a mosaic breast pin.

Even with Mary and their younger grandchildren absent, Mr. and Mrs. Custis celebrated a traditional Arlington Christmas in grand style. As master of the house, Custis chose the Yule log for the fireplace. It was then carried in by two slaves and placed on the andirons in an old ceremony from Mount Vernon called "Bringing in Christmas." The house was hung with evergreens, the sideboard filled to every edge with fine silver and china and delicious food, and the driveway busy with carriages coming and going day and night.

Mary and the four youngest children arrived at Arlington in January; Captain Lee stayed behind to buy more stone for the construction work at the harbor. On February 10, 1846, at the age of thirty-seven, Mary gave birth to her seventh child, a girl, named Mildred Childe Lee after Captain Lee's sister living in Paris.

There were no serious complications after the delivery, but Mary remained weak and exhausted for weeks. By the time Robert came to visit in April, she was feeling better, but she remained at Arlington when he returned to Fort Hamilton after only a short stay. As he did every year, Robert urged her to leave the coast during the hot summer months for the more healthful air of the mountains and to come back to him as soon as she was able. "I hope you will make your trip up the country at once," he wrote her on May 3, "and then come on as soon after as you can. I am very lonesome & solitary & want to see you all very much. Besides, those 'chillen' can't do without their Papa." Furthermore, he longed to meet his newest child, to kiss her "fragrant mouth & feel that little heart fluttering against mine."

Mary was just starting to pack up for Fort Hamilton when word came that Congress had declared war on Mexico. The root of the problem was a disagreement over the boundary between the newly admitted slave state of Texas and the sovereign nation of Mexico. The American government placed the border at the Rio Grande, while the Mexicans insisted that it was the Nueces River, a hundred miles to the east. American blood had been shed in the disputed territory in April, but the conflict had simmered unsteadily until May 13, when Congress passed a declaration calling for war.

Mary knew that, as an engineer in the middle of an important assignment, her husband would not be called to fight right away, if at all. But as an army wife, she also knew that promotions and opportunity were rare in peace and plentiful in war. The invasion of Mexico was the first significant American military engagement since the Battle of New Orleans forty-six years earlier. She resigned herself to the fact that Robert would want to go where the action was. In fact, within a month of the congressional declaration, Lee wrote to his immediate superior in Washington, Colonel Joseph G. Totten:

> In the event of war with any foreign government I should desire to be brought into active service in the field with as high a rank in the regular army as I could obtain. If that could not be accomplished without leaving the Corps of Engineers, I should then desire a transfer....

To his wife he admitted that he had reservations about the war. In a letter written on May 12, he confessed, "I wish I was better satisfied as to the justice of our cause, but that is not my province to consider, & should my services be wanted I shall promptly furnish them."

Mary decided to wait at Arlington until the matter of Robert's duty assignment was settled; it scarcely made sense to go to the trouble and expense of moving back to Fort Hamilton—particularly with a wagonload of children, the youngest only three months—until she knew what Robert would do. The wait lasted three months more. On August 19, 1846, Captain Lee was ordered to report to Brigadier General Robert E. Wool in San Antonio, Texas.

Robert gave up their rented house in Brooklyn and shipped the furniture back to Arlington. He also returned to Washington to spend time at the War Department and get ready for his journey. Mary welcomed him with a mixture of pride at his patriotism and fear for his safety. Ever dutiful, the captain drew up his will, leaving all his property to his wife for life, to be divided after her death among their children, with special mention of Annie, who he thought would need particular care because of her disfigurement and blindness in one eye. Lee's salary and allowances were about $1,300 annually; income from his mother's legacy yielded about $2,000 per year more.

Mary and the family would live with her parents indefinitely until Robert's return. After all too short a visit, Mary bid her husband a tearful farewell, entrusting his safety to the hand of God.

CHAPTER TWELVE

MEXICAN VIGIL

$\mathcal{C}$aptain Lee began the long journey to San Antonio with a trip by rail to Wheeling, Virginia. He continued by steamer to New Orleans and then sailed across the Gulf of Mexico to Port Lavaca, Texas, along with his Irish orderly, Jim Connally, 66 mules, a group of army volunteers, and $60,000 in government funds he had been entrusted to deliver to General Wool. From Port Lavaca he rode horseback inland to join the garrison in the old Spanish colonial city of San Antonio de Bexar.

Back at Arlington, Mary began the vigil so familiar to military wives—waiting for news and for her husband's safe return home. At the regular morning and evening family devotional times, Mary lifted up heartfelt prayers for Robert's safety.

Once more the arrival of the mailbag from Alexandria became the high point of the day as Mary and the children scanned the pile of envelopes for the captain's familiar handwriting. He was unable to write as often as he wished, but his letters were long and interesting, combining descriptions of the exotic Texas landscape with assurances that he missed them all terribly and could scarcely wait to see them again. He wished that he had his four girls on maneuvers with him "to wrap up in my blankets each night. What a comfort they would be to me…. But I am afraid Millet [Mildred] would kick too much."

Whenever the mailbag arrived with a letter from Mexico, the children sat wide-eyed as Mary read the next chapter in the unfolding adventure: of Robert meeting up with his brother Smith, who was serving in the navy on the steam warship *Mississippi*; of sailing to Veracruz to mount an assault on Mexico City; of tasting battle for the first time after eighteen years as an officer. He described the gun shells, "so beautiful in their flight and so destructive in their fall. It was awful! My heart bled for the inhabitants. The soldiers I did not care so much for, but it was terrible to think of the women and children."

During the summer Mary had all seven children at home, from Custis, now fourteen, down to the newborn Mildred, or "Milly." Daughter continued her French studies, and to encourage her further in appreciating the refined pursuits appropriate for eleven-year-old ladies, Mary bought her a piano so she could take lessons.

The children loved the lawns, gardens, and woods of Arlington and declared them far better than the Brooklyn shore. With the tools he got for Christmas, Custis built a tree house. The older children loved playing with their father's horse, which Robert had left behind in the care of their grandfather. To replace it for the Texas campaign, Captain Lee bought a horse in New Orleans.

In September, Mary received a stark reminder of the far-off conflict. Robert sent word that their cousin Markie's father, Captain William G. Williams, had been killed while leading an assault on the city of Monterrey. He also sent Williams's bloodstained belt for Mary to present his widow as a token of honor and sacrifice.

Christmas 1846 found Mary somewhat distracted and quieter than usual. All the traditional holiday trappings were there, but her thoughts were half a continent away with her husband. On Christmas Eve, Robert wrote Mary from Saltillo, Mexico:

We have had many happy Christmases together & this is the first time we have been entirely separated at this holy time since our marriage. I hope it does not interfere with your happiness, surrounded as you are by father, mother, children, and dear friends. I therefore trust that you are well and happy, and that this is the last time I shall be absent from you during my life. May God preserve & bless you till then & forever after is my constant prayer.

Lee also wrote the two oldest boys, Custis and Rooney:

I hope good Santa Claus will fill my Rob's stockings tonight, & that Mildred's, Agnes' & Anna's may break down with the good things. I do not know what he will have for you & Mary, but if he only leaves you half of what I wish you, you will want for nothing. I have frequently thought if I had one of you on each side of me riding on ponies, such as I could get you, I would be comparatively happy.

Mr. Custis had given Robert a knife and fork set of Washington's to use during the war. At an improvised Christmas dinner for senior officers, Lee set them at General Wool's place and was pleased to see that they were "passed around the table with much veneration & excited universal attention."

In the spring, Mary took some of the children for an extended visit to Audley, the estate of her cousin Lorenzo Lewis. Lorenzo's mother, Mary's Aunt Eleanor, had recently moved there from Woodlawn following the death of her husband. But instead of the relaxing time she expected, Mary was pressed into service helping to nurse Lorenzo through a serious illness. The "high spirits and exuberance" of the Lee children on holiday became a liability as Mary did her best to tend to the baby, keep the other boys and girls outside as much as possible, and comfort Lorenzo on his sickbed.

Despite all she and the others could do for him, Lorenzo steadily declined. Drawing fully on her own limited reserves of strength, Mary worked diligently to prepare his soul for death even as she struggled to help him live. He asked Mary to write his will, which he dictated in a weak, halting voice.

Lorenzo called for his son Washington, a cadet at Virginia Military Academy, but the boy could not reach home before his father died. Mary wrote him the details of his father's last days and gave him some advice. As the oldest son, Washington stood to inherit his father's property, including slaves, and Mary admonished him to treat them with compassion: "Let no motive of worldly interest induce you to act an unkind or ungenerous part toward them. I well know what a trial they are, but think we are little disposed to make allowances for their peculiar ignorance and debased condition...."

Of the sad events that spring, Aunt Eleanor wrote a friend, "Dear Mary

Lee was a most tender & efficient nurse & a source of great comfort to him. Her pure unaffected piety had great influence in preparing him for a life beyond the grave—in his delirium he always submitted to being controlled by her." With Robert's life at risk on the battlefield, Mary must have wondered whether she would ever have the assurance of knowing that he was equally prepared to meet the end and whether she would have another opportunity in this life to help him make ready.

While Mary was comforting Lorenzo, Captain Lee was fighting in Cerro Gordo, a valley town blocking the American army's advance. From there Robert wrote Custis, "You have no idea what a horrible sight a battlefield is." The memory of innocent victims of war haunted Lee. He had come upon a girl standing beside a wounded Mexican drummer boy trapped under the body of a dying soldier. Perhaps he thought of the girls he had seen frolicking on a St. Louis lawn not many years before, or of his own daughters:

> Her large black eyes were streaming with tears, her hands crossed over her breast; her hair in one long plait behind reached her waist, her shoulders and arms bare, and without stockings or shoes. Her plaintive tone of *'Mille gracias, Signor,'* as I had the dying man lifted off the boy and both carried to the hospital, still lingers in my ear.

During the war with Mexico, which ended in a decisive victory for the United States, Lee earned three brevet promotions in five months: to the rank of major effective April 18, to lieutenant colonel August 20, and to colonel September 13. Marked as a rising star, he was transferred to the personal staff of General-in-Chief Winfield Scott. In official reports, Scott described Lee as "the gallant, indefatigable Captain Lee," one who was "as distinguished for felicitous execution as for science and daring." After the Battle of Churubusco on August 19, where Lee led his men in battle for thirty-six hours or more without sleep, Scott described his action as "the greatest feat of physical and moral courage performed by any individual in my knowledge."

Mary knew little of her husband's exploits and honors because he wrote of them only obliquely or not at all in his letters. He never mentioned the recognition he received for his bravery and resourcefulness in action.

Nor did he describe his narrow escape when an American sentry mistook him for a Mexican and fired. The shot passed harmlessly between his torso and left arm. What Mary learned came for the most part from reading official accounts in the Washington newspapers.

In addition to following the war news, Mary kept up with local politics. In the summer of 1846, Congress authorized the return of the Virginia portion of the District of Columbia, which included Arlington, to the state. Mr. Custis was very much in favor of the move. As a resident of Virginia, he could vote in national elections, while as a resident of the District, he could not. Despite his keen interest in politics, the "child of Mount Vernon" had never voted for president.

Mary also read the papers to keep up with the grain market, and she followed the price fluctuations that now, after a couple of years of rare prosperity, were making her father's life miserable. Confident that 1847 would bring a banner market for his harvest in England, Custis had held back as much of the crop as he could the year before. But instead of going up, prices plummeted, and by the middle of the summer he was so deeply in debt that he had to borrow money for basic living expenses.

By fall of 1847 the picture had improved. Though prices remained low, the crop at the White House was so plentiful that he was able to pay off some of his creditors. He also received several orders from New York shipbuilders for timber from "the Devil's Shipyard," the ancient oak forest of Romancoke.

As his longtime financial troubles continued, so did Custis's public standing as a great patriot and living symbol of America's heroic early years. In May of 1848 he enthusiastically accepted an invitation from the Washington National Monument Society to help mark the arrival of the cornerstone for the dramatic marble obelisk to be built in honor of the first president. Originally designed in 1833 as a shaft towering more than 500 feet high encircled by a colonnade and thirty-three statues (one for each state), the monument had been simplified by omitting the colonnade. When finished, it would be prominently visible from the Arlington portico.

On the appointed day, Custis crossed the Potomac to Washington to accompany the twelve-ton marble block from the freight yard to the building site near the east bank of the Potomac. On June 10, 1848, the *National Intelligencer* reported:

The citizens turned out in great numbers and manifested the deep interest they felt in the erection of the proposed monument by spiritedly dragging the stone to its destined place. Among these was observed the venerable G. W. P. Custis, who seemed to be inspired by the same enthusiasm which animated the patriotic citizens who assisted on the occasion.

By September of that year, the fighting in Mexico was over, and in answer to Mary's faithful prayers, her husband had survived. She and the children continued their vigil through Christmas as they waited for peace negotiations to be concluded. Finally, on February 2, 1849, a treaty was signed.

When General Scott returned from the front, Mary went to see him in Washington. Robert had hoped to return home with the general but had stayed on at the request of General William Orlando Butler, the U. S. Army commander in Mexico. Scott received Mrs. Lee graciously at army head-quarters, complimented her husband "in the highest possible manner," and assured her that he would do all he could to return Colonel Lee to her safely as soon as he could. In April the official word came through: Robert was coming home. On June 9, Colonel Lee sailed for New Orleans from Veracruz with Jim Connally and Grace Darling, a sturdy mare he had bought in Texas and ridden throughout the campaign.

Mary's wait was all the harder those last few weeks. She watched with envy as ranks of blue-uniformed veterans, their faces tanned and creased by the Mexican sun, marched from Georgetown to Arlington Spring to cele-brate their homecoming. Crowds arrived by steamer almost every day for picnics in honor of returning heroes. Mary longed to see Robert and to feel his arms around her once more.

As preoccupied as she was, Mary still made time to travel to Baltimore to help Robert's sister Anne Marshall, who was in poor health. She had lost the use of her right hand and then seriously injured the left. She was almost helpless, unable even to feed herself. Mary gave her what relief she could, attending to household duties, encouraging her sister-in-law, and praying for her to be strengthened, uplifted, and healed.

Back at Arlington, Mary received word that Robert, after his long voyage from Mexico up the Mississippi and Ohio Rivers, would take the train from Wheeling and arrive at the Washington station June 29. Mary spent days planning his welcome: making sure the house was clean and inviting, carefully selecting the clothes she would wear, stocking up on his favorite foods, and double- and triple-checking the supply of fresh buttermilk, his favorite bedtime snack.

At last the day came. On the twenty-ninth, Mary dressed in her Sunday best and decked the children out in their finery as well. Custis, nearly sixteen, looking less like a boy and more like a man every day, already talked of following his father into military service. Young Mary Custis, scarcely two weeks from her thirteenth birthday, was cool and austere; eleven-year-old Rooney was still the free-spirited rowdy of the bunch. Annie and Agnes, nine and seven, were inseparable playmates. Rob, four, had spent almost half his life without his father at home and scarcely remembered him. Mildred, walking, talking, and cutting teeth at age two, remembered nothing at all.

Mary laid out Robert's favorite summer clothes, freshly washed and pressed—a special luxury for him after twenty-one months in uniform and twenty days en route from Mexico. Mr. Custis sent his coach to the station, and Mary watched at the window for the first glimpse of it winding up the hillside to the house. As the day went on, every member of the household, sometimes several at once, stood looking for a time down the drive where it disappeared over the hill, watching for the top of the Arlington coach to rise into view.

Hours dragged by, and the coach did not return. Then suddenly, their dog Spec began barking and tore across the portico and down the driveway toward a figure approaching the house on horseback. Everybody had been watching for the coach and had paid no attention to the horse and rider heading toward them. Even at a distance, Mary recognized Robert.

Drawing mightily on her self-control, Mary waited patiently in the front hall, letting the children run up and greet their father first and watching him reach down and scoop baby Mildred up with a chuckle of delight. Then husband and wife embraced; God had returned him safely to her arms at last.

Looking around, Colonel Lee saw a handsomely dressed little boy with carefully curled hair standing shyly to the side. Robert thought he was his namesake. "Where's my little boy?" he teased, approaching the child, hands open wide to grab him, and lifting him playfully into the air. Only it was not little Rob at all, but Rob's friend Armistead Lippitt, who was visiting that day with his mother. The colonel quickly straightened out the case of mistaken identity, but it took a few minutes for his youngest son to warm up to this strange new admirer.

Robert had changed. He had shaved off his whiskers and moustache, which Mary had thought were "exceedingly becoming." As she held him close that afternoon of his return, she noticed that the lines were etched deeper on his face, which was darkly tanned, and that his hair had its first flecks of gray. She did not see these signs of maturity as distractions; if anything, she thought they made him more handsome than ever.

With the whole family together once again, the next few months were particularly happy for Mary. And, as usual, she was relieved to have Robert share the parenting duties for a while. She knew her weaknesses: She was too easily circumvented or finessed by crafty children who eventually got their way. Robert was just the opposite. He insisted on exact and immediate obedience, and he got it. Mary was more than ready to let him be the disciplinarian and take a rest from struggling to execute the parenting advice and admonitions he had sent by mail for months—now years—at a time while he was away.

The children, especially the younger ones, were shy around their father for a while, but he quickly won their hearts. Many mornings some of them would bound into their parents' room, climb into bed with them, and snuggle up for a story. During the day, Mary watched from the portico or the garden as they romped on the lawn together or played with Grace Darling. Robert told the children about the horse's daring and showed them the seven round scars she carried, one for each time she had been shot by Mexican soldiers.

In the evenings, around the fire after tea, Mary listened along with the older children as the colonel told of his travels and the sights he had seen, without ever lingering on his battle experiences. He also read aloud from the novels of Sir Walter Scott that Mary loved, sometimes from the very books he had read aloud in the same room when they were courting. In exchange for entertaining his audience, he playfully insisted that the children take turns tickling his feet. When the tickler became distracted or dozed off, Lee stopped abruptly and exclaimed with mock seriousness, "No tickling, no reading!" The offender and one or two others would squeal with laughter and the tickling—and the reading—would continue.

On Sundays, the whole family went to Christ Church in Alexandria, where they sat in Robert's favorite place, to the left of the pulpit up in the gallery. Independent-minded Daughter made the trip riding sidesaddle, holding her little brother Rob in front. Following them came Mary, the colonel, and the other children in the coach, with old Daniel perched on the driver's box, where it seemed he had been forever.

On July 4, 1849, the cornerstone was laid for the Washington Monument. Mr. Custis, Mary, and Robert no doubt attended the ceremony and heard "the venerable Custis" quoted from the rostrum. A large equestrian portrait by the old gentleman was displayed (to scant applause) in the banquet room of the National Hotel, where the official dinner was held afterward.

Lee spent the summer traveling and working in Washington; his father-in-law spent it trying to get another Whig president elected. Colonel Lee's former commander in Mexico, General Zachary Taylor, was running against Democrat Lewis Cass and the Free Soil candidate, former president Martin Van Buren. The key issue was whether or not slavery should be extended to the territory acquired from Mexico as a result of the war. Van Buren, a New Yorker, was adamantly opposed, while Cass and Taylor played both sides of the issue.

Mary kept a close watch on the election. She thought General Taylor was the best man to reconcile all parties and declared that if the Whigs, with their war hero candidate, could not defeat the disorganized Democrats and the disaffected Free Soilers, "they must be very weak indeed."

Ultimately, Taylor was the right candidate for the time: a popular figure who was opposed to the extension of slavery, but who owned more than a hundred slaves and thought it should remain legal where it was traditionally practiced. In his "rich, full-toned voice," Mr. Custis proclaimed that he, a grandfather, would cast his first vote in this election and that it would be for General Taylor, who, he said, was "much like George Washington."

With Cass and Van Buren dividing the traditional Democratic vote, Taylor was elected. Though he was away on business at the time, Colonel Lee was listed as one of 230 honorary managers at President Taylor's inaugural ball on March 5, 1849. Another name on the list was the "Hon. A. Lincoln," a one-term Whig congressman from Illinois, who had declined

Taylor's offer of an appointment as territorial governor of Oregon and returned to his law practice in Springfield.

Although her father attended General Taylor's inauguration, Mary decided to go only if the weather was nice. She had been to the inaugural ceremony four years earlier and had seen "nothing but a crowd of umbrellas moving along." Two months into the new administration, she and the colonel dined with President Taylor at the White House, after which the old general gallantly handed Mrs. Lee into her carriage.

Colonel Lee and General Taylor had fought a war together; now they each went forward into new phases of their lives. While Taylor embraced the challenges and perquisites of the presidency, Lee prepared for another duty station. Colonel Lee's next engineering assignment was the construction of Fort Carroll, on Soller's Point near Baltimore. Between the fall of 1848 and the following April, he spent time there, as well as in Massachusetts and Florida, where he inspected possible fort locations around Key West.

While he was away, Mary was a single parent again. She told her friends that the details of her life at home must seem dull and "devoid of all interest" to them. "You know what a monotonous life I lead," she confided, "and how very stupid the fitting up of 7 children with winter clothes must make one, & all their little smart sayings are only interesting to a parent's ear." Like generations of mothers before and afterward, she worried that the routine of child rearing was dulling her interests and intellect.

Even so, Mary kept up her active correspondence with cousins and friends in Virginia and elsewhere. She wrote to Caroline Peters, then visiting in New York, asking her to shop for a new kettle and commenting on a salmon-colored dress Caroline had seen at "Mr. Macy's" that she could wear in the fall. Mary also kept up her reading, particularly Samuel Taylor Coleridge and Robert Southey—perhaps the latter's *Life of Wesley,* his biography of Thomas More, or his translation of the medieval Spanish epic *El Cid.*

That summer Mary was unable to do her accustomed traveling because, once again, she was pressed into service as a nurse. Over the winter her father had caught some intestinal disorder he could not seem to shake, and she felt obliged to stay with him. Robert was sick too; on a visit home in July he came down with malaria. Out of concern for the children, he went away to Ravensworth to recover. He was still suffering when he left on official business for New York and Newport, Rhode Island. He asked Mary to accompany him, but she thought she ought to stay with her father.

Late in October, Mary spent a bittersweet day at Mount Vernon. Though still in the Washington family, the old estate was sadly neglected. Walking through the grounds and past Washington's tomb, she viewed the scene with an artist's—and a patriot's—eye:

> It looks lovely & mournful with all the touching reminiscences of by gone days & the Master spirit who presided there & whose image always fills my imagination tho' I never saw him. It was a soft, beautiful day & the falling leaves seemed to accord well with the decaying state of all things around me. But the hero sleeps calmly, undisturbed by the surrounding ruin, & well he has earned his repose crowned with undying glory and honor.

Mount Vernon was not the only estate suffering from neglect. That summer, a visitor from Boston took away an indelible impression of a gracious but seemingly disorganized hostess and her historic but somewhat unkempt surroundings:

> We had tea in the Washington teacups, and Mrs. Lee took me into the tangled, neglected gardens, full of rose-buds, and allowed me to pick my fill of the sweet dainty Bon Silene variety, which she told me blossomed all winter.... Mrs. Lee had the face of a genius: a wealth of dark hair, carelessly put up, gave her fine head the air of one of Romney's portraits. She was most lovely and sympathetic.

It was typical for Mary to use the historic Mount Vernon tea service and share her beloved roses, while being somewhat careless about her own looks. It reflected the priorities—service and relationships over appearances—that had been consistent throughout her married life. With her limited energy, she was forced to make choices; the older she got and the less energy (and more children) she had, the more obvious the consequences of her choices became in her personal appearance and her household. The same visitor also noted a plow rusting in the field and chunks of plaster fallen from the portico columns.

Mary had not been surprised when her oldest son told her in the spring of 1849 that he wanted to be a soldier like his father. She knew that Custis admired Robert's bravery and patriotism and hoped that her son would make as fine an officer as her husband. Her Aunt Eleanor Lewis was a good friend of the president, and she wrote to him on young Custis's behalf asking for an appointment to West Point. President Taylor's reply filled Mary with understandable pride both as a wife and mother. "The son of Col. Lee, whose father has done so much in Mexico in contributing to our success there, and who deservedly stands so high with all who knew him as a soldier, a man and a gentleman, is unquestionably entitled…to an appointment at the Military Academy."

While Custis was waiting for his appointment, Colonel Lee went to his new duty assignment in Baltimore to find a house for his family. Even with seven children, there was plenty of room for them at Arlington. Mildred had moved in with Annie and Agnes across the hall from their parents; Rob joined his brothers in the front bedroom next to Mama and Papa; Daughter kept the fourth upstairs bedroom all to herself, and her sisters seemed content to let her have it. Finding a house in Baltimore with comparable space would be a challenge.

The house Lee finally settled on in Baltimore was cramped—his and Mary's bedroom, he said, was "hardly big enough to swing a cat in"—but convenient to the worksite. The home was still under construction, so Mary and the children made plans to join Robert in the fall. Finally in October 1849, they left Arlington for a new three-story brick townhouse at 908 Madison Avenue in Baltimore.

In a break from tradition, Mary did not bring any of the Arlington house slaves along to help with the housework and mind the children. In light of the high-profile abolitionist activity in Baltimore, her husband had advised against it. As well as Arlington slaves were treated, and as sincerely as both Mary and Robert thought slaves should one day be free, the colonel was still concerned about how exposure to such radical ideas might affect them.

The house on Madison Avenue, owned by Robert's Uncle William Wickham, had the signature Baltimore marble steps, with a long entrance hall running from front to back on one side of the first floor. Four rooms in a row opened onto the hall; bedrooms and servants' quarters were upstairs. Because it was a townhouse, with other houses on either side, only the rooms in the front and back had windows.

Though spacious by city standards, the house seemed dark and cramped to the Lees. The children missed their little individual garden plots at Arlington, but at least there was room in back for Grace Darling, and also for Santa Anna, a pony Lee bought in Mexico and had shipped directly to Baltimore. Spec was along too, as were several of the cats from Arlington that Robert and Mary enjoyed having around.

Once the family had settled in as comfortably as their close quarters would allow, the Lees began to attend Mount Cavalry Episcopal Church. They also looked forward to meeting new friends through Robert's sister Anne and her husband, Judge William Marshall. In Baltimore, just as in Washington, family connections were invaluable for gaining introductions.

CHAPTER THIRTEEN

EARTH IS NOT OUR HOME

*T*hrough her sister-in-law, Mary was soon introduced into Baltimore society. Judge Marshall, who had been U.S. District Attorney for Baltimore, had many prominent and influential friends, including Jerome Bonaparte Jr., nephew of Napoleon. They all soon affirmed that well-read, well-spoken, and aristocratic Mrs. Lee was a popular addition to dinner tables and drawing rooms throughout the city.

The Lee children grew accustomed to the sight of their parents leaving for an evening out. As was his lifelong habit, the colonel appeared immaculately dressed and groomed and invariably on time—many people thought he was the most punctual man they had even known. Mary, on the other hand, had never shared her husband's commitment to the clock and showed no hint of changing her ways as she got older. The engineer and the artist remained of different minds on the matter.

Robert ribbed Mary good-naturedly. As their son Rob later recalled, his father was "always in full uniform, always ready and waiting for my mother, who was generally late. He would chide her gently, in a playful way and with a bright smile. He would then bid us good-bye, and I would go to sleep with this beautiful picture in my mind, the golden epaulets and all—chiefly the epaulets."

Custis, still awaiting his appointment to West Point, continued at school in Alexandria, while the rest of the older children were schooled in Baltimore. First Rooney, and then Rob, began attending a school run by a Mr. Rollins; Daughter started her classes at one of the four "female academies" in town; Mary taught Annie and Agnes at home.

During the spring of 1850, Mary read in the Baltimore newspapers of a crisis in Washington over slavery that threatened to boil over into sectional conflict. California had forced the issue by demanding to be admitted to the Union as a free state. Proslavery forces claimed this would upset the delicate balance established by the Missouri Compromise of 1820, which had prohibited slavery in new states north of 36°30' but allowed it in states to the south. About half of California was below that latitude, and slaveholders believed that having so much free-state land in their region would start a war of attrition that would undermine their right to carry their slaves into new territories.

A Southern convention was scheduled for June in Nashville, and careful observers warned that the representatives who met there would be prepared to commit their states to secession from the Union.

Throughout the spring and summer, Kentucky Senator Henry Clay, who had engineered the Missouri Compromise thirty years before, fought for five congressional bills he hoped would defuse the crisis, including one that admitted California as a free state and a counterbalancing one that remanded fugitive slaves living in free states to their masters without trial or evidence that the claimant actually owned the slave.

Mary saw danger from extremists on both sides of the argument. In her view, abolitionists were impractical and dangerous agitators who trampled both property rights and state's rights, while secessionists were rash, short-sighted people too eager to part with a Union that Mary considered precious and indivisible.

Mary's father made public appeals for compromise, and to show his appreciation, President Taylor attended a ceremony on July 4, 1850, where Custis dedicated a stone in the Washington Monument that was a gift of the city and people of Washington. The day was blazing hot, and that night the President fell ill. Five days later, he died, the second President—and the second Whig—to die in office. Mr. Custis was an honorary pallbearer at his funeral.

President Taylor died without appointing Custis Lee to the Military

Academy, but with help from his father's old friend and commander General Scott, he was accepted before the month was out and entered West Point in July. Daughter spent the summer with relatives, and Annie and Agnes went to Arlington. At the end of the summer, Mary allowed them to remain at Arlington with the understanding that their grandmother would be their teacher. Mrs. Custis, however, reported that the only subject they were diligent in was "cutting up paper into babies & dresses & articles of furniture" and leaving them strewn around the house.

It was the first summer in many that Mary's plans were not dictated by what she thought was best for her children and most practical for herself as a mother—which was, invariably, the familiar comforts and lifelong friends of Arlington. That year she stayed with Robert and their three youngest children in Baltimore, trading the gardens and luxuries of the family estate for the heat, flies, and mosquitoes of Madison Avenue.

There was, however, a little taste of home in the neighborhood, at least in name. Lit by newfangled gaslights, Mount Vernon Place was a quiet public park that featured a small cylindrical monument to Washington, and Mary often took the children there to play. She thought it especially beautiful in the moonlight. When her mother came up for a visit, the two of them went there to watch the little ones run, roll hoops, and play with other neighborhood children. Mildred, the baby, had become "quite a little woman," Mary decided. "She sings a great many songs…and is a most finished coquette."

During their time together that summer, Mary and Mrs. Custis read and sewed during the day, and Mary also painted. With her mother, Mary kept an eye on current clothing styles and looked to her friend and cousin Caroline Peters for the latest fashion news from New York. She ordered "zephyr cloth," a lightweight worsted, for herself and her mother and seven yards of "any little *cheap* trimming that would answer to trim Annie & Agnes' joseys." In the same letter she asked about the latest looks in sleeves and shawls. Baltimore may have had its gaslights and the world's first telegraph, but New York still led the way in style.

In December the Lees took their traditional Christmas trip to Arlington. After the colonel returned to his work at Fort Carroll, Mary and the children stayed on until Robert expressed his concern that Daughter would miss the beginning of the school term. "We must not for our own pleasure lose sight of the interests of our children," he admonished Mary.

Mary, Daughter, Rooney, Rob, and Mildred returned to Baltimore later in the winter. Not long after, Mrs. Custis hired a governess, Susan Poor, to live at Arlington and teach Annie and Agnes. The girls, their parents, and their grandparents all came to like her very much, and she returned their affections. Colonel Lee expected Miss Poor to teach the girls "to write a good hand & to be regular, orderly, & energetic in the performance of their duties…to sing…to sew and knit" and take "regular exercise."

In Baltimore the Lees always seemed to have a house full of company. In April 1851, after visiting Custis at West Point, Robert returned home earlier than expected, arriving by train before dawn. Mary had invited some of her Randolph cousins to visit while her husband was away. So when he let himself in, came upstairs, and tapped at their bedroom door, she jumped out of bed, padded to the doorway, and whispered that he could not come in because cousin Emma Randolph was sleeping in his spot. Down the hall, he discovered that Daughter had cousin Cornelia Randolph sleeping with her and that Mildred and Rob were sleeping with Rooney. "I did not venture to examine farther into the house," Robert wrote Custis of his homecoming. "After a reasonable time we all assembled at the breakfast table & laughed over the adventures of the morning."

Custis got off to an unpromising start at West Point. Mary saw that her oldest son would be compared constantly with his father. But Custis had had a much easier upbringing and was not so accustomed to hard work; nor did he have his father's sense of duty and responsibility. Few men did.

As the end of the 1851 school year approached, Custis promised to renew his commitment to succeed at the academy, and Mary had every reason to believe that his first year would end on a note of optimism. Instead, liquor was discovered in Custis's room, and he and his roommate faced the possibility of expulsion. Custis insisted he was innocent, and an inquiry failed to find any evidence that he knew the liquor was there. Nevertheless, the investigators decided he should be held responsible for what went on in his room, and he received eight demerits. Considering what could have happened, the punishment was light. Determined to clear his name, Custis worked harder than ever and ended his first year ranked second in the class, just behind a Bowdoin graduate from Maine, Oliver Otis Howard.

Mary might well have spent another summer with Robert in Baltimore, but in 1851 her beloved Aunt Eleanor was seriously ill. Mr. Custis's older sister had turned seventy-two that spring and was feeble and frail. Mary took the children to Arlington and then went on with her mother to Audley to help care for Aunt Nelly.

While Mary stayed at Audley, the children played in the woods and gardens of Arlington, spent time down at Arlington Spring, and visited and were visited by numerous cousins. They watched with interest the rebuilding of the floor of the great Arlington portico. Their Grandpa Custis had originally built it out of wood as a way to save money without taking anything away from its magnificent appearance. Now he replaced the wood floor with hexagonal tiles fired across the river in Washington. From the portico, where they often gathered to catch the summer breeze off the river, the children could see the city extending beyond the Potomac and into the distance.

Aunt Eleanor recovered to the point that Mary felt she could return to Baltimore. In addition to Custis being away at the academy and Annie and Agnes taking their lessons from Miss Poor, Rooney was now enrolled in school in Virginia. So only Daughter, Rob, and Mildred returned to the Madison Avenue townhouse at summer's end.

To Mary's delight, her father came for a visit in September. Ever the student of history, he toured Fort McHenry, where a British bombardment had inspired Francis Scott Key to write "The Star Spangled Banner." He also attended a meeting promoting Irish nationalism and gave an impromptu speech. Colonel Lee was surprised at the large crowd the old man drew and the enthusiastic applause that followed his rousing remarks.

Having spent the summer as nurse to Aunt Eleanor, Mary was pressed into service again that fall when Rob and Mildred came down with whooping cough. With the help of their nursemaid Eliza, she restored the children to health. Mildred insisted that her broken doll, Angelina, needed treatment too, and Mary dutifully attended to it by "having the upper half of her cranium cemented on."

As the children grew older and her own parents became more infirm, Mary cherished Christmases more than ever. Clearly, there would not be many more holidays that they would all spend together. Mary invited her parents to Baltimore for Christmas, but they declined to make the trip. Custis had to remain at West Point through the holiday season, so Mary wrote to him about her plans:

I have been trying very hard to persuade your Grandpa and Grandma to come and spend Xmas with me, but as yet without success. If they will not, we shall go down there. We shall all think of and wish for you, when enjoying ourselves together. It seems a pity that in this short life we should be so much separated from those we love; yet all is meant to teach us that earth is not our home, that only in heaven are we to look for perfect bliss. There parting and sorrow are alike unknown.

In the same letter, she admonished her nineteen-year-old son to work hard and pray hard:

Your Papa gave me a fine account of you. One report of you I like not, that you cannot help getting demerit marks. I will quote the reply of the peasant to Kossuth: "Nothing is impossible to him that wills it," only adding that in resisting evil we all need the aid of a higher Power, the author of all our good resolutions and desires, to enable us to accomplish them.

This assistance we can all obtain by prayer, earnest prayer; and why should we not pray to One who is always more ready to hear than we to ask? Why should we slight our highest privilege? Look into your heart, my son, and see if it is often lifted up to Him who made it and who has bestowed upon you so many blessings, far more than you deserve.

Christmas that year was bitterly cold. The family waited more than an hour at the Baltimore train station on Christmas Eve day because the train was delayed by snow and ice. Arriving in Washington at last, they found Mr. Custis, Rooney, and Daniel, the old Mount Vernon coachman, waiting. After exchanging warm greetings all around, Mary, her maid, Daughter, and the younger children squeezed into the coach with Mr. Custis for the trip home, with baggage packed in every available corner. Robert and Rooney walked alongside in the snow.

At home there was a grand reunion with Annie and Agnes. That night the children could hardly be coaxed into bed; they were too excited and too busy making plans for the morning to sleep. Before daylight they were up and about, examining the contents of their stockings. Even in wealthy families, Christmas gifts of the time were modest, and each member of the Lee household got a stocking filled with fruit, candy, and various trinkets, plus a few other toys and thoughtful mementos. Cascading into their parents' room before the sun was up, the children excitedly showed off their presents. Mildred was the most thrilled of anyone with her gift—a new doll to replace Angelina, whose "broken cranium" had led to her demise.

Mary, Robert, Daughter, and Rooney went to church later in the day. Rooney brought his ice skates along and skated home on the canal with friends after the service. Suppertime brought the traditional Christmas feast on the Mount Vernon sideboard, beginning with turkey and ham and ending with plum pudding and mince pies.

Because of the extreme cold, the children and various friends and cousins who visited over the holidays spent most of their time inside. As the colonel wrote to Custis at West Point, "The beaux have successfully maintained their reserve so far, notwithstanding the captivating glances of the belles. The first day they tried skating, but the ice was soft and rough, and it was abandoned in despair. They have not moved out of the house since."

In January, Mary and Robert returned to Baltimore with Daughter, Rob, and Mildred. Within weeks, all three children and Eliza, the maid, came down with the measles, and Mary suddenly found herself with four bedridden and miserable patients to attend to. Robert went back to his duties at Fort Carroll, and his wife once more assumed the role of nurse. Mildred recovered first and was soon hosting tea parties for her new Christmas doll, which she called Jenny Lind after the famous Swedish soprano then on a tour of New England. Rob and Eliza recovered next, enabling the servant to take over some of Mary's nursing duties during Daughter's long convalescence.

May of 1852 brought another change of assignment for Colonel Lee and the prospect of more changes for Mary and the children. Lee received orders to assume command of his alma mater, the United States Military Academy at West Point, where Custis Lee was just finishing his second year as a cadet. Mary evidently looked more favorably on this move than she had on the earlier ones in her marriage. Like Baltimore and Brooklyn before it, West Point would be a place where her family could be together—even more together than in the recent past because Custis would be there too.

Furthermore, it promised access once again to New York shops and entertainment and easy travel by train to Washington and Mary's parents.

Though it was a prestigious appointment, Colonel Lee at first tried to
have his orders changed. Honest and transparent, he disliked military politics and feared that West Point would be a hotbed of professional jealousy,
intrigue, and suspicion. He was reluctant to take the job, but in the end he
humbly accepted the post, effective September 1.

The family returned to Virginia for the summer, while Colonel Lee finished the last of his duties in Baltimore and prepared a new home for them
at West Point. When Mary and the children arrived at Arlington, the gardens were nearing their peak, their color and fragrance enveloping visitors
who walked along the pathways. Little Mildred was only six and scarcely
remembered living in this immense fairyland of beauty and elegance; to
her, home was a red brick townhouse in Baltimore. Sisters Annie and
Agnes, who had been living there with their grandparents, welcomed her
with a crown of red roses, which she wore with delight.

Mary could see that her father was in fine form. The Romancoke and
White House estates had produced bumper crops of wheat, and an equally
good corn crop was on the way. The weather was perfect, prices were high,
and Mr. Custis had had his most successful growing season in years. He
built a new river dock at Arlington Spring so visitors could land even at low
tide. As a result, attendance that season surpassed 20,000—an all-time high.
School children came in groups as large as 300 for a picnic and a swim.

A local guidebook showcased the spring as an inviting stop for
tourists:

Very near the river, rising at the cool of a venerable umbrageous
old oak, is the famous Arlington Spring, to which thousands resort
in the summer months, and where preparations have been made
by the hospitable proprietor for their welcome reception. Small
buildings are here erected in which any articles of the company
may be safely deposited; the best ice is always abundant; and all
conveniences are provided on an ample sheltered platform, with
commodious seats for a participation in such meals or refreshments as the party may have provided. Here are still, retired walks,
inviting lawns, shaded by beautiful groves, and the finest view of

the river and city imaginable. The fine manners and instructive conversation of the venerable proprietor often add to the life and social enjoyment of those who seek from the dust and crowds of the city a few hours relaxation and retirement amid the charm of this cool and quiet spot.

The only sorrowful episode in the idyllic summer was the death of Mary's Aunt Eleanor on July 15. Wash and Nelly had grown up at Mount Vernon, and her death left Mr. Custis the last living link with Washington's immediate family. Mary thought it fitting that Aunt Nelly was to be buried at Mount Vernon, and she accompanied her parents there for the funeral.

A little more than a month later, on August 23, Colonel Lee left Baltimore for West Point. Mary knew he expected her to join him there as soon as possible, but her mother was sick again, and she sensed that their time together was growing short. Mrs. Custis was sixty-four, well beyond the average life span of the day, and had been in and out of ill health for years. The colonel was lonesome, but he agreed that Mary should remain with her mother until she was better.

When Mary finally arrived at West Point in the fall, she found the superintendent's quarters to be a large, comfortable, two-story house with an iron fence around the yard, a stable for the family's two horses, Grace Darling and Santa Anna, a garden with a pond, and a greenhouse, where Mary lost no time in planting cuttings she had brought from the gardens at Arlington. She furnished the house with a red velvet parlor suite she bought in Baltimore and with Custis family furniture. She also brought a good deal of family silver and china in order to entertain dignitaries and other visitors to the Point in a manner befitting the superintendent's wife.

Official visitors were frequent, and sometimes they came with little or no notice. If ten people appeared at the house at dinnertime, Mary huddled with the cook to figure out how to serve them with whatever was on hand. Sometimes the soup was a little on the thin side, but in the eyes of her guests, Mary's graciousness and the elegance of her table more than made up for it.

Not long after she settled in, Mary was brimming with enthusiasm about the new garden she was working on and looking forward to her mother coming to see her handiwork the next spring or summer:

I should be glad to have any seed you have. They can be sowed very late here. I have been planting some flower roots today. We have a very good and industrious gardener & by the time you come, my flowers will be in full perfection & West Point in full beauty. Would I could be with you this spring to assist you in your labours; but as it seems to be decided I am to stay here, you must come on to me as soon as possible. Do not be any later than the middle of July.... Cloudy today, fine time to plant out my roses....

The garden occupies part of our mornings. I have been taking all of the flowers out of the greenhouse & putting them in the grounds.

Mary also went walking along the rocky trails outside the Point, fascinated by the unfamiliar wildflowers that seemed to grow out of solid rock along the cliffs overlooking the Hudson. She even climbed to the top of a local landmark called the Crow's Nest in search of new varieties.

As they had in the past, Annie and Agnes stayed at Arlington to study under Miss Poor. Milly and Rob enrolled in the school for officers' children on the post, and Rooney went off to boarding school thirty miles downriver in New York City. Daughter began at the post school but shortly withdrew and enrolled in Pelham Priory, a school for girls in Westchester County. With a strong emphasis on moral development, the school offered courses in European history, Latin, Greek, and Bible study, along with art, piano, and harp lessons.

Pelham was a somber place. It was made out of an old estate built to look like a castle, and its classrooms had dark stained-glass windows, armor, and carved high-backed chairs. Despite the surroundings, eighteen-year-old Mary seemed to enjoy her time there. She began signing letters to her parents at West Point "Marielle"—certainly more worldly and exotic than plain "Mary."

The colonel could not leave West Point during Christmas that year, and Mary remained at the Point with him to take charge of the holiday entertaining expected of the Superintendent. Rooney and Daughter joined them, leaving only Annie and Agnes, still with their grandparents, missing from the family picture.

On Christmas night, Mary hosted a "little party" of about thirty cadets and the young ladies who lived at the Point. At nine in the evening they gathered in the superintendent's quarters for a supper of cold turkey, ham, olio, stewed oysters, pheasants, lemonade, ice cream, jellies, and cakes. With garlands festooning the hallways and mantels, youthful laughter filling the house, lamps and candles shining in every room, and the family silver gleaming on the sideboard and dining table, it must have seemed to Mary as much like Christmas at Arlington as possible.

Though they missed their family and looked forward to spending the summer at West Point, Annie and Agnes had a wonderful Christmas with their grandparents. They were up at twenty minutes to five, digging into their stockings and trying to be the first among all the children, including the black ones sharing in the festivities, to shout, "Christmas gift!"—meaning that the others were supposed to offer a present. They also enjoyed playing with Grandpa Custis, who allowed them to pretend that they were Indians exploring the large, still-unfinished ballroom and to make houses and stables from his paintings and the old Mount Vernon furniture.

As spring approached, Mrs. Custis's health continued to decline, and Mary encouraged her parents to come to West Point for the summer so she could continue her duties as official hostess while looking after her mother. To her surprise, they agreed, and Mary immediately began making plans to meet them in New York for several days of sightseeing.

It was not to be. On Sunday, April 24, Mary received a telegram telling her that her mother was gravely ill and to come to Arlington immediately. She left West Point by train for New York, changed there for Washington, and after traveling through the night Monday, arrived at Arlington before breakfast Tuesday morning. She came too late. Mary Lee Fitzhugh Custis had died early Sunday morning, a little more than a day after her sixty-fifth birthday.

On Thursday, she had complained of a headache. Headaches were not uncommon for her, and when the doctor examined her the next day, he said that it was nothing life threatening—perhaps a mild stroke. One day later the doctor was back, and this time his diagnosis was completely different: She was fatally ill, with possibly only hours to live. Mr. Custis summoned his daughter from West Point, both by letter and by telegram.

Mary's mother knew that the end was near. Asked if she had any message for her daughter, she said that she was concerned at "how terribly she will be shocked when she hears this." Seeing Annie and Agnes hovering in her doorway, frightened, confused, and in tears, Grandma Custis motioned them to come to her and had them climb up onto her bed.

The household servants stood around their mistress weeping. As her husband knelt on the floor beside her bed in prayer, Mrs. Custis tried to comfort Annie. "How can you cry so?" she asked weakly. As her breathing grew ragged and faint, she recited the Lord's Prayer softly. The next breath was shallower than the one before, the next one shallower still, and then there were no more. It was 1:20 on Sunday morning.

To twelve-year-old Agnes, it was all like a bad dream. A few days later in her journal she wrote, "How lonely it is to feel you haven't a Grandma any more. I know she died a Christian & to think she is with our Savior in Heaven. They tell me we must not wish her back, but this is the first person I loved that has ever been taken from me & it will seem so hard."

Old Mr. Custis was paralyzed with grief, incapable even of deciding where his wife should be buried. Mary took charge. As soon as breakfast was over, she rang the bell her mother had used nearly every day of her married life to signal that daily prayers were about to begin in the parlor. In a remarkable show of self-control, she gathered the family and servants for a brief service. Then she went out into the garden, among the new light-green leaves and flower buds of spring, to select a burial site.

Just beyond the flower garden, which Mary could see from her bedroom, was a gentle slope descending to the river. She picked a spot there. Because her father was so shocked by his sudden loss, Mary decided that the funeral would be private, attended only by members of the extended family and servants. The day after her arrival, the service was conducted in the front hall of the house. Four slaves, including the old coachman Daniel and Mrs. Custis's favorite gardener, Ephraim, carried the casket from the house to the gravesite.

Before the service, Mary had gathered bouquets of spring flowers from the garden; now she handed them out to onlookers as they formed a procession. She and the girls walked immediately behind the coffin, followed by relatives and servants. As the casket was lowered into the grave, Mary threw her flowers on top of it—the sight of flowers always reminded her of her mother—and the other mourners followed suit.

Mr. Custis stayed inside, too distraught to go to the graveside. "How changed is her recent home," wrote the anonymous author of his wife's obituary, who was very likely Custis himself:

> The stately mansion is still there: the lofty halls, the hospitable board; the park, the lawn, the beautiful garden, the pleasant walks; the trees, the shrubs, and the flowers she loved so well are still there, decked in green, and blooming in all their wonted fragrance and beauty…. The venerable bereaved husband is there, but he feels that he is *alone*.

In its fifty years, Arlington had had only one mistress; now Mary had somehow to assume her mother's role. Mary Custis Lee was the new lady of Arlington.

CHAPTER FOURTEEN

BLESSINGS
AND BURDENS

ith her husband busy at West Point until the end of the school year, Mary took sole responsibility for her father and for managing the household in the two months following her mother's death.

On June 21, Mary served as hostess when Mr. Custis received a condolence call from the president of the United States and his wife. In March, Custis had attended the inauguration of Franklin Pierce, a Democrat who had beaten the Whig candidate, Colonel Lee's old mentor General Winfield Scott, by promising to uphold the Compromise of 1850. No doubt Mary returned the Pierces' sympathy at her recent loss with comforting words of her own. In January the president's eleven-year-old son, Benjamin, the only one of his three children to survive infancy, had been killed in a train wreck.

Pierce's years in office were marked by great prosperity for the nation as a whole, and in the first half of 1853, Mr. Custis had been able to pay off some of his debts and make a few improvements to the estate. About the time his wife died, however, he realized that the year was not going to be as prosperous as he had hoped. His loneliness made his financial difficulties all the more worrisome.

"Weak and dispirited as I am," he wrote his overseer at the White

House plantation, with slight exaggeration, "these [financial] disappoint-
ments annoy me very much. I have not to accuse myself of any extrava-
gance—I have not owned a saddle horse to ride for 6 years—I have not
drove a nail into my unfinished house."

Mary lovingly supported her father and did as much possible in the
midst of her own bereavement to ease the emotional strain on him. She was
at a loss, though, to know how to help him with his financial affairs. As a
woman, she was not privy to her family's financial details; as her father's
daughter, the details she knew sometimes simply escaped her.

That summer something else commanded Mary's attention—something she considered much more interesting and important than account
books.

Waiting as patiently as she could for Robert to arrive from West Point,
Mary had taken comfort from his touching expressions of solace. One letter
in particular gave her hope that her mother's death had been a catalyst for
deepening Robert's commitment to Christ. He wrote:

> May God give you strength to enable you to bear and say, "His will
> be done." She has gone from all trouble, care and sorrow to a holy
> immortality, there to rejoice and praise forever the God and
> Saviour she so long and truly served. Let that be our comfort and
> that our consolation. May our death be like hers, and may we meet
> in happiness in Heaven.

Early in July 1853, Robert arrived, bringing Mildred and Rob with
him. Soon after, Rooney and Daughter joined the family from their respective schools. On July 17, the Lees went to Christ Church in Alexandria, as
they did most Sundays when they were in town. This Sunday was one of
the most glorious days of Mary's life: Robert had decided to be confirmed.

It was the answer to prayers that Mary had begun lifting up even before
she and Robert had become engaged. His mother had been a woman of
unquestioned faith and piety, and Robert certainly was a kind, reverent
man. He had always been a faithful churchgoer and had even served on the
vestry at Fort Hamilton. Still, the question had lingered—burned—inside
her: *Had her husband given his life to Christ? Had he been born again as she
had?*

Now there was no doubt in her mind. That Sunday, Bishop John Johns, the Episcopal bishop of Virginia, delivered a sermon on the text, "And Simon Peter answered him, Lord to whom shall we go? Thou hast the words of eternal life." It was an unequivocal call to Christ. After the sermon, along with Annie and Daughter, Robert went forward, knelt at the communion rail, and was confirmed by Bishop Johns. Mary's husband was now, without a doubt, one of God's own. If anything could have offset the pain and emptiness of losing her mother, this was it.

After a round of summer visits, including a trip to Ravensworth, Mary and the family returned to West Point. She even convinced her father to leave a neighbor in charge of his estate and accompany them. The children said good-bye to their pet rabbits, snug in their new pen in the garden, and everyone walked over to Mrs. Custis's grave for one last visit, gathering flowers along the way to decorate the site. Agnes knelt to kiss the ground, which, she wrote in her diary, "returned not my affection, so I walked sadly away."

The family took the express train to Baltimore and spent several days with Lee's sister Anne before continuing on by rail to New York. From there they went by river steamer to West Point. Mary had her maid Eliza with her, and with help from the girls, they soon had the house in order for the round of receptions and dinners that would mark the beginning of the new school year.

Along with her duties as the superintendent's wife, Mary had to contend with three very homesick members of the household: Annie and Agnes, who had lived the last two years with their grandparents, and her father, who, it seemed, spent every waking moment wondering what was going on at home. Wet weather had made hay scarce, and he was worried about fodder for his livestock. A railroad was being planned to Leesburg, and he fretted about his plans to sell some parcels of land for the right-of-way.

Hoping to distract his father-in-law from Arlington matters, Robert took him to Niagara Falls; later in the summer, Mary escorted him to New York for a few days of sightseeing. She planned to travel with him back to Arlington in November, but the old gentleman could not wait. Before September was out, he had written the coachman to meet him in Washington and had gone home on the train alone.

The Lees spent the Christmas holidays at West Point. Even in winter the Point was a beautiful place. The superintendent's house was near the middle of a row of houses facing the parade ground, with cliffs rising up majestically behind them. Nearby were several walkways and overlooks where sightseers could look across the river and see a magnificent landscape covered with a blanket of snow miles across, soft and shimmering in the winter sun.

Mary celebrated Christmas surrounded by her husband, her children, and dozens of cadets and young ladies grateful for the warm yet elegant dinners and receptions she gave. Some of the most popular were a Christmas Eve party and, later in the week, a buffet supper with games for schoolchildren. With help from Eliza and a local hired cook, Mary oversaw decorating the Christmas tree and the preparation of one grand meal after another.

Among the cadets Mary entertained that season, a number would go on to distinguished careers, though not necessarily military ones. Custis's classmates Jeb Stuart, John Pegram, Archie Grace, and Otis Howard became generals; James McNeill Whistler, whose friends called him "Curly," lasted two years before being dismissed for poor academic performance and too many demerits, though he was first in his art class.

True to tradition, the children were up before daylight on Christmas Day, with seven-year-old Mildred bounding into her older sisters' bed at four in the morning. Christmas was on a Sunday that year, so even Custis was able to spend the time with the family. At dinner, Mary could look down the table and see her husband and every one of her children, laughing, exchanging stories, and joyfully celebrating the season together.

Later during the winter, Mary nursed Mildred through another bout with whooping cough and did her best to soothe a rather grumpy Daughter, who had a serious foot injury that kept her from ice skating, riding, or even walking outside. Agnes was homesick for Arlington, especially after her cousin Markie Williams, who was living there for the winter, sent her pressed crocuses from the garden. Agnes also longed for the "dear old servants," her pet bunnies, chickens, cats, pigeons, and "in fact everything in & near home."

In May, Mary took Mildred and Daughter (using crutches and wearing a buckskin boot) with her to Arlington to help her father prepare for a trip to Europe, where he planned to visit the Marquis de Lafayette's home at La

Grange, France. Mr. Custis finally seemed to have recovered from the shock of his wife's death and was making public appearances again. He dined at the White House, where he presented President Pierce with the British and Hessian colors surrendered at Trenton and Yorktown. He suggested they be displayed at the Patent Office with other war memorabilia. Eventually, despite the enthusiastic preparations he had made, the old gentleman decided he could not make an ocean voyage and canceled his plans.

By summer's end the Lees were back at Arlington, and with the approach of another school year, they organized a caravan to transport Daughter, still crippled by her mysterious foot ailment, back to the Point. The colonel and Rooney carried her to the train, Annie carried her crutches, and Agnes carried everybody's coats. At every station where they changed trains, they created a sensation as the conductor, seeing the invalid, called for porters. As Agnes later wrote, "Instantly two or three great men would rush up & lift us, cloaks, crutches, dogs & people up or down whether we would or no." Mary avoided this circus train and came along later with her father and Mildred.

Though Mr. Custis was restless at times during his trip to the Point, Mary had a pleasant visit with him while she continued her established routine of entertaining, sewing, reading, painting, and daily Bible study and prayer, including morning prayer at the post chapel.

Robert had to be at his desk at seven, so breakfast was at six-thirty. The colonel was punctual as ever; Mary, as ever, was less concerned about the time. The difference between husband and wife was always obvious but never a cause for discord. As their son Rob wrote later about the West Point years:

> My father was the most punctual man I ever knew. He was always ready for family prayers, for meals, and met every engagement, social or business, at the moment. He expected all of us to be the same.... I never knew him late for Sunday service at the Post Chapel. He used to appear some minutes before the rest of us, in uniform, jokingly rallying my mother for being late, and for forgetting something at the last moment. When he could wait no longer for her, he would say that he was off and would march along to church by himself, or with any of the children who were ready.

In June, Custis graduated first in the West Point Class of 1854 and was assigned to the Chief Engineer's Office in Washington, where his father had served. Mary was doubly pleased: first, that her oldest son was first in his class and, second, that he would be able to live at Arlington and look after his grandfather while she tended to her duties at the Point.

When Lieutenant Custis Lee escorted his grandfather home from West Point to Arlington in October, the old gentleman found an unpleasant surprise waiting: an overdue lien for almost a thousand dollars from a man he had never met. Both the debt and its late payment were the fault of a former manager of the estate, Francis Nelson. When he thought he would be traveling to Europe, Mr. Custis had asked Robert to help him sort out the estate books. Lee had suggested then that he hire an accountant, but the books were still a muddle. Now Robert again suggested that his father-in-law hire a professional accountant and warned him to get a careful and complete reckoning from Nelson, whose accounts had not been reconciled in eleven years.

That fall, five Lee children were at home at West Point: Rob and Mildred, attending the post school; Annie and Agnes, continuing their studies with tutors; and daughter Mary, still hampered by her injured foot. Custis was in Washington, and Rooney, unable to secure an appointment to West Point, had enrolled at Harvard College.

Mary hosted Christmas parties at West Point for another season, followed by New Year's celebrations and an elaborate Valentine's Day party. Her sympathy for the young, homesick cadets and the acclaim she received as a hostess prompted her to have more parties than ever. In fact, Agnes confided in her journal, "We have had so many, averaging more than one a week, that the whole family are heartily sick of them."

Well into her third year at the Point, Mary had much for which to be thankful. Her husband was successful and content in his duties; her father had recovered from her mother's death; her children (with the possible exception of independent, strong-willed Daughter) were growing up filled with a sense of purpose and Christian responsibility; her own success as official hostess and surrogate cadet mother was assured; and her health—so precarious during her childbearing years—was by all accounts remarkably good.

Then, in the spring of 1855, Colonel Lee received a new assignment from President Pierce's secretary of war, Jefferson Davis. To protect settlers on the Western frontier, Congress had authorized two cavalry regiments, and Davis appointed Lee second in command of the Second Cavalry. The transfer meant changing from a staff position to an officer of the line. For the first time in twenty-five years of military service, Lee would command a fighting unit.

The colonel seemed to be of two minds about the change. On one hand, he wrote Markie Williams at Arlington: "The thought that my presence may be important to or necessary to my children is bitter in the extreme. Still, in a military point of view I have no other course, and when I am obliged to act differently, it will be time for me to quit the service." On the other hand, he admitted, "The change from my present confined & sedentary life, to one more free & active, will certainly be more agreeable to my feelings & serviceable to my health." For Mary, the change meant that once more she and the children would be separated indefinitely from their husband and father.

Lee was relieved of his command at West Point on March 31, and the family left a week or so later. Mary supervised packing up the household. She cleaned out the house from top to bottom so that on the last night nothing was left but the beds. Friends stopped in to say good-bye, and the entire cadet corps surprised them with a visit to wish them well, singing their renditions of "Home Sweet Home" and "Carry Me Back to Old Virginny."

As much as the family had missed Arlington, it was hard to bid farewell to their friends at the Point. Annie and Agnes had once cried for the sight of their grandmother's garden; the day they boarded the open boat on the Hudson to go back there, they cried for the Academy as they took one last look at it through the pouring rain.

The family spent several days sightseeing in New York and then visited Robert's sister in Baltimore, where they also saw old friends from their days in the Madison Avenue townhouse. Daughter Mary stayed on with her Aunt Anne, and the rest of the family continued toward home. Old Daniel was waiting for them at the train station in Washington. As the coach turned up the familiar drive, Agnes expressed what they all felt: "It seemed an age before we dashed around the garden fence. I sprang out on the steps, kissed Grandpa & Cousin Markie, ran out to tell the servants how d'ye do & then wandered all over the house."

With her husband leaving and her father feeble, much of the responsibility for maintaining Arlington fell to Mary. Seeing that matters would be in the hands of two people he knew all too well, and whose artistic and literary skills far outweighed their understanding of or interest in accounting and management, Robert arranged to make matters as easy as possible for Mr. Custis and Mary while he was away.

Recently, and especially since Mrs. Custis's death, the Arlington house had deteriorated considerably, and Robert now did some refurbishing. Lee himself paid for all of it, even before it was completed. It was his way of honoring his mother-in-law, thanking his father-in-law for housing his wife and children, and making everyone more comfortable in his absence.

Robert made plans to finish off the big room to the left of the front hall where Mount Vernon relics had been stored for more than thirty-five years. Originally it was to have been a ballroom, but Mr. Custis had never followed through with his plan. Now Robert transformed it into an elegant parlor. He also ordered a new furnace for the house and designed and ordered a monument for Mrs. Custis's grave—a plinth of marble, "perfect in every respect," carved with a wreath of her favorite flowers, heartsease and lilies of the valley.

The lilies in Arlington's garden were particularly beautiful that spring. Mary had cultivated cuttings from Arlington the whole time she lived at West Point, and now she was surrounded once more by the flowers that reminded her so of her mother. Besides the lilies of the valley, there were white lilacs and fragrant honeysuckle perfuming the air, locust blossoms, bluebells, mock oranges, and the fruit trees in bloom between the house and the river. And of course there were roses of every color and description, including her favorite, the moss rose.

Once again the children had their own plots for growing their favorite things. Agnes pitched in with an enthusiasm worthy of her mother and grandmother, even—to cousin Markie's dismay—manuring the beds herself. With the help of other servants, including "swarms of small Ethiopians" weeding, hoeing, and trimming, the old gardener, Ephraim, carefully tended the flower gardens, kitchen garden, and lawn.

On April 18, 1855, Lee, now a lieutenant colonel in the cavalry, left for Louisville, Kentucky, to join his regiment. He was appointed temporary commander in the absence of Colonel Albert Sydney Johnston, who, once he arrived, would be Lee's superior officer. Before Robert left Arlington, Mr. Custis presented him with George Washington's service sword. Mary's father had planned to leave it to him in his will, but he decided that Robert should have it for his first field command.

Mary took over the household, watching with satisfaction as the workmen repaired and painted the walls of her beloved home and installed new marble mantels from New York in the parlor. She had a refreshing sense of self-sufficiency at being able to live largely off the bounty of the fields and gardens of the Custis estates, instead of depending on merchants as she had at West Point, where everything was "enormously high": beef 15¢ a pound and "very indifferent," eggs 25¢ a dozen, with other groceries in proportion. Furthermore, there were plenty of slaves to manage all the work, whereas she had paid her waiter at West Point $18 a month and the cook half that amount.

Mary continued the family tradition of teaching the children of slaves to read. She resumed classes in the same room on the north end of the house where she herself had learned as a young girl and where she had once taught her own children and their generation of "little black scholars." Annie and Agnes did most of the teaching now: reading, writing, and spelling, though they thought that their little pupils weren't always quite as attentive as they should be.

In addition to the usual array of visitors during the summer, Mary and her father received visits from several West Point graduates who stopped by to pay their respects to their former commandant's family. The colonel's brother Smith, just returned from naval duty with Commodore Matthew Perry in Japan, came as well, bearing an exotic Oriental tray for Mary, kimonos and lacquered boxes for the girls, and a Chinese kite for Rob.

It rained that Fourth of July, so Mary and the children elected to stay home and watch the annual Washington fireworks from the portico. Only Mr. Custis braved the storm to cross the Potomac and attend the festivities in person. Sitting on cushions and shawls, the others watched expectantly from their hillside perch for the traditional display. But except for a few weak fizzles, the fireworks failed on account of the dampness.

The family had enjoyed a more successful outing in June, when Mary took the younger children with her to visit her Stuart cousins at Cedar Grove, a large plantation sixty miles downriver, a five-hour steamer voyage.

Mary had taught her children by word and deed to treat slaves humanely, and they were disturbed by the demeaning way Cedar Grove slaves were treated. In a letter, Annie reported with astonishment that slaves were commanded to carry passengers ashore from the riverboat on their backs. Even her host, "over six feet and quite stout," was ferried to dry land from the shallows "on the back of a rather small Negro."

Returning to Arlington after a ten-day visit, Mary hired dressmakers from Washington to come over and make up travel wardrobes for Annie and Agnes. She had decided to send them away to school and wanted them to look their best. On September 12, Daughter, back from Baltimore, escorted her sisters by carriage to Alexandria, where they joined three cousins and various members of their families for a journey down the Shenandoah Valley to the Virginia Female Institute in Staunton.

This highly regarded school, run by Mr. and Mrs. Daniel Sheffey with oversight from the Episcopal Diocese of Virginia, was popular with aristocratic families throughout the South. Tuition and board was $240 per year, plus $60 for piano lessons, $20 for art and each foreign language, and $2.50 annual pew rent at Trinity Episcopal Church two blocks away.

Meanwhile, back at home, at her husband's suggestion, Mary put Daughter in charge of teaching Rob and Milly. Lee expected that his oldest girl would chafe at the task—Daughter was developing into an impatient sort. In a letter to Mary about the matter, Robert wrote, "She must exert her self control & ingenuity by making it agreeable as well as instructive.... As much can be accomplished by the *suaviter in modo* [gentleness in manner] as the *fortier in re* [resoluteness in action]."

Robert's letters—first from Louisville, then from St. Louis, then from Kansas—reinforced Mary's assurance that his public profession of faith in Alexandria had been genuine and that his spiritual life now had a deeper, richer cast. He confided:

I am content to read my Bible & prayers alone & draw much comfort from their holy precepts & merciful promises, though I feel unable to follow one, & utterly unworthy of the other. I must still pray to that glorious God, without whom there is no help, & with whom there is no danger. That He may guard & protect you all, and more than supply you in my absence, is my daily & constant prayer.

When the Second Cavalry was posted to Texas, Mary braced herself for a long separation, though she expected it to be less of a trial than earlier stretches of single parenting. Mildred, the youngest, was almost ten now, and the three oldest children were grown—a far different family landscape than during the Mexican War years, when she had all seven to look after without a father in the house.

It was a pleasant surprise for Mary when, before reporting to his Western post, Robert received orders to sit on a series of courts-martial in locations that gave him a chance to visit Arlington. He arrived on November 27, and Mary and her father, with the children trailing behind them, proudly showed off the refurbishing that had been done throughout the house. There was new paint and plastering, new heart of pine floors, and, of course, the new parlor. The room was furnished with the red velvet furniture Mary had bought in Baltimore and a collection of Arlington pieces, including a cup and saucer from General Washington's state china. A houseguest of the time pronounced it "a beautiful & noble drawing room, very handsomely furnished."

Annie and Agnes came home for Christmas. Over the past three years, Mary had seen her two middle daughters transformed from gangly pre-teens—all arms, legs, and teeth—into graceful and sophisticated young ladies.

Agnes herself had recognized the transition. In January 1854 she complained in her diary that "young as I am I must sit up & talk & walk as a young lady and be constantly greeted with, 'Ladies do this & that & think so,' all as if I were twenty." Little more than a year later, as a wise woman of fourteen, she had written of her first meeting with the new plebes, or first-year cadets, at a reception hosted by her parents. "They were very nice boys. It hardly becomes *me* to call them boys, but, though young in years, my residence at W. P. has given me the experience of an ancient & enables me to look down upon young people generally from a great height!"

Now Agnes and Annie recounted tales of the new frontiers they had encountered in algebra, chemistry, political economy, and other unfamiliar subjects, plus the novel challenge of classroom exams, which they had never had before. They reported that the boys at nearby schools were hopelessly juvenile compared with the mature and disciplined cadets at West Point.

Though their academic schedule was rigorous—six hours of classes, two hours of individual study, Bible study before breakfast, and chapel afterward every day—the girls found time to make friends and have fun. One afternoon at school they burned a piece of bristol board from art class and used the ashes to paint "ferocious moustaches and eyebrows" on each other. Agnes went so far as to wear hers down to supper, but she hastily wiped it off at the last minute with a handkerchief when they all thought Mrs. Sheffey was about to come into the room.

A day or two before Christmas, Daughter went out back to the servants' quarters to visit Old Nurse, only to find that she had died in her sleep. As a child, she had been the slave in charge of watching for General Washington and running to open the gate for him. With her death, there were only two Mount Vernon servants left, and one more link with the old days was gone.

Colonel Lee spent most of his time at home trying to untangle Mr. Custis's estate accounts. Although his base salary had never exceeded $3,000 a year, Robert had grown wealthy by carefully guarding the inheritance his mother had left him and by investing wisely in banks, railroads, canals, and state bonds. His father-in-law, on the other hand, spent a fortune without ever seeming to know where it went. He put the management of his estates in the hands of careless men and held them accountable for nothing. Lee found over $6,000 worth of errors in the overseer's books and more than that much again in questionable charges.

When Robert set out for Texas in February 1856, he made it clear to Mary that she was in charge of the household. En route to San Antonio, he reminded her, "As regards your household arrangements & what concerns your father's comfort & welfare, as well as your own, you must yourself act & not rely on him or wait on me."

Mary may not have managed her accounts as accurately as the colonel would have, but she rose to the task before her, dealing with bank accounts and stock transactions, paying for the children's schooling, and seeing to the family's financial needs.

The month Robert left for his new assignment, Mary was in relatively good health, as she had been for many years. But sometime in the spring of 1856, she began noticing an ominous stiffness in her joints. Her disability came upon her suddenly and her condition worsened rapidly. It was the worst flare-up of illness since the months of complications following Daughter's birth in 1835.

Mary's pain, swelling, and stiffness came and went, but even when she was feeling her best, she walked with great difficulty and could hardly climb the steps to her bedroom. Her doctor prescribed various drinks and pills, but all they did was leave her constipated. Her joints, particularly in her right hand and arm, pained her constantly. Although she continued writing letters, the writing grew small and ragged on the page.

She explained something of her condition in a letter to her brother-in-law Carter on July 17:

I have been confined to my room & bed most of the time more than 4 weeks with rheumatism in my knee & have tried every thing my sapient Dr. could suggest, without effect. This is a complaint I never had before in my life & I am anxious to check it at once—for I cannot resign myself willingly to this state of inaction.

Mary loved swimming, and exercise and warm water were the two best treatments available for her condition, so Carter suggested that she visit a particular spring. But Mary replied that she could not make the trip, "for I am such a cripple that I do not feel able to undertake the difficulties I must encounter in getting to that famous spring of yours. I fear too that the baths are too cold & I must go either to Bath or to the Warm Springs."

By the time Annie and Agnes returned from Staunton in July, Mary had been bedfast for a month. The girls always looked forward to seeing their mother waiting on the portico to greet them when they arrived home for the summer. When they turned up the driveway that year, they were surprised that she was absent and truly alarmed to discover how crippled she was. "Oh! How strange it seemed not to see Ma waiting for us," Annie wrote to a schoolmate, "but she [has] been an invalid upstairs for nearly a month with rheumatism."

Mary wondered how much she should tell her husband about her illness. Robert was in Texas dealing with the Comanches, and she saw no reason to alarm him. There was, after all, nothing he could do to help her. So she wrote of the children, the neighbors, the money she spent, and the bank deposits she made. She did mention that she planned to visit the mineral springs on the recommendation of her doctor and asked Robert's advice about making financial arrangements to pay for the trip. From the Texas desert, Robert wrote back:

> At this distance I can do nothing for you. You must make your own arrangements and carry out your own plans. I am at a loss however to know where you will get funds for your journey, as it seemed from your letter that you have deprived yourself of those you had in your possession before you knew how you could replace them.

In August, Mary traveled to Warm Springs, two hundred miles by train southwest of Washington, accompanied by Daughter, Rooney, and Rob, who, she explained to Robert, seemed most of all the children "to require some renovation." Annie and Agnes stayed home to look after Grandpa Custis, and Mildred left for a visit to Cedar Grove. After several weeks of warm mineral pools and cool mountain air, Mary felt refreshed and moved around somewhat more freely with less pain.

With Robert away, her father in good hands, and the weather in Washington still sultry, Mary would have liked to stay longer at the springs. But Rooney had to get back to college for the fall term, and she felt she could not make the trip home in her "helpless state" without him. The family returned to Arlington just in time to get Annie and Agnes off to Staunton and Rooney back to Harvard. Rob went to board during the week at a nearby school and came home on the weekends. Daughter left on a round of visits. Having lived in Baltimore and New York, she was easily bored with country life.

In her letters, Mary gave Robert the details of her financial transactions that she thought might interest him. She had solved the question about travel funds on her own. "Mr. Marbury having very kindly said he would receive my check, I got money enough for my journey," she wrote. There was $500 in the bank and two checks for $200 each that she would "put away at present." As for other account activity, "I will know from Mr. Marbury whether any other deposits have been made & inform you in my next." With a check Robert sent for $400, on her own initiative she bought bonds in the Orange & Alexandria Railroad, which were "selling very *low* just now."

Mary also gave him a little fuller account of her illness. Annie had already told her father what she knew, so the secret was out. Whatever benefit the hot springs had given her hadn't lasted.

My visit to the Springs only served to bring out & diffuse the disease, which the Dr. says is very favorable & that *now* he can cure me, but my progress is slow & he advises me to ride & walk about. The riding is very pleasant & does not tire me, but I walk very unsteadily & not often without a crutch. My general health is perfectly good, nor do I suffer much pain except when I move suddenly. I trust in my next letter I may be able to give you more cheering accounts.

Sadly, Mary would never again be able to give her husband a very cheering account of her condition. Seasons of change were upon her, as they were upon her country. And neither would ever be the same again.

CHAPTER FIFTEEN

SEASONS OF CHANGE

*D*espite her infirmities and all the distractions they caused, Mary kept herself up to date on the presidential election of 1856. In 1854 the Kansas-Nebraska Act had nullified the Compromise of 1850 by providing for "popular sovereignty"—the right of the citizens of new territories to decide whether or not to allow slavery there. The Act brought the slavery issue, once thought settled through compromise, back into national politics and fractured the American two-party system.

Along with a decade of riptide immigration, this political fragmentation resulted in the demise of the Whig Party, the birth of the Native American and Republican Parties (among others), and the division of the Democratic Party into two wings, northern and southern.

The election of 1856 was a three-cornered contest. The Know-Nothing Party, made up of radical anti-Catholics who promised to keep the Irish and other foreigners out of America through strict immigration laws, nominated former President Millard Fillmore, who was also endorsed by the foundering Whigs. The Republicans, in their first national election, backed John C. Frémont, a senator from California known for his trailblazing journeys west in the 1840s, who ran on a radical platform of "Free Soil, Free Labor, Free Men." The Democrats selected James Buchanan, a former Federalist, senator from Pennsylvania, and ambassador to Russia and

England, who ran on a "Save the Union" theme, promising to "arrest the agitation of the slavery question at the North and to destroy sectional parties." Buchanan, with his conciliatory stance, won the election over his polarized and polarizing challengers.

As ever, Mary was steadfastly opposed to the idea of slavery but accepted it in practice because she believed that without education or property, freed slaves would be unable to make their way in the world. After Buchanan's victory, but before his inauguration, Mary received a letter from Robert that closely mirrored her views on the issue. The only difference between their opinions was that Mary still supported the efforts of the Colonization Society to return willing slaves to Africa, while Robert did not. On December 27, the colonel mused at length about the South's "peculiar institution":

> In this enlightened age, there are few I believe, but what will acknowledge that slavery as an institution is a moral & political evil in any country.... I think it however a greater evil to the white than to the black race, & while my feelings are strongly enlisted in behalf of the latter, my sympathies are more strong for the former. The blacks are immeasurably better off here than in Africa, morally, socially & physically. The painful discipline they are undergoing is necessary for their instruction as a race, & I hope will prepare & lead them to better things. How long their subjugation may be necessary is known & ordered by a wise merciful Providence. Their emancipation will sooner result from the mild & melting influence of Christianity, than the storms and tempests of fiery controversy....
>
> While we see the course of the final abolition of human slavery is onward, & we give it the aid of our prayers & all justifiable means in our power, we must leave the progress as well as the result in His hands who sees the end; who chooses to work by slow influences; & with whom two thousand years are but as a single day. Although the abolitionist must know this, & must see that he has neither the right or power of operating except by moral means & suasion, & if he means well to the slave, he must not create angry feelings in the master; that although he may not

In this Washington family portrait, George Washington Parke Custis is at left and his sister Eleanor, Mary's Aunt Nellie, stands between the general and Mrs. Washington. Both children grew up at Mount Vernon after their father's death in the closing days of the Revolutionary War. Their grandfather was Daniel Parke Custis, Martha Washington's first husband.

G. W. P. Custis was a popular orator, a gracious host, and an enthusiastic but uninspired painter and playwright. He built Arlington as a monument to General Washington and filled it with artifacts from Mount Vernon. Lavish entertaining and careless financial management kept him perpetually in debt.

On her way to St. Louis during the spring of 1838, Mary had her portrait painted in Baltimore by William Edward West. She was 29 and the mother of three children. She had already suffered from debilitating illnesses that gave her a deep regard for the preciousness of life.

Lieutenant Robert E. Lee also sat for a portrait by West during the Baltimore visit of 1838. Mary sent back to Arlington for his dress uniform; the artist painted Lee's face while waiting for it, then added the epaulettes and other details later.

Arlington as it appeared in the 1850s when the Lees lived there. Even before the house was completed in 1817, it was famous for its Washington memorabilia and a magnificent view of the capital across the Potomac River. The monumental Doric columns were 23 feet high, yet the steps were made of wood to save money.

Mary's mother, Mary Lee Fitzhugh Custis, loved flowers and paid special attention to the elaborate rose arbor on the south side of the house. Mary could see the garden from her room and looked forward to spring there from as early as she could remember until she left the house in April 1861.

Fearful that Confederate forces would attack Washington from the hills of Arlington, the Union captured the house and grounds in the opening weeks of the war. Warned of the invasion in advance, Mrs. Lee and her children escaped. She never spent another night there. In May 1864, the property was turned into a military cemetery by Secretary of War Edwin M. Stanton.

By the time this photo was taken, about 1868, Mary was almost completely confined to a wheelchair by rheumatoid arthritis. Though her hands were misshapen and in constant pain, she still wore her wedding band and continued sewing tirelessly to raise money for charity.

Mary made exquisite doll clothes from her old ball gowns. Some were for fund-raising and others were for children of friends. This dress was made for Rose McDonald, whose father was on the faculty of VMI, and who later wrote a biography of Mrs. Lee.

After General Lee became president of Washington College, the trustees built a house for his family with wide porches on three sides so Mary could sit outside in her wheelchair. Students paused as they walked by in hopes of seeing the general pushing her chair, which he claimed as his special privilege.

One of Mary's most successful fund raising projects was hand tinting inexpensive pictures of General and Mrs. Washington, General Lee, and herself.

She raised one thousand dollars in a single summer for her church building fund, selling them to friends at the hot springs where she had gone for arthritis treatments.

In June 1873, Mary returned to Alexandria for the first time since the war to visit her dear Aunt Maria Fitzhugh (far right), whose husband's death in 1830 had led to Mary's religious conversion. This photo was taken on the porch of the Fitzhugh townhouse, where Mary's parents had been married in 1804.

Near the end of her life, Mrs. Lee posed for a formal portrait in her widow's cap. She continued living in Lexington after her son Custis took over as president of Washington College following the general's death. Until her final illness she remained a devoted mother, a generous and cheerful neighbor, and a tireless supporter of her church.

approve the mode by which it pleases Providence to accomplish its purposes, the result will nevertheless be the same; that the reasons he gives for interference in what he has no concern, holds good for every kind of interference with our neighbors when we disapprove their conduct....

Robert hoped that the new president would "extinguish the fanaticism North & South, & cultivate love for the country & Union, & restore harmony between the different sections."

With the excitement of the presidential election over, Mary, slowed by her infirmities, spent a quiet Christmas at Arlington with her father and all of her children except Custis, who did not get Christmas leave. Various family members accepted invitations to parties at other houses, even one on Christmas Day, which made the big white house seem all the quieter. It was a far cry from the year before, when she and the colonel had hosted one party after another at West Point.

And then there was her father, whose moods had begun to swing back and forth from a state of ennui to a wild, almost childish exuberance. Mary continued in charge of the house and family matters, though she relied on Robert's long-distance advice when she could get it. When the new furnace quit working properly, various servants tinkered with it, but they only made matters worse. Mary wrote to Robert for counsel. He suggested she ask the manufacturer to repair it and then let only one servant, his trusted valet, Perry, tend it.

As best she could, Mary continued to manage the family financial affairs in a way her husband would approve, but she was not always up to his precise standards. He wrote her that a check he had drafted on his account had been returned, even though she had deposited money in the account. "You must be very particular, dear Mary, when you deal in money matters," Robert admonished her. "You know I cannot draw upon a bank unless I know *where* the money is & its *exact* amount." After his check was returned, he reminded her again that neither of them could "give checks on banks & not have [an account balance] to meet them. People may think I am endeavoring to *swindle*."

In the spring of 1857, Mary made plans to travel again to the mineral springs in the summer. Meanwhile, she maintained a mother's keen interest in Annie and Agnes, away for their spring term at the Virginia Female Institute, which by now the girls had christened "Staunton Jail."

Agnes had been sick off and on at school for months, first with painful swelling in her fingers and feet, and later with chills—classic symptoms of rheumatic fever. In the fall of the previous year she had come down with chicken pox, and now in the spring she contracted roseola. Nevertheless, she made the highest grade possible—a six—in all twenty-one of her subjects, including algebra, chemistry, logic, theology, philosophy, geography, French, and piano. Her mother wrote her often and sent new clothes and boxes of their favorite foods to both girls.

The biggest news from Staunton that season was of a religious revival that began in March and swept through the student body. Mary judiciously encouraged her daughters' religious stirrings—always supportive, yet always willing to let the Lord move at His own pace. In the midst of Annie's search for religious renewal at school, Mary counseled:

> I had long hoped that the spirit of God was moving in your heart, tho' I felt disappointed that you should so long delay to come forward and declare yourself on the Lord's side. Now that you have experienced His love and the sense of His forgiveness, why should you hesitate? God will give you grace to persevere. He will confirm & strengthen you & enable you to pass over any obstacle. From the moment that you devote your all to Him, He is pledged to preserve you & His word cannot fail. You may have many a struggle, but you must conquer in the end. I would advise you to go to the communion. You would feel strengthened in your resolve. You must consult your minister. The hungry & starving are invited to that holy feast & are satisfied while the rich are sent empty away.... 'Tis not the righteous, [but] sinners Jesus came to call.... Remember what He says, "Those who seek me early shall find me." The promises of God cannot fail. Therefore *seek* Him with all your heart....

On Easter Sunday, 1857, Bishop John Johns, who was visiting Staunton that day, confirmed Agnes, just as he had Robert, Daughter, and Annie nearly four years earlier. Later in the service, kneeling next to Annie, Agnes received her first communion. Mary lifted up deeply felt prayers of thanksgiving that another member of her family had given her heart to Christ.

Mary wrote that she was overjoyed to "hear that God has sent his spirit into your heart & drawn you to himself," and asked her daughters' help in praying for members of the family who did not yet know Christ as their Savior:

> You must pray for your sister & for your brothers who are out of the fold of Christ. Think what a happiness to your Mother to be able to present *all* her children at the *throne* of God & to be able to say, "Here I am Lord & the children Thou hast given me." Pray for your Mother that she may be more faithful in her prayers & example...
>
> You must aid me and pray for your poor grandfather whose heart seems as far as ever from his God. Oh, I am often tempted to despair of him. Could I only believe, all things are possible to him who believeth. But it is hard, very hard, for the old to turn to God....
>
> I heard from Rooney recently. Would that he could be brought to give his heart to his God. It would save me from many anxious thoughts for him. It is the only real safeguard from the snares and temptations of the world....

Mary faulted herself for complaining about her own infirmities when she should be rejoicing that God had given three of her daughters the precious gift of salvation and that she had seen her husband come to Christ after years of praying for him. She wrote:

> You must pray for your brothers & sisters & for your poor mother that she may become more perfected in her Christian course & not yield to the irritations produced by the constant petty cares & vexations which annoy her.

Besides her physical difficulties, one of Mary's vexations was her youngest child, Mildred, whose temper and behavior were "most improper." Mary knew only too well her parental shortcomings as a disciplinarian. She had confessed them in years past, and she owned up to them again as Mildred—"Precious Life" to her doting father—made a difficult transition from girlhood to adolescence. "I feel how much to blame I am for permitting [her to behave as she does]. May God be merciful to her & change her heart before Satan has taken possession of it."

While Mildred was throwing tantrums at home, Rooney struggled academically and personally at Harvard. Robert thought that his second son spent far too much time and money "running about amusing himself." The lingering disappointment at not following his father and brother to West Point may have had something to do with it. Rooney asked his mother if he could request a direct commission in the army from his father's old mentor, General Winfield Scott.

Mary wrote her husband for advice, but his answer had not arrived by the time General Scott offered Rooney a commission as a second lieutenant in the infantry. Rooney was disappointed. He wanted to be in the cavalry like his father and wondered whether he should decline the post. Finally he asked his mother to decide for him.

General Scott was a dear family friend, the Lees had a proud tradition of military service, and Rooney seemed headed for a dead end at Harvard. So Mary, mindful of her son's "warm & affectionate heart, but too careless & reckless a disposition," accepted the commission on her son's behalf. Though he had not wanted the infantry at first, Rooney was beside himself with excitement at his mother's decision and made plans to leave Cambridge for good at the end of the school year.

In May, while Rooney was still at Harvard, Annie became so sick that the school authorities at Staunton decided to send her home before the end of the term. Doctors at Arlington diagnosed her condition as overwork and "a weak stomach." Rooney came home in June to accept his commission, and Agnes arrived from Staunton soon after. Daughter, who had been unmoved by her father's earlier requests that she return from her long visit in Philadelphia to help her mother manage the household, came home as well.

That summer, Robert's sister Mildred died in Paris, where her family had lived for years. After her death, her husband, Edward Childe, and daughter, Mary, came to Arlington for a visit, and Mrs. Lee invited her niece to travel with her to the springs that summer. When it came time to go, only Annie and Mary's maid joined them. Custis was stationed in Florida; Rooney was preparing for his first military assignment; and Daughter, Agnes, Rob, and

Mildred wanted to stay home and entertain the summer company.

Determined to find a cure for her vexing illness, Mary planned a long trip to Berkeley, Virginia, also known as Bath. When she and her companions arrived, they all marveled at the new swimming pool, more than sixty feet long. It was for the gentlemen, but the ladies had a fine big one of their own, with a swing built over it, poolside seats, and broad stairs that made it as comfortable as possible for Mary to get into the water.

Bath was on the rail line, which made the trip relatively easy, and at the spring there was an elegant hotel with four hundred rooms. The mineral-laden water buoyed Mary's stiff, painful limbs and relieved her suffering, at least temporarily. An excellent swimmer, she took it upon herself to teach Annie and her niece Mary to swim, but she wasn't very successful. She finally gave up and turned the job over to a young girl at the hotel.

At Berkeley, Mary got a letter from Custis saying he had been ordered to California. He was traveling from Florida to New York to catch a steamer around Cape Horn, and, to his mother's disappointment, he would have to embark without seeing her. Fortunately for them both, he was delayed in reaching New York and missed his ship. The next one wouldn't sail for some days, so Custis had time to visit his grandfather at Arlington and then to come on to his mother, who had not seen him in two years.

When Custis arrived at Berkeley, there was a happy reunion, but behind his newly grown beard, Mary could see a sick and exhausted young man. Secretly she wrote Custis's commander, General Totten, asking him to give her son "a little time to recruit his health and visit his friends." The general quickly telegraphed his consent, along with revised orders for Custis to sail from New York on August 5, nearly two weeks away.

At Bath, Mary also learned that Rooney, a freshly minted second lieutenant, was engaged to marry his cousin Charlotte Wickham. Charlotte's parents had both died of tuberculosis, and her grandmother had raised her at Shirley, the ancestral home of Colonel Lee's mother. Mary and Robert both thought Rooney was too immature to marry and that Charlotte's health was too delicate. But they soon gave their blessings. As Mary commented hopefully, "A virtuous attachment is often a great safeguard to a young man."

Impatient with the progress she was making at Berkeley, Mary decided to move to a nearby farm with a small sulphur spring that came highly recommended. Her stay was short. The modest farmhouse where they slept was infested with bedbugs, the food was terrible, and the landlady was grumpy. So they traveled on to another more traditional spa, a comfortable resort hotel at Jordan Springs, near Winchester, Virginia.

After taking the waters there, Mary and her fellow travelers went to visit her cousin Esther Lewis at Audley. Mary would have liked to stay longer, but she had promised her father she would take him to the annual exhibition of the U.S. Agricultural Society in Louisville, Kentucky.

In 1855, Mr. Custis had gone by himself to the annual meeting in Philadelphia and received a "storm of applause" from the audience of two thousand when he was introduced at the formal dinner. Thus encouraged, he had told Mary that he wanted to attend the Virginia State Fair in Richmond in the fall of 1856.

Mary believed that her father was too frail to make the trip, and she had tried to dissuade him until the minute he was packed up and seated in his carriage. Even then, standing in the driveway in the cool air of an autumn morning, she continued making her case. Finally, realizing how tired he really was, Mr. Custis had climbed out of the coach and walked back inside.

When she arrived home in early September 1857, Mary saw at once that her father was too sick to travel. His illness—which the doctors called "a minor bilious complaint"—did not seem life threatening, but it hung on stubbornly. During the first week in October, he was confined to bed with influenza, which developed into pneumonia. It was more than the old man's frail body could bear. He called for a minister, spoke calmly and frankly about the end that awaited, and expressed regret that he had never taken communion.

"God have mercy on me in my last moments," he whispered. "I am so thankful I leave a pious family. Lay me beside my blessed wife."

On October 10, 1857, after four days in his sickbed, George Washington Parke Custis died peacefully. Mary and other family members stood around his bed, and according to Mary, the spirit of her mother was close by. Mary described the moment in a letter to Benjamin Lossing, a writer and illustrator who had long admired Mr. Custis and his famous estate:

Though almost from the commencement of his brief illness convinced he must die, yet no feeling of terror betrayed itself. With a heart overflowing with affection to all around him, patient, gentle, humbly as a little child did he implore that mercy which God has promised to the merciful, & we all felt that ministering angels were around that death bed & even that *her spirit* hovered near who had so long & so faithfully prayed for him.

Just that spring, Mary had written her daughter Annie that it was "very hard for the old to turn to God." But now she sensed that the years she and her mother had spent praying for her dear father had borne fruit in his last moments.

In contrast to his wife's quiet, private funeral service, G. W. P. Custis's was a great public affair. On a bright, crisp autumn day, six slaves carried the mahogany coffin from the drawing room of the mansion to the gravesite next to Mrs. Custis's. A brass band played, their instruments glistening in the sunlight, the sound echoing off the hills to the west. The Washington Light Infantry was there, as were veterans of the War of 1812 in their old and faded uniforms. Altogether, more than a thousand people crowded around the grave as the funeral service was read.

Newspapers throughout the country carried Mr. Custis's obituary. The *National Intelligencer* echoed the sentiments of many:

> Thousands from this country and from foreign lands who have visited Arlington to commune with our departed friend, and look upon the touching memorials there treasured up with care of him who was first in the hearts of his countrymen, will not forget the charm thrown over all by the ease, grace, interest, and vivacity of the manners and conversation of him whose voice, alas!, is silent now.

News of his father-in-law's death reached Robert in Texas on October 21. He immediately applied for a two-month leave to go home and help Mary straighten out her father's tangled business affairs. In typical Custis fashion, the will, dated March 26, 1855, had been drawn up without an attorney. Of the four executors, only Colonel Lee was legally qualified for the position; he alone would have to shoulder the burden of settling the estate. Lee considered that high position of family trust sufficient to leave his military duties for a while.

While Robert made the two-and-a-half-week journey from San Antonio, Mary began gathering her father's papers and arranging them as best she could. Among them she found his unfinished "Recollections."

Almost as long as Mary could remember, Mr. Custis had written memoirs of his years at Mount Vernon and published them from time to time in a local newspaper, with the idea of someday collecting them all into a book. Although he had insisted several times that he was finished with them, late in life he had returned to the project with renewed passion.

Custis bemoaned the loss of Washington's type of patriotism, piety, and purity of motives in the federal government and hoped to rekindle the faded fires of selfless resolve he considered essential for preserving the philosophy that had brought America into existence. He wrote his "Recollections" to remind people how they had achieved what they had, so they could understand how to safequard the sacred birthright of freedom.

Mary shared her father's veneration for Washington's ideals and believed that they were being compromised and threatened by a new breed of political leader who, never having had to make sacrifices or humble himself, had lost sight of the simple, selfless goals of the American Revolution.

She was convinced that she could complete her father's book from the articles and notes he left behind. There was no better way to preserve Washington's—and her father's—legacy than for her to write a book citing their accomplishments and upholding the values they had treasured.

Thanksgiving week, little more than a month after her father died, Mary informed her friend Benjamin Lossing:

> It is my purpose as soon as I can command the time to make a minute investigation of all his papers to see what materials I can collect for his Memoirs of Washington. I fear they are much disconnected, but they should be preserved—a brief memoir of his own life, the letters of his adopted father to him while at college & many other little incidents of a private nature shewing forth more fully the domestic character of Washington, whose mind seemed to embrace every duty.... Would that my memory served to relate all I have heard both from him & his sister Mrs. Lewis....

In the months that followed, Mary went to work on her literary project. She had started something similar years before in St. Louis. Now she had plenty of time, a treasury of reference material, and no need to work in a converted closet to keep the pens and paper away from little hands. Nevertheless, progress was slow because her father's papers were in such disarray and because her arthritis made it steadily more difficult for her to write.

As she gathered together her father's notes, Mary sent pictures and paintings to her agent in Philadelphia, Derby & Jackson, to be engraved for illustrations. She also wrote a biography of her father to go in the front of the book and did some careful editing. As she explained:

I have found some scraps of papers I send you from which you may glean some passages of interest. There are many speeches at the Irish [St. Patrick's Day] Celebrations which contain bursts of real eloquence, but are otherwise so *denunciatory* of England that I do [not] think it desirable to publish them at this day.

She also quoted a brief note from Washington, which its owner was trying to sell her for $150, adding with irony, "We have I suppose given away several hundred autographs and are too poor to buy one at that price."

By the end of 1859, Mary had finished her father's memoirs and was proofreading typeset copy from the publishers. She was very pleased with the book, longwindedly but descriptively entitled *Recollections and Private Memoirs of Washington, by his Adopted Son, George Washington Parke Custis, with a Memoir of the Author, by his Daughter.* She suggested only a few changes to correct minor inaccuracies.

Recollections was published to favorable reviews. Her old friend William Seaton, editor of the *National Intelligencer,* in which many of her father's stories originally had been published, hailed it as a "splendid memorial to Washington" and "a worthy tribute of a distinguished lady to her eloquent and honored father...clear, concise, and interesting." A London edition was also released, to somewhat less favorable reviews. The *Atheneum* found it "unavoidably uninteresting" because George Washington himself was "as uninteresting a character as one can easily conceive." Nevertheless, sales were gratifying on both sides of the Atlantic.

During the two years that Mary worked on her book, the sectional strife over slavery grew increasingly violent. After the passage of the Kansas-Nebraska Act, Kansas had become a battleground between pro-slavery and antislavery forces, and on May 21, 1856, a number of abolitionists were murdered at Lawrence. The next day, Charles Sumner, an abolitionist senator from Massachusetts, delivered a speech on the Senate floor entitled "The Crime Against Kansas," in which he vilified a number of men, including South Carolina senator Andrew P. Butler. On May 24, John Brown and his band of fanatical abolitionists killed five proslavery adherents at Pottawatomie Creek, Kansas, in retaliation for the deaths at Lawrence. That same day back in Washington, Butler's kinsman, Representative Preston Brooks, entered the Senate brandishing a cane and beat Sumner senseless.

Between 1856 and 1860, "bleeding Kansas" and the bloodied senator were just two in a series of events—all connected to the question of slavery—that edged North and South ever closer to fratricide. By the fall of 1860, when Republican candidate Abraham Lincoln was elected president, many Southerners were already convinced that civil war was inevitable.

Mary's book was published near the time of Lincoln's election, and she hoped its message would fall on fertile soil. "If the public would give more attention to the memory and precepts of Washington, they would not be ripe for disunion," she wrote. "I will still hope 'til the storm breaks over us.... God knows how it will all end."

In addition to her work on *Recollections,* Mary's time between her father's death and the election of Lincoln was taken up with affairs at Arlington. She was now not only the lady of Arlington; she was also its owner. By the time her husband fulfilled his legal and financial obligations as executor, the two months he had allotted for settling her father's estate would stretch into two arduous, frustrating years.

CHAPTER SIXTEEN

TOWARD THE ABYSS

*A*long with everyone else who knew him well, Mary had long recognized that her father "was not very methodical in the management of his affairs." A clearer picture of just how unmethodical he was emerged after Robert arrived at Arlington and Custis's will was unsealed.

One matter Lee had to deal with quickly was the provision his father-in-law had made to free his slaves. Mr. Custis had directed that all 196 slaves on his estates "be emancipated by my executors...said emancipation to be accomplished in not exceeding five years from the time of my decease." Nevertheless, a rumor circulated among the slaves that old Mr. Custis had meant for them to be freed as soon as he died and that the true terms of his will were being kept secret long enough for them all to be sold.

Newspapers in Chicago, Boston, New York, and other abolitionist cities picked up the story. Some of them reprinted a mock obituary from the *Chicago Tribune* that read in part:

He was early united in marriage to Miss Mary Lee Fitzhugh...[who vindicated] her woman's nobility by avoiding the society of her husband for many years previous to her death, on account of his notorious licentiousness—a licentiousness which was strictly Virginian in its impartiality for color.... Thousands who have visited

Arlington to look upon the memorials there treasured up...will not forget the mortification excited by the thought that George Washington Parke Custis was the keeper of these memorials, and that he could even have passed a moment in the society of George Washington.

Colonel Lee wrote a polite letter to the *New York Times,* which had run a story about the Arlington slaves, explaining that there were no provisions for freeing the slaves immediately, that the will was filed at the Alexandria County Courthouse, and that they and anyone else were welcome to go there and read it for themselves.

Mary was less diplomatic on the subject. To a friend she declared:

Scarcely had my father been laid in his tomb when two men were constantly lurking about here tampering with the servants & telling them they had a right to their freedom *immediately* & that if they would unite & *demand* it they would obtain it. The merciful hand of a kind Providence & their own inertness I suppose prevented an outbreak.... We should be most deeply indebted to their *kind friends* the abolitionists if they would come forward and purchase their time & let them enjoy the comforts of freedom *at once.*

The remaining provisions in the will gave his daughter Arlington House and the surrounding 1,100-acre plantation, 63 slaves, the mill at Four Mile Run, and other lands in Alexandria and Fairfax Counties, together with her father's "horses and carriages, furniture, pictures, and plate." Upon Mary's death, everything she had was to go to her oldest son and Custis's namesake, George Washington Custis Lee. All the Washington silver and memorabilia were to remain with the house "entire and unchanged." Colonel Lee received only a city lot in Washington.

Rooney inherited the White House plantation; Romancoke was left to Rob. Each of the four granddaughters had a legacy of $10,000, to be raised from the proceeds of plantation operations and by selling various other tracts of land. The colonel already knew that those properties were deeply in debt. It would be years before they would earn enough to pay off their creditors and generate $40,000 more to pay the granddaughters their due.

Even with the labor of the slaves, he faced the impossible task of making the properties profitable in five years or less, after which the slaves would be gone.

Taken individually, White House and Romancoke were self-sufficient. But Arlington, always the showplace, was awash in red ink. Tradesmen came calling with claims totaling more than $10,000 against the Custis estate. Because the records were so muddled and incomplete, Robert had no idea how much Mary really owed. Nor did he see how she would ever be able to run the plantation in his absence.

"Every thing is in ruins & will have to be rebuilt," Robert confided to Mary's aunt Maria Fitzhugh a few days after his arrival from Texas. "I feel more familiar with the military operations of a campaign than the details of a farm." Lee considered resigning from the army to run Arlington, especially if his sons decided not to leave their own careers to manage their new properties. He was granted a year's extension of his two-month leave of absence, to December 1858.

Robert seemed to be in constant motion as he juggled the cares and minor crises of the various family estates: paying bills, hiring overseers, preparing the fields for planting, selling crops and standing timber, resolving boundary disputes, reconciling accounts, having buildings and fences repaired, and hiring out surplus slaves to other plantations—all the time wondering what effect his extended absence from duty would have on his military career.

Mary worried about the amount of work Robert faced. She also kept a wary eye on the slaves' activities. Arlington was a high-profile target, and abolitionists kept trying to stir them up. Now that the slaves would have to be freed in five years, it was crucial that they work diligently during that time to generate the money to pay off the estate's debts and obligations. But Mr. Custis had owned many more slaves than his property could profitably employ, and they were not accustomed to work. When Robert went to the White House and Romancoke to reorganize the slaves' duties, he discovered that they saw no reason to work any harder than they ever had. As Mary wrote a friend:

The servants here have been so long accustomed to do little or nothing that they cannot be convinced of the necessity now of exerting themselves to accomplish the conditions of the will, which the sooner they do, the sooner they will be entitled to their freedom. What they will do then, unless there is a mighty change wrought in them, I do not know. But at any rate we shall be relieved from the care of them which will be an immense burden taken from our shoulders.

On another occasion she asserted, "It will be a great relief to me when they are all gone, for they are much trouble and no profit."

Summer weather brought the usual crowds to Arlington Spring, and Lee did his best to make them as welcome as before. A newspaper reporter wrote that he had never seen "better order, heard less noise, or enjoyed more quietude" at the picnic grounds. On the Fourth of July more than 2,000 people came to celebrate the day with speeches and fireworks; later in the month the German Music Festival was a "mammoth" affair, with music, dancing, gymnastics, and "an abundance of good cheer in the shape of well-brewed lager, nothing stronger being allowed."

The hot weather prompted Mary to resume her search for relief from her tenacious ailment. Though she had written Robert that she had been seeing a doctor, visited hot springs, and often walked with a crutch, he had still been shocked to see her so crippled and weary when he came home after her father's death. Her right hand and arm were sometimes completely useless. The pain in her joints kept her from sleeping. Swelling in her feet and ankles came and went. Some days she could scarcely write or even hold a pen, though she had labored away bravely at her desk, working on her book or corresponding with friends, the writing sometimes tiny and jagged, other times a nearly illegible scrawl.

In August 1858, Mary set out for a visit to another spa, this time with Annie, still in delicate health herself after her illness at school, and Robert, who left his duties managing the estate long enough to escort them to Hot Springs, at the foot of Warm Springs Mountain, eighteen hours from Arlington by stagecoach. A large, elegant hotel called the Homestead had been built there, near a series of twenty mineral springs where 100-degree water flowed year-round from deep inside the earth. There were cottages and bathhouses, good food and pleasant company. Colonel and Mrs. Lee and their daughter spent a month there before returning to Arlington.

Having been granted another extension of his military leave, this one until May 1, 1859, Lee moved ahead with an engineer's precision and sense of purpose to make the Custis properties solvent. He plowed every cent he made from operations back into improvements. The only exception was $235 he spent to buy a grave marker for Mr. Custis. Like the one for Mrs. Custis, Robert designed it himself. Made of white marble, it was a miniature Washington Monument—or more accurately, a model resembling what the monument would look like when it was completed. About five years earlier, construction had ground to a halt due to partisan bickering, and the elegant marble shaft was less than one-third finished.

Though he was on leave from his cavalry unit in Texas, Colonel Lee was called up for court-martial duty at West Point and was away through Christmas. It was a somber celebration that year. The weather was terrible; Mary and Annie were sick; and Custis, Rooney, and Robert were all away. But by New Year's Day, Robert was back, bringing presents for all the girls—watches for Daughter and Agnes, games for Mildred, and a golden thimble, pins, and hair decorations for Annie.

A few weeks later, Rooney came home from his duty station in California. After a taste of military life, he had decided to resign his commission, marry his fiancée, Charlotte, and move to the White House plantation his grandfather had left him. The wedding was March 23 at Shirley, in the same magnificent hall where Robert's parents had been married in 1793. Though she would have enjoyed the celebration and the pleasure of seeing the first of her children wed, Mary was too sick to travel. Agnes, Annie, and their father went, promising to bring back a complete account of the festivities.

The flowers at Arlington that spring were exceptional, and Mary spent as much time as she could outside. It was impossible for her to tend them the way she had always loved to do. Kneeling and getting up again were painful and exhausting, and her hands were too stiff to hold a rake or trowel. But she absorbed as much of her beloved garden as she could—the sights, smells, breezes, the warmth of the sun—by sitting in the middle of it and directing Ephraim, Old George, and the rest of the gardeners in their work.

There was a painted wooded arbor covered with pink and red honeysuckle and yellow jasmine where Annie, Agnes, and Mildred all enjoyed sitting to read. Sometimes they made necklaces from the jasmine blossoms or tied them into chains to put between the folds of sheets in the linen press, which gave the beds the fragrance of flowers and fresh earth and sunlight.

Mary sat on a chair near the arbor, a large white sunbonnet hanging by a ribbon down her back, watching intently as the gardeners planted, pruned, fertilized, and cut the roses. She always paid special attention to her favorite moss roses. The colonel liked safronia roses best, and every morning before breakfast he gathered four perfect buds and placed one beside each daughter's plate—the smallest at Mildred's and on up to the largest at daughter Mary's.

Far away from the idyllic gardens on the south lawn, rumors continued to swirl about the Arlington slaves. On June 24, the New York *Tribune* reported, in the form of "anonymous letters," that three runaway slaves had been captured and returned to the estate, which was true. But the paper embellished the story by insisting that Mr. Custis had fathered fifteen slaves on the place. The paper, owned by abolitionist Horace Greeley, also reported that Colonel Lee had ordered the three captured slaves whipped and that Lee himself had given the woman in the group thirty-nine lashes—a particularly vicious accusation, as female slaves were sometimes stripped to the waist and brutally abused by the men who whipped them.

Publicly, the Lees ignored the story, though Robert wrote a friend, "No servant, soldier, or citizen that was ever employed by me can with truth charge me with bad treatment." A family friend wrote to the newspaper, "I am no advocate of slavery in any form and have no other interest in noticing this matter than...defending the reputation of an accomplished gentleman and estimable man like Col. Lee." Mary was particularly irritated that the escaped female slave was a maid of hers who always had fine clothes and "fared as well as my daughters."

Still looking for a cure for her arthritis, Mary considered visiting a resort in Canada known as St. Catherine's Well, where the water was supposed to have remarkable restorative powers. The colonel had bought barrels of water from the spring for Mary to drink, but it seemed not to help. The water tasted unpleasantly salty, and she soon came to dread every glassful. Nevertheless, Robert promised her that he would send her anywhere she wanted to go that might help her. He began to fear she would never be well again.

Instead of traveling to Canada that year, Mary went to Capon Springs, near Winchester, Virginia. Agnes, who had been having pains in her eyes and face, also went. Robert accompanied them and stayed a while to see if the "pure air and healing waters" gave his wife any relief. Mary enjoyed both the mineral baths and the company of friends, some of whom she saw year after year. There were some encouraging results: By the time Mary returned to Arlington, she had a healthier complexion, a heartier appetite, and walked with less pain and more easily, though still slowly.

In May, Colonel Lee's leave was up, and he requested another extension until the end of the year, which his old friend General Scott quickly approved. Rooney and Charlotte were settling in at the White House, the Custis accounts were nearly straightened out, farm improvements had been made, debts had been paid, and everything seemed headed toward a full resolution. Lee did not expect to have every last detail of his work as executor completed when he returned to Texas, but in the fall of 1859 the end appeared to be in sight at last.

The morning of October 17, Robert was making his way through the day's paperwork, filling out an application for more fire insurance on the mansion and stables, when Lieutenant Jeb Stuart came riding hard up the Arlington drive. Stuart had been a cadet at West Point when Lee was the superintendent, and the dashing young officer had become a family friend and frequent visitor. But this was not a social call. Stuart brought a message from Secretary of War John Floyd: Lee was to report to the War Department immediately.

Robert bid Mary a hasty farewell, and she watched as, still in his civilian clothes, he galloped after Lieutenant Stuart. Only later did she learn what happened in the tumultuous few days that followed.

On the night of October 16, John Brown, whose fanatical followers had murdered five men in Kansas three years earlier, led a raid on the U.S. Army arsenal at Harper's Ferry, Virginia. Backed by a group of Northern abolitionist businessmen, Brown planned to free the slaves by force and establish a refuge for them in the Allegheny Mountains.

To carry out his grandiose scheme, Brown planned to equip a slave army with twenty thousand weapons stolen from the Harper's Ferry arsenal. Leading a band of twenty-two men, some white and some black, Brown seized the unguarded facility from the handful of soldiers on duty and then sent raiding parties to neighboring farms to bring back hostages and incite a slave insurrection.

By the night of October 17, local townspeople had formed a militia and surrounded Brown's force. When Colonel Lee arrived around ten o'clock, the few remaining invaders and their hostages were barricaded in the firehouse. Under Lee's orders, Lieutenant Stuart demanded that Brown and his men surrender. When they refused, Lee's men broke down the firehouse door, capturing Brown and six of his disciples. Thirteen hostages were released unharmed, among them Lewis W. Washington, an ancient cousin of the first President, who, during earlier negotiations for their release, had shouted from inside, "Never mind us, fire!"

John Brown was convicted of murder, treason, and inciting slave insurrection. He went to the gallows on December 2. Because of numerous warnings that armed vigilantes would come to rescue Brown at the last minute, three thousand state troops, plus four federal companies commanded by Colonel Lee, stood by on the day of execution.

To Mary and other Southerners, Robert had done his duty and done it admirably—he had protected American lives and property from lawless marauders—but many Northerners considered Brown a martyr to the cause of human freedom. In Boston, Ralph Waldo Emerson declared to thundering applause that Brown was a new saint that would "make the gallows glorious like the cross." Such sympathy for Brown drove the psychological wedge between North and South even deeper.

After John Brown was hung, Colonel Lee prepared to return to Texas at last. Before he left, he was able to have his son Custis transferred from California to Washington, where he could look after Mary and the estate. He left for San Antonio in February 1860, taking a copy of Mary's *Recollections* with him.

The next month, with Custis home to watch over the girls, Mary went to the White House to visit Rooney and Charlotte, who were expecting their first child. Mary had not seen the place in thirty-five years. Though the original house had been demolished and another one built, Mary still associated White House with her great-grandmother, the beautiful, rich young widow Martha Dandridge Custis, who had married Colonel George Washington there just over a hundred years earlier.

Mary was pleased that the old slaves remembered her and welcomed her so warmly. She wrote to Agnes that "they make so much over me that I do not know what to do…. They call me Mistress and always ask after your Papa as *Old* Master, which I told them they must not do as he considered himself quite a young man yet."

Before March was out, Charlotte gave birth to Mary's first grandchild, a boy. His parents decided at once to name him Robert Edward Lee.

With the baby safely arrived and Charlotte recovering well, Mary began planning what had become an annual pilgrimage. Though the drinking water from St. Catherine's Well had failed to provide a cure, she still thought that she might benefit from treatment there. The various Virginia springs had given her no lasting benefit, and she kept hearing about this particular salt spring and its restorative powers.

Writing from San Antonio, Robert reinforced her decision, "What I most desire is that you should do all in your power to recover your health…. As to your domestic affairs, you must not worry yourself about them." The colonel had mellowed considerably in the years since he had chided her playfully, but with more than a hint of reproach, about her lazy housekeeping.

Robert may have mellowed, but Mary's ability to run a household had also improved. From the White House she had sent Annie detailed instructions for spring-cleaning. Whether she was home or not, she suspected that if she did not organize the annual cleaning, no one would. She wanted the heavy winter curtains taken down and stored in the attic as always, the rugs rolled up, the heart of pine floors given their yearly coating of dark stain made from walnut bark, and a long list of other chores done.

Toward midsummer, with Custis as escort, Mary, Agnes, and cousin Markie made the two-day train trip from Washington to Niagara by way of Baltimore, New York, and Elmira. Mary wrote Annie that Niagara Falls was a disappointment:

Man has done all in his power to mar its sublimity by building workshops & mills down to its very edge. I…lament that it had not been left in its wild state with trees & rocks overhanging the shore. This busy life of man does not accord with the sublimity of the cataract. How grand it must have been when the Indians first wandered on its shore!

St. Catherine's was twelve miles from the falls and filled with hotels and boarding houses for the visitors who came to take the famous waters. In Mary's eyes it was a "pretty little village," with stores selling Indian artifacts and other attractive souvenirs, though "the inhabitants never appear even at the doors. The place looks very much as if it had fallen into Rip Van Winkle's sleep." After a short stay in a hotel that Mrs. Lee pronounced "intolerably stupid," the group went to a more satisfactory place, "a sweet little vine covered cottage." Sundays they attended the local Anglican church, where they joined the rest of the congregation in prayers for "the sovereign lady Queen Victoria."

Mary was astonished both at the number of runaway slaves around the town and how badly the Canadians treated them. "There are a great many runaways here," she observed, adding:

> The white people say that before long they will be obliged to make laws to send them all out of Canada, so I see no place left for them but Africa. I am told they suffer a great deal here in the long cold winters. After enticing them over here, the white people will not let their children go to the same schools or treat them as equals in any way. So amalgamation is out of the question, tho' occasionally a very low Irish woman marries a black man.

The mineral waters at the resort tasted terrible, but Mary gamely pursued her course of treatment, beginning with a daily wineglass full of the salty concoction two hours before breakfast, followed by exercise. Annie was sick at home, and Mary suggested the same treatment for her, using water from the barrels Robert had bought earlier. "It is very nauseous," she warned her daughter, "but you can wash your mouth after taking it. Try one glass for a while and if it seems to do you good, increase the dose."

As she swam and drank at St. Catherine's Well, Mary sent a steady stream of instructions home to Annie, just turned twenty, and sixteen-year-old Rob, about keeping house and getting fourteen-year-old Mildred ready for school in the fall. The youngest Lee child had always been educated at home, but her parents thought her lessons there were now too unstructured for a young lady in need of some discipline and control. This year Mildred would attend a small boarding school in Winchester, Virginia.

Mary rose early at St. Catherine's and attended to her correspondence while Agnes and Markie were still asleep. Some days she could write only a page or two on account of her hands, but she almost always wrote something. One typical letter to Annie mentioned the work expected of the slaves. In part, it read:

> Tell Rob I depend upon him & Uncle Charles to attend to outdoor concerns, the garden & the park & to keep the [slave] children at work. Do see that they water my flowers. The latter part of next week I want Billy & Ephraim to wash a bag of wool & Nurse must see to the dyeing & putting it away & when Sally & Patsy have done knitting they can pull [card] it. Daniel must haul some manure for Ephraim's strawberry bed. When you get tomatoes enough, have some cans filled & sealed up. Old George picks them & Nurse must do them with someone to help her seal them up. I shall not put up so many as I did last year as there is some left. You had better lock up the key to my cellar as the wine there is a tempting article.

Mary also instructed Annie to get Mildred's wardrobe ready for the school term. If she needed any new underclothes, Annie was to buy thick cotton at twelve and a half cents a yard. "You had better have her dresses & gowns made also & see if you or your sister have anything that will do for her, as there will be no time when I return to make anything for her."

Mary was frugal with her clothing budget, but, as always, wanted her children well dressed:

> I think she had better have ruffles of the same sort round the necks of both her calico dresses as they are fashionable, youthful, and will save her much trouble.... Tell Mildred almost all of the ladies have ruffles on their dresses made of the same material as the dress. They are very pretty with a little cord in the middle.

And there were other items the schoolmistress had specified: "Each pupil must bring with her a list of her clothing, which must be marked with her name in full; half a dozen towels, also marked; over-shoes and an umbrella."

Mary also sent words of motherly encouragement. "I hope you will find your duties at home more pleasant than you anticipate, as there is always a satisfaction in the performance of duty while in all things else there is a certain disappointment."

With the season drawing to a close, Mary left St. Catherine's for New York City, where Agnes and Markie stayed behind to visit friends, then rode all night on the train to get to Arlington before Mildred set off for school. To Mary's disappointment, she discovered that Mildred had found an escort and left without waiting to say good-bye to her. Mary wrote to her daughter at once. "Perhaps it is as well that you went under such a good escort & I am glad you are so much pleased. I am sure, if you conduct yourself as a lady should do, you will meet with every kindness."

With Custis as her only steady companion through the fall, Mary felt more alone at Arlington that she ever had. There were visitors, of course, and letters from Robert and the children. She also spent some time making revisions for a second edition of *Recollections*, which continued to sell well both in the United States and England, despite further unflattering reviews in London that called the work "bulky and uninteresting," "turgid and bombastic."

Mary anxiously followed the presidential election of 1860—the prospects of a Lincoln presidency filled her with concern. This was only the Republicans' second presidential race, but the Democrats were divided between Buchanan's vice president, John C. Breckinridge, and Senator Stephen Douglas of Illinois. The Southern Democrats wanted Breckinridge because he believed that the abolition of slavery in the western territories was unconstitutional; the Northern wing preferred Douglas, who endorsed popular sovereignty.

Both Democratic candidates ran in the national election, as did John Bell, whose Constitutional Union Party stood for "the Union and the Constitution," however construed. With the vote split so many ways, the presidency went to the Republican candidate, Abraham Lincoln, who stood squarely against extension of slavery into the territories.

On December 20, 1860, little more than a month after the election, South Carolina voted to secede from the Union. Newspapers were filled with predictions and dire warnings, claims and counterclaims, rumors of anarchy and revolution. At Arlington five days later, Christmas was less festive than usual. Mary was uneasy: What would a Lincoln presidency bring? "Things wear a very gloomy aspect now that the Republican party in Congress threw cold water upon all the conservative movements," she wrote. Snow fell on Christmas Eve, followed by days of bitterly cold temperatures.

Recollections continued to sell steadily. But as the political situation around her deteriorated, Mary knew the value of having whatever money was due her well in hand—in cash. She had managed her household affairs for many months at a time without help from anyone, and she now inquired of her agent whether she could expect any more proceeds:

I do not know, my dear Sir, whether in these troubled times I am to expect any further payments upon the *Recollections*. It would be very acceptable at this time, but I write especially to say should there be any such, I do not care to have a note at 4 months subject to discount, but will wait 'till it becomes due.

In January, Mary revealed her anxiety in a letter to Mildred at school:

I do not feel much in my heart to go anywhere, viewing constantly the sad state of my country. We must be more earnest in supplication to that Almighty Power who alone can save us. This is all we poor women can do.... Prepare yourself for usefulness & devote all your powers to the service of God. There is no such thing as an indolent Christian.

As the political atmosphere became increasingly unstable, Mary looked for points of agreement between North and South and watched with horror as her beloved country marched, in her husband's words, toward "anarchy or civil war." How could the nation of Washington and Adams be so intent on tearing itself in two?

Mary found no peace as she pondered the issue. She was a slaveholder who despised the institution of slavery. Her slaves would be free within two years. She loved her country; she also loved her dear native state of Virginia. She deeply respected the government her husband had devoted his entire career to serving, but she also felt sure that citizens should be free to manage their affairs in whatever way they thought was best.

On February 4, 1861, a month before Lincoln's inauguration, representatives from South Carolina, Georgia, Florida, Alabama, Louisiana, and Mississippi met in Montgomery, Alabama, and announced the formation of the Confederate States of America, a republic dedicated to "states' rights and individual liberty."

Mary was not optimistic, as she stated frankly to Mildred:

With a sad and heavy heart, my dear child, I write, for the prospects before us are sad indeed. And as I think both parties are in the wrong in this fratricidal war there is nothing comforting even in the hope that God may prosper the right, for I see no right in this matter. We can only pray that in His mercy He will spare us.

On February 22, Mary crossed the river to attend the annual Washington's Birthday parade and festivities, but President Buchanan abruptly called it off for fear of some public disturbance. Returning home, she hosted her own party at Arlington instead. Among the guests were Henry and Charles Francis Adams, grandson and son of former president John Quincy Adams. Of the company at the elegant dinner, Charles recalled years later:

A daughter, Miss Agnes, I thought extremely attractive. We had some young officers of artillery there. A few months later we were all arrayed against each other; and I fancy there must have been fully half-a-dozen future generals and colonels about the Arlington table that day.

The next day the president-elect arrived in the city. Lincoln's life had been threatened, so he traveled in disguise, took a roundabout route by train, and reached the capital in the middle of the night. Mary recorded the event:

The papers are filled with Mr. Lincoln's arrival in Washington and this week will I presume decide our fate as a nation. I pray that the Almighty may listen to the prayers of the faithful in the land & direct their counsels for good, & that the designs of ambitious & selfish politicians may be frustrated, especially that our state may act right & obtain the merit promised in the Bible to the peace makers.

Like many Southerners, Mary blamed Lincoln for fanning the flames of war. If he had "consulted his own happiness and been a true and disinterested patriot," he would have resigned before taking office. "Nothing he can do now will meet with any favour from the South," she concluded.

Meanwhile, Colonel Lee was heading home from Texas. On February 1, the state had seceded from the Union and declared itself an independent republic, which it had been for nine years before its admission to the United States in 1845. Mary's old beau Sam Houston, former president of the Republic of Texas and governor of the state in 1861, strongly opposed secession and was driven from office. Within weeks, Texas joined the Confederacy.

Unsure of his official status, Robert went from his post to San Antonio. There he learned that his superior had turned over U.S. military equipment to the Texas militia and left town. Colonel Robert E. Lee, United States Army, was on alien soil. He changed into civilian clothes and, after a few days, left for Washington and consultations with General Scott.

Like his wife, Colonel Lee hated the thought of war. But his allegiance was clear. From San Antonio he wrote to a friend, "I still think…that my loyalty to Virginia ought to take precedence over that which is due the Federal government.… If Virginia stands by the old Union, so will I. But if she secedes (though I do not believe in secession as a Constitutional right, nor that there is sufficient cause for revolution), then I will still follow my native state with my sword, and if need be with my life."

At least for now, however, Virginia held firm for the Union.

CHAPTER SEVENTEEN

A DEATHLIKE
STILLNESS

*M*ary waited impatiently for Robert's return from the frontier
and felt herself flooded with relief when he arrived safely at
Arlington the afternoon of March 1, 1861. At fifty-four, he still
looked younger than his years. Mary, on the other hand, had aged rapidly. She
seemed more infirm by the month, her feet and ankles swollen constantly,
hips stiff and painful, and hands beginning to look gnarled and twisted.

Mary had already seen the effects of national upheaval in running her
household. Union and secessionist forces were jockeying for control of
institutions and public forums all over the state, and when both of them
tried to take control of the banks in Virginia, the banks closed their doors.
Mildred needed warmer clothes at school, and her mother could not withdraw any money to buy her some.

Mary explained the situation to Mildred and suggested how she could
keep warm:

> I hope you will be able to get along with what I have sent you, as
> times are very hard & the banks are all suspending payment. You
> could wear your calicoes when the weather is *not severe* with a *josey*
> over them—& if your arms are cold it is well just to pin up under
> your sleeves the legs of stockings.

Mary had no fear for her own safety. Even so, when Custis had to leave the estate on business for a few days, he insisted that Markie's brother, Orton Williams, stay in the house and look after the ladies. Orton, a frequent visitor who had a growing affection for Agnes (and she for him), was a junior member of General Scott's staff in Washington. But he made no secret of his eagerness to get a commission in the "Army of the Southern Republic."

Events moved more and more rapidly toward war. On March 16, Lee was commissioned a full colonel, replacing his brevet rank. President Lincoln himself signed the commission. On April 4 by a majority of more than two to one, the State of Virginia voted not to secede from the Union. On April 8 the President ordered the navy to resupply the federal garrison at Fort Sumter in Charleston, South Carolina, despite demands from rebel forces that the fort be abandoned. On April 12, South Carolina troops opened fire on the fort.

Lincoln immediately called for 75,000 volunteers—including Virginians—to squelch the insurrection. Jefferson Davis, who had been elected president of the Confederacy, responded with an order for 100,000 volunteers of his own.

Amidst these ominous events, Mary wrote a friend:

> Only God can stay the waves of anarchy & disunion & make the passions of men subservient to His will. We of the South have had great provocation, yet for my part I would rather endure the ills we know than rush madly into greater evils—& what could be greater than the division of our glorious Republic into petty states, each seeking its private interests & unmindful of the whole.

On April 18, President Lincoln, through his friend and confidant Francis Preston Blair, offered Lee a general's stars and command of the volunteer troops being raised to put down the Southern rebellion, but Lee declined. The next day, Virginia voted to secede from the Union, and Colonel Lee knew that, as a United States Army officer, he would soon be ordered to fight against Virginians. That he could never do.

Mary trusted her husband to make the right decision and vowed to support him whatever he did. Into the evening of April 19 she watched with sympathy and concern as he walked in the rose garden and paced through the house thinking about what course of action to take. Finally, leaving Mary to attend to guests who had gathered at the house to discuss Virginia's secession, Robert went upstairs to their bedroom.

The guests left one by one, her bedtime came and went, but still Mary heard her husband pacing the floor above, sometimes dropping to his knees in prayer. She left him alone and waited patiently until after midnight, when he descended the stairs with two letters in his hands. "Well, Mary," he said. "The question is settled. Here is my letter of resignation and a letter I have written to General Scott."

Fully aware of the importance of the moment, Mary answered, "Whichever way you go will be in the path of duty. You will think it right, and I shall be satisfied."

Robert handed her the letters to read. The first, to Secretary of War Simon Cameron, was a single sentence:

Sir:
    I have the honor to tender the resignation of my commission as Colonel of the 1st Regt. of Cavalry.
    Very resp'y Your Obedient Servant
    R. E. Lee
    Col. 1st Cav'y."

The other letter was longer and, Mary knew, ever so much harder to write. It was an explanation of his decision, written to the mentor and friend who had once called him "not only the greatest soldier of America, but the greatest now living in the world." Lee requested that Scott recommend acceptance of his resignation. "It would have been presented at once," he wrote, "but for the struggle it has cost me to separate myself from a service to which I have devoted the best years of my life, and all the ability I possessed.... Save in defense of my native state, I never desire to again draw my sword."

Two days later, Lee accepted a commission from Governor John Letcher as major general and commander in chief of the Virginia Provisional Army.

More than anyone, Mary knew what a patriot her husband was and what agony it was for him to give up the military career he loved so dearly.

His Virginia command was strictly defensive; the last thing on earth he wanted to do was harm the country he had cherished and faithfully served for fully half his life—even longer than he had been married.

The Northern papers interpreted Lee's actions differently. The visceral attack of one article in particular infuriated Mary. It numbered her husband among the "ingrates and traitors" who had resigned their Union commissions, and it dragged her into the matter as well:

> Lee once professed to greatly venerate the memory and example of the great Washington. He even married the daughter of George Washington Parke Custis... [who] never tired of writing and eloquently portraying the virtues and eminent deeds of the Father of his Country.... [If Custis] could have lived until now, he would have good cause to be bowed down in grief and sorrow to behold his son-in-law following in the footsteps of Benedict Arnold.

To a Washington newspaper editor and family friend, Mary penned a reply, trusting that it would make its way north. She couched her response not in the shrill tone the paper had adopted, but in the thoughtful, incisive words of the well-educated, well-read woman she was. It was as clear and straightforward a statement of the Southern cause as would ever be written:

> I do not know, my dear sir, what your feeling may be *now* towards the South, and this unhappy difference which has destroyed our glorious Union forever.... I have lived seven of the happiest years of my life in the North and have admired its institutions, its energy, its progress; have never denied the great advantages they possess [over us with] their free labor, or attributed to the people the mad ravings of a few fanatics. I had no sympathy with the hasty course of South Carolina and prayed and hoped for the Union...till the course of the Administration left us no alternative but to retire and defend our lives, our fortune, and our sacred honor, and I assure you there is *but one voice* now in the South.
>
> The idea of coercing a free people into *Union* is perfectly absurd, and there is a spirit here that will not be coerced. There is a perfect

military despotism now at Washington.... I pray daily to God to avert civil war, yet cannot conceive why Lincoln has assembled such an army if it is not his intention to *attempt* to *crush* the South.... I have but one great consolation now, that my dear parents are both laid low in their graves, where but for my children I would most gladly lay beside them.

The provocation was about to grow much greater. From his vantage point at military headquarters in Richmond, Lee could tell that his wife and her property were in danger, and he urged her to move to a safer place. Mary knew something of the situation too. The same incendiary newspapers that had attacked her husband insisted that the Arlington estate, on a high bluff directly across from Washington, was "a nest of traitors," an obvious place for launching a rebel attack on the Union capital that should be taken and fortified against the enemy as soon as possible. Mary reeled from the shock of the accusation that her home—built in honor of Washington—would be used to attack the country he had helped found.

About the same time, she had a revealing firsthand look at the government's efforts to turn public opinion against her husband and to justify confiscating her property. She happened to be in Washington when the New York 7th Regiment paraded into town. To Mary the whole affair looked like a trumped-up effort to incite both the soldiers and the public. As she later recalled:

Not a cheer was raised even from a small boy, and with sullen and downcast countenance they marched to the President's House, where some faint huzzars were raised, I was told, by men hired for the occasion. As I was going out of town, one of the members of the Reg. who I had known at West Point came to the door of my carriage to greet me. [I asked,] "What are you doing here in this guise?" He replied, "We were summoned here to defend the Capitol which we were told was in imminent danger & expected to see Jeff Davis with an army of at least 30,000 men on the Arlington Heights." I replied, "Come over and judge for yourself. I will secure you against capture."

Over the next two weeks Robert continued to warn Mary to move, but she could not bring herself to leave. On April 26 he wrote from Richmond:

I am very anxious about you. You have to move and go to some point of safety, which you must select. The Mount Vernon plate and pictures ought to be secured. Keep quiet while you remain and in your preparation. War is inevitable, and there is no telling when it will burst around you. Virginia, yesterday, I understand, joined the Confederate States. What policy they may adopt I cannot conjecture. May God bless and preserve you, and have mercy upon all our people....

Robert wrote again on April 30—"You had better prepare all things for removal, that is, the plate, pictures, etc. and be prepared at any moment"— and yet again on May 2—"I want you to be in a place of safety.... We have only to be resigned to God's will and pleasure, and do all we can for our protection...." But in the end, it was not her husband's constant prodding that galvanized Mary into action, but an unexpected visit from Orton Williams, grandson of her aunt Martha Custis Peter.

One sunny afternoon, a house servant answered the knock at Arlington's huge oak front door to find Orton, dressed in his United States Army uniform, waiting impatiently in the shade of the portico. At twenty-two, he was fresh faced and fair skinned, with dark, penetrating eyes like Mary's. Except for his sense of urgency, his appearance would have been no surprise. He was courting Agnes, and his face was as familiar to the servants as their masters' were. Flushed with the urgency and import of his message, Orton rushed upstairs wide-eyed into Mary's bedroom, where she sat at her easel copying an oil portrait of her son Rob.

Mary was startled at his appearance and even more amazed at his message. "You've got to get out now. Union troops are ready to take Arlington Heights."

Orton did not have to tell her who had dispatched him from Washington. Freshly commissioned a Union lieutenant, the young soldier was still on General Scott's staff despite his Southern sympathies. Now in command of the Union forces, Scott had sent Orton on this secret, personal mission to warn his friend's family that Federal troops were on their way to occupy the house. Robert's old friend was warning Mary to get out while she still could.

As suddenly as he had arrived, Orton rushed out of the room and back down the stairs. His warning spurred Mary to begin planning her departure immediately. But the next morning, she looked out her bedroom window after a sleepless night to see him emerge from the woods and move quickly through the garden to the house. He brought heartening news: The invasion had been delayed.

A few days later, Orton went to resign his commission in order to join the Confederacy. He was offered a position as an instructor in cavalry tactics at West Point if he would stay with the Union. When he refused, he was sent to prison on Governor's Island. As Mary reported to Robert, "All his assurances that he considered himself bound in honor not to reveal anything & that you & I had advised him to remain in the U.S. service as long as he could & be of use to Genl. Scott were not credited."

By now, Mary had no doubt that the Federals were looking for an excuse to invade Virginia:

> They are anxious at present to keep up an appearance & would gladly I believe have a *pretext* for invading Virginia soil.... Capt. Townsend & Col. Thomas, who had remonstrated with him in the most urgent manner, told [Orton] he would be branded as a traitor of the deepest dye & no one would believe that he had not [visited Arlington] to betray all their plan of operations of which he had been made cognizant.

Beginning her preparations at last, Mary moved quickly to safeguard as many belongings as possible. The family silver, Washington's personal papers, and Custis and Lee family papers were packed in two crates and sent by rail to Robert in Richmond. Books and engravings were locked away in closets. Carpets and drapes—including a set of damask draperies from Martha Washington—went into the attic. The famous punch bowl with its ship painted on the bottom, the Washington state china, and the other Mount Vernon relics were securely crated and locked in the cellar.

On May 8 paintings, wine, food, clothes, housekeeping supplies, and the Arlington piano were loaded up, and daughter Mary and Agnes traveled with them to Ravensworth, where Aunt Maria Fitzhugh had offered to let them all stay as long as they needed to.

The next day, Mary wrote Robert:

> I suppose 'ere this, dear Robert, you have heard of the arrival of our valuables in Richmond. We have sent many others to Ravensworth.... I was very unwilling to do this; but Orton was *so* urgent & even intimated that the day was fixed to take possession of these heights, that I did not feel it was prudent to risk articles that could never be replaced.

She also wrote General Scott, who had sent her a gracious message asking for an account of Lee's activities in Richmond. She cut an article about his arrival there from the Richmond newspaper and sent it in reply. Indirectly, she thanked him for warning her about the coming occupation, but she also made it clear that she was leaving Arlington only because withdrawing to a point of safety would ease Robert's mind a little.

> My dear General:
>
> Hearing that you desire to see the account of my husband's reception in Richmond, I have sent it to you. No honors can reconcile us to this fratricidal war which we would have laid down our lives freely to avert. Whatever may happen, I feel that I may expect from your kindness all the protection you can in honor afford.... If you knew all, you would not think so hardly of me. Were it not that I would not add one feather to [my husband's] load of care, nothing would induce me to abandon my home. Oh that you could command peace to our distracted country!

Mary was alone in the house now except for Custis and the servants. Rooney was with his family at the White House, and Annie was there as well, helping with the baby. Rob and Mildred were at school; Daughter and Agnes were already at Ravensworth. Robert was with his men, and there was no telling when, or if, she would see him again.

The spring weather had been unusually chilly and wet, and the flower gardens had started the season far behind schedule. On April 10, Mary had written Mildred that it was still too dark and cold for most of the flowers. "We have had some lovely callas in the greenhouse & those parma violets, but there is so little sun very few things bloom." The road to Alexandria had been so muddy that she had not gone to church in four weeks. Now, a month later, the gardens had blossomed magnificently.

Returning to her writing desk after an early morning walk around the garden on her crutches, Mary poured out her feelings to Robert about her treasured surroundings and the uncertain prospects for the future:

> This is a lovely morning. I never saw the countryside more beautiful, perfectly *radiant*. The yellow jasmine is in full bloom & perfuming all the air, but a deathlike stillness prevails everywhere. You hear no sound from Washington, not a soul moving about. We may well exclaim, "Can such things be? Can man thus trample upon all his Creator has lavished upon him of love & beauty?" I think the hours and years must be commencing when Satan is to be let loose upon earth...and while we must feel that our sins both personal & national merit the chastisement of the Almighty, we may still implore Him to spare us & with mercy not in wrath to visit us.

How could Mary explain to a fifteen-year-old girl what was happening? Mildred had written from Winchester asking for more money and more clothes, wondering about her cats, relaying news of happenings at school, and talking about plans for the summer. She had been away since before the Confederacy was formed, and, through no fault of her own, had no real idea of what was going on. The night of May 9, at the end of the lovely spring day she had described to her husband, Mary wrote Mildred a starkly honest assessment of the family's prospects:

> My dear little girl,
>
> I received your very amusing letter & am glad that you have spirits to be happy. We, alas, are very sad now. We have received information from a friend that the government troops are to take possession of these heights in a few days, & as they will not I suppose be allowed to remain here if the South can dislodge them, I fear this will be the scene of conflict & my beautiful home,

endeared by a thousand associations, may become a field of car-
nage God forbid.... Except to relieve the mind of your Father and
brother & leave them...to perform their duty, I would not stir
from the house even if the whole Northern Army were to surround
it. The zealous patriots who are risking their lives to *preserve* the
Union founded by Washington might come & take the [great]
granddaughter of his wife from her home & desecrate it, for whatever I have thought, and even *now* think, of the commencement of
this horrible conflict, *now* our duty is *plain*—to resist unto death.

The government has proved itself so false & treacherous that
we have nothing to hope. The men who are at the head of it seem
to be without honor & without pity & I believe it would give them
[satisfaction] to lay waste our fair country.... In God is our only
hope.

I have sent all our silver & valuables to Richmond & some
other things to Ravensworth where we are going in a few days &
will remain till we see what is to be done & the rest of our effects
must take their chance. I do not know what to do with Bub [a
cat].... Poor fellow, he comes up to see me every morning in my
room & gets in my bed. I shall be very sorry to leave him [with the
servants] but hope he will escape harm & if this alarm should not
be true, I shall come down & see after him.

I cannot attend to your little wants now, & if they are indis-
pensable & you have spent all your money, ask Mrs. Powell [the
schoolmistress] to advance you some.... Make the best of your
time as we may not be able to send you to school another year....
May God bless you. Pray for your country that it may yet be
delivered.

Rooney and Custis both requested and received commissions in the
Virginia army. Seventeen-year-old Rob wanted one too, but his parents
thought he was too young. Custis was leaving for Richmond in a few days,
and Mary waited until he was ready to go so he could escort her to
Ravensworth on the way.

Meanwhile, she got another letter from Mildred, who complained
about a bonnet she had received and said that she needed money to pay

back schoolmates she had borrowed from. She still failed to see the gravity of the situation. On May 11, Mary replied:

> I must confess I was both hurt & mortified that a *daughter* of *mine,* at a time when her Father's life is in peril, her home in danger of being trampled over by a lawless foe, if not leveled to the ground, should allow a disappointment about a *bonnet* to be so *deep* in her mind....
>
> All is gloom & uncertainty & I see nothing before me but war. I would have greatly preferred remaining at home & having my children around me, but as it would greatly increase your father's anxiety, I shall go to Ravensworth & await the issue of events.

The same day, Robert wrote Mary from his Richmond headquarters:

> I am glad to hear that you are at peace, and enjoying the sweet weather and beautiful flowers. You had better complete your arrangements and retire further from the scene of war. It may burst upon you at any time. It is sad to think of the devastation, if not ruin, it may bring upon a spot so endeared to us. But God's will be done. We must be resigned.

In another letter on May 13, he wrote:

> Make your plans for several years of war. If Virginia is invaded, which appears to be designed, the main routes through the country will, in all probability, be infested and passage interrupted. The times are indeed calamitous. The brightness of God's countenance seems turned away from us, and its mercy stopped in its blissful current. It may not always be so dark, and He may in time pardon our sins and take us under his protection.

On May 14, the Virginia army joined forces with the Confederacy, and Robert Edward Lee's command was transferred to the Confederate States of America.

One morning, Mary watched as two Confederate officers rode up the drive, across the lawn, and around the property, almost as if they were scouting for something. She hoped that the Confederates were planning to build some kind of fortification to protect the area, but the men did not call at the house, and they never returned.

There were other telltale signs that something was about to happen. River traffic increased exponentially almost overnight, and the Potomac was suddenly crowded with transports, cargo vessels, tugs, and ships of every size and description. A number of Arlington slaves disappeared under cover of darkness, gone without a trace. And Washington newspapers reported that Union troops were set to commandeer Arlington Heights any day.

At last the moment came when, with the family pets distributed among the slaves and the house keys turned over to a trusted personal maid, Selina Grey, a daughter of Old Nurse, Mary had nothing left to do but get into her waiting carriage and drive away. And so on a beautiful morning in the middle of May, 1861, Mary Custis Lee took one last walk—slowly and stiffly, leaning on her crutches—through the garden her parents had laid out more than half a century before, now awash in the colors and fragrances of spring. Here was her mother's favorite spot. And here were little plots where each of the girls had planted whatever pleased them. Mildred's was smaller than the rest because she used part of her space to bury her cats in when they died. Mary stooped slowly, stiffly, and cut a moss rose from the arbor.

At the foot of the rolling lawn was the river, and across it Washington City glistened in the sun. There was the Capitol. Her great-grandmother's husband had laid the cornerstone while her father watched, and now a new dome was under construction, begun under the auspices of Jefferson Davis what seemed like a thousand years ago. There was the Washington Monument, whose cornerstone her father had helped haul through the streets, a marble stub stalled by partisan discord at just over 150 feet.

As Custis helped her into the carriage, Mary saw tears in the servants' eyes through the tears in her own. A shake of the reins, and the carriage wheels began to roll. Mary braced herself as best she could for the ten-mile ride to Ravensworth and watched her home slowly disappear behind the hillside. Then she looked down at the freshly cut rose in her lap: a rose of Arlington. She wondered when she would ever see another one.

For more than a week there was an eerie calm about the estate. The slaves continued their duties in the house and on the grounds. Meals were served, livestock tended, furniture dusted, gardens kept. The commander of Virginia troops in Alexandria was instructed not to disturb the house so as not to provoke the Federals, but reports flew that rebels were mapping out fortifications and that an artillery battery was being installed to lay siege to Washington.

At last, on the clear, moonlit night of May 23, more than ten thousand Federal troops crossed the Potomac across the Long Bridge and the Aqueduct Bridge to the Virginia shore. They fanned out across the countryside, skirmishing from time to time with Confederate pickets. Settling into makeshift campsites, many of them had a view of a magnificent white mansion, which they understood belonged to the "ex-Colonel Lee."

CHAPTER EIGHTEEN

HOMELESS

*R*avensworth was a natural refuge for Mary, its lawns and welcoming rooms as familiar to her as Arlington. She had visited her maternal grandparents there since before she could remember; later she often brought her own children to see their Fitzhugh cousins. She had named Rooney after her Uncle William, who inherited the plantation from his father.

The Fitzhughs of Ravensworth were related to Mary's husband as well; Mary's Uncle William was a cousin of Robert's mother, Ann Carter Lee. Robert too had visited Ravensworth as a boy. He was at his mother's side when she died of tuberculosis at the Fitzhugh townhouse in Alexandria within days of his graduation from West Point in 1829; and she was buried in the family cemetery on the Ravensworth grounds.

The house was not nearly as impressive as Arlington, but it was large and comfortable: a frame structure with a long, two-story porch across the front, set in a magnificent stand of old oaks. The landholdings, at 22,000 acres, were twenty times Arlington's.

Mary went there, as she wrote Mildred at school, to "await the issue of events," hopeful of returning home within a few weeks. She was both saddened and irritated at word of the celebrations in Washington after the western shore of the Potomac was "secured" by Union forces. She was equally upset at reports of celebrations in Richmond when Virginia's secession vote was ratified and its membership in the Confederacy became official.

Now that his mother was safely situated, Custis made plans to serve as an engineer in the Confederate army. Rooney had already left his wife and new baby at the White House to accept a commission in the cavalry. Rob, still at the University of Virginia, again begged for permission to enlist. From West Point years earlier, Mary had written to a cousin about a mother's helplessness in protecting her sons from the dangers of the world. Now her observations were more relevant than ever:

> The only hope we can entertain for our sons, exposed as they always are to dangers & snares both for body & soul in every situation, is to trust them to Almighty God & pray that His Spirit may fill their hearts & purify them so that they may be preserved from the Evil One.

Soon Agnes went to join Annie at the White House, and Custis's departure left daughter Mary in the unaccustomed position of being her mother's only companion. The two of them waited impatiently at Ravensworth for news of their home, hoping any day to hear that the invaders had gone and they could return. The newspapers were no help; the Virginia papers had been shut down, and Mary believed that the Washington papers were printing nothing but rumors. Mail delivery became erratic, though just after arriving at Ravensworth, she and Agnes had received a letter from Markie Williams, who was studying art at Cooper Union in New York.

The war had separated Markie from her brother: After being paroled, Orton had joined the Confederacy, while Markie stayed loyal to the Union. Even so, she still loved the Lees and feared for their safety. She admitted that she wept at hearing the account "of the last days at dear, dear Arlington."

News of Mary's home came at last, and the first reports were encouraging. General Charles W. Sandford, the officer in charge of the occupying forces, had not disturbed the house, but had set up his headquarters in three tents on the lawn. Troops made camp in the surrounding area, staying clear of the house and gardens, though they cut down trees by the dozen for firewood.

Two days after he arrived, General Sandford posted a guard around the house, reinforcing his earlier orders that nothing was to be harmed and no servants disturbed. Visitors began arriving from Washington to see the famous house, including poet Charles Russell Lowell and President Lincoln's son Robert. With Robert was presidential secretary John Hay, who mentioned the house in his diary. "I do not know when it was built," he wrote, "but it was evidently in its day a grand affair."

As the days wore on and the novelty of their situation wore off, troops became steadily bolder about approaching the servants and entering the house. The gardens were still "a mass of flowers" surrounded by "luxuriance and beauty," according to one newspaper report, yet keeping the soldiers away from "General Lee's property" (as everyone called it, though it belonged to his wife) became an impossible task.

Finally, after Union soldiers had killed his pets and threatened his wife, an overseer from the estate traveled to Ravensworth to report to Mary. She listened as the man, tears streaming down his face, recited a litany of abuses he was powerless to stop. His story released a flood of pent-up emotion in Mary. There was no more denying the unvarnished truth: The country to which she and her family had devoted their lives had confiscated the only home she had ever known—a home built to honor the very hero she was now accused of betraying.

Mary wrote immediately to General Sandford, her handwriting level and even, her disdain and resentment seething through her accustomed genteel courtesy:

It never occurred to me Gen'l. San[d]ford that *I* could be forced to sue for permission to enter my *own house* and that such an outrage as its military occupation to the exclusion of me and my children could ever have been perpetrated by anyone in the whole extent of this country.

I had been warned by an anxious friend that such a design was in contemplation nearly a month ago & advised to remove to a place of safety all my property that was of any value. Still *incredulous,* I complied with his earnest entreaties in regard to the Mt. Vernon relics, plate, & pictures that we could never replace, & after a visit of about 10 days to a friend in Fairfax was preparing to return to enjoy the season of all others most delightful and prepare for the reception of my younger children, who will soon be returning from their different schools, when I was informed that the whole place as well as the mansion was occupied by Northern troops....

So I am left homeless, not even able to get or send to Alexandria where my funds are deposited to obtain means for my support.... The whole country is filled with men, women & children flying in terror.

The South, she continued, never believed the story that Arlington Heights had to be occupied by Federal troops in order to keep the Confederacy from attacking the capital. Had the South wanted to launch an offensive on Washington, they could have fortified the heights months before.

However, I forget that I am a suppliant and cannot trust my pen to write what I feel. You have a beautiful home & people that you love, & can sympathize perhaps even with the wife of a "traitor & a rebel!" I implore you by the courtesy due to any woman and which no brave soldier could ever deny, to allow my old coachman by whom I send this letter to get his clothes & give some letters to my manager relative to the farm & etc....

After requesting passes for various slaves who made regular visits to their families in Washington, Mary concluded, "I will not trouble you with any further requests, only pray that God may ever spare you & yours the agony and inconvenience I am now enduring. Respectfully, M. C. Lee."

Mary sent the letter by Daniel as soon as it was ready. General Sandford had been relieved on May 28, two days before Mary wrote to him, and so it was his replacement, General Irvin McDowell, who received her letter and answered it the same afternoon.

The sight of the heading alone made Mary flush with indignation: "Head Qrs. Dept N. E. Virginia/Arlington May 30, 1861."

McDowell explained that he had replaced Sandford in the field and was replying in his stead. Then he assured her:

With respect to the occupation of Arlington by the United States troops, I beg to say it has been done by my predecessor with every regard to the preservation of the place. I am here temporarily in camp on the grounds, preferring this to sleeping in the house, under the circumstances which the painful state of the country places me with respect to its proprietors.

One of his command, he explained, lived in the downstairs of the house to "insure its being respected."

I insure you, it has been and will be my earnest endeavor to have all things so ordered that on your return you will find things as little disturbed as possible.... Everything has been done as you described with respect to your servants, and your wishes, as far as they are known or could be anticipated, have been complied with. When you desire to return, every facility will be given you for so doing.

I trust, Madam, you will not consider it an intrusion if I say I have the most sincere sympathy for your distress; and that, as far as it is compatible with my duty, I shall always be ready to do whatever may alleviate it.

In a postscript, he added that the occupying forces had been ordered not to enter the house when they arrived if the family was still there.

Writing to her husband that evening, Mary confided, "I fear there is nothing but the special protection of Heaven which can save [Arlington] from ruin." Unknown to her, a letter from Robert was already on its way with a reminder that the sovereign hand of God was guiding everything. "I fear we have not been grateful enough for the happiness there within our reach," he wrote, "and our Heavenly Father has found it necessary to deprive us of what He has given us."

That night, Mary also wrote at length to her cousin Caroline Peters, whose recent letter to Mary had been especially welcome at a time "when the friendship of some is apt to wax cool." Mary warned that she could not write details of her location or plans for the future because of the threat of "espionage" and the unsteady state of the postal service. But she pulled no punches in assessing the national dilemma:

One thing is certain, that the South will resist unto death. I think when the government has exhausted itself upon us, the North itself will revolt against the despotism it had aided to uphold. I am glad Kentucky is allowed to remain neutral & wish that the Border States had been all able to unite to prevent the war, but it is the will of Heaven perhaps to chastise us for our sins. Oh, may we submit & perchance the Lord may turn away His anger from us.... A little concession on both sides might have adjusted all in the beginning, but now the South has but one course left....

Tho' every hearth in the South is open to me however humble, still I feel desolate & houseless most especially as the time approaches to have all my children assembled at that happy season when they come home from vacation, but I will try to say from my heart, "God's will be done to me & mine" even should He slay us.

General Lee wanted Mary and Daughter farther from the skirmish lines and was concerned at the reprisals the Federals might visit on Ravensworth if they learned that the Lee family was there. So, while she considered her long-term plans, Mary accepted invitations to visit several friends and relatives during the spring and early summer. After two weeks or so, she went on a round of travels to visit the widow of her Uncle Calvert Stuart at Chantilly, Randolph kin at Eastern View, and cousin Edward Turner and his family at Kinloch. She traveled back and forth among some of these places several times, with daughter Mary helping her in and out of the old Arlington coach and Daniel driving her, as he had since she was a girl.

Mary wrote Mildred to plan to meet her at Kinloch when school was out for the summer. Instead of focusing her letters on her vagabond lifestyle or threats posed by war, she dwelt on mundane matters that lent a sense of normalcy to her routine and to Mildred's life. She told Mildred that she had received her report card, "which much gratified me," and instructed her to pack her things and store them there in boxes with her name, since no one knew whether or not they could send her back to school next year. She also told her to be sure to bring her music with her to Kinloch, "as they have a piano there." She made her customary reference to styles and fashions, including an ironic mention of a Zouave, a short, fitted, embroidered jacket. Similar to a type worn by fancifully uniformed French Algerian soldiers, it had also been adopted by a unit of Federal troops now camped on the Arlington grounds.

Even more than usual, Mary took care in these uncertain times to look after her children's spiritual needs. When Mildred confessed doubts and fears about her spiritual worthiness and her faith, her mother was quick to respond:

> Do not be discouraged because you see so much in yourself that is vile & sinful. That is the sure work of the Holy Spirit. Before His influence was shed into your heart, you could see none of your faults. It was like coming into the parlor some cloudy morning. All the dust & litter of the room would *not* be *visible*. But let a bright ray of *sunshine* gleam in & how you would see every particle of dust! So the Holy Spirit has shined into your heart & you are astonished at what you see there. He shows all these defilements to you that He may cleanse them & daily you must pray for his purifying influence....
>
> Do not doubt for a moment His power & His willingness to receive you.... He will keep you safe. He will never leave you nor forsake you. He will give you peace & joy the world knows not of.

Mary recalled her own spiritual conversion more than thirty years earlier, just after she and Lieutenant Lee were engaged:

> When first I was brought to feel my sinfulness... I was for some weeks very miserable. I could not feel willing to give up *all* for God. The world had such a strong hold upon me & the Tempter whispered to me, "Banish these thoughts. They will only make you unhappy." But I could not get rid of them & it was only when, after many prayers & tears, I was made to feel willing to give up *all*, even my life, if God should require it, that I obtained joy & peace.

Those same divine gifts of assurance and peace brought Mary a change of heart about the home she had left behind. During her first days at Ravensworth, she had expected to return to Arlington any day and fretted constantly about what was happening to her property in her absence. But on June 6, a houseguest at Chantilly noted in her diary that "Mrs. Genl. Lee" now saw matters differently. She said she expected to be away from her home "for an indefinite period" and that she was happy and confident about the future. "I never saw her more cheerful," the diarist observed, "and seems to have no doubt of our success."

In July, Mary welcomed Mildred to Kinloch. Days later a letter came from cousin Markie, who had secured permission from General Scott to remove her own clothes and other personal belongings from the bedroom at Arlington that she had shared with Daughter off and on for years. It was the first eyewitness account Mary had received of their home since the overseer had reported to her a month earlier.

The letter was heartbreaking. As Markie had passed along the drive, she had seen soldiers camped everywhere. "I was blinded with tears & choked with sorrow," she wrote. "The poor house looked so desolate." She went upstairs, locked herself in her old room, and had a long cry alone before packing up her trunk. Going into the attic to look for some letters, she found one of Mildred's favorite cats, Tom Titta, who "rubbed his little head against my dress in the most affectionate way. I took him up, covered him with tears & kisses. Oh! How many fond associations of the past did that poor little cat bring up." Markie also passed on greetings from the house servants, who all gathered around to see her and send messages to the Lees. "Who in their wildest dreams could have conjured all this last summer? It was but one year ago that we were all there, so happy & so peaceful."

Stories of marauding Northern soldiers circulated everywhere, and Mary heard firsthand the story of one man, probably a neighbor near Ravensworth, whose life had been threatened by "perfectly lawless" New Jersey troops. The whole sorry state of affairs "only wants the guillotine to complete it," she concluded. Mary also heard rumors of "marches & counter-marches" in the region and felt certain that "some crisis is approaching."

She was right. On Sunday, July 21, 1861, Federal troops—under the command of General McDowell, whose men were camped in Mary's front yard—attacked a Confederate force commanded by General P. G. T. Beauregard that was stationed along a creek known as Bull Run, between Manassas and Sudley Springs. Neither side was prepared for war. The Northern troops were supposedly on duty for the defense of Washington, but their three-month enlistments were almost up, nothing much had happened, and the public wanted action. Lincoln decided to give it to them.

The battlefield was forty miles from Kinloch; even so, Mary could hear the sounds of cannon fire that morning. She waited impatiently for news of the outcome and was elated and relieved when she learned that the South had driven the Yankees from the field in a rout and that none of her family had been there. Had the Confederates known the extent of their victory, they might have marched into Washington on the spot; but they did not, and by the time they realized what they had achieved, it was too late to take advantage of their success.

Excited as they were by this early, decisive victory, the sight of wounded men in ambulances the next day gave the family members at Kinloch a taste of the shattering reality of war. Rain poured down in torrents as some of the injured were taken to a makeshift field hospital at Blantyre, an estate nearby. Daughter Mary and Mildred volunteered as nurses there. Mildred in particular seemed a startling contrast to the grim surroundings. "She was dressed in a blue riding habit," a volunteer later remembered, "very pretty and so fresh and fair."

In midsummer, Mary left Kinloch for a brief visit with her cousin Mary Meade and then went on across the Blue Ridge Mountains to Audley, the Lewis estate that had once been the home of Mary's beloved Aunt Nelly, her father's sister Eleanor. Not only was the weather cooler there, but it was also farther from the battlefront and only a few miles from Winchester, where Mary still hoped to send Mildred back to school in the fall.

Mary wrote Robert for advice on where to send their daughter, but he replied, as he had from duty stations in the past, that he was in no position to tell her what to do. He instructed her to decide "as you think best about Mildred. I am unable to help you, even about your own movements.... Everything within the seat of war must be uncertain." Mildred did go back to school in Winchester, but the loss of war had already touched that quiet town: One of the schoolmistress's sons had fallen at Manassas.

Cloudbursts that began just after the Battle of Manassas continued day after day. One soldier swore it rained thirty-two days during August that year. Although the wet weather aggravated her painful arthritis, Mary wrote letter after letter, unsure if they would ever reach their intended recipients. She had also started knitting socks for General Lee and enclosing them in her letters. There were few newspapers or books for her to read and no opportunities to paint or garden, so knitting became a pastime that produced a sense of accomplishment, along with a comforting reminder of home for the general.

Once Mildred was back at school, Mary thought she would try to take a trip back to Hot Springs, Virginia, for another round of mineral baths. The general advised against it, warning her that the season was past and the weather there was already too cold. Eager for any chance to relieve her symptoms, Mary replied that she wanted to make the trip anyway. Rob, still on vacation from school, escorted his mother and Daughter to the baths. It was a wonderful respite from her wandering, unsettled life to stay put and be pampered for a while, and Mary enjoyed several weeks of swimming and socializing before the cold weather put an end to her visit.

As a faithful correspondent and newspaper reader all her life, Mary was hungry for reliable news of her husband, her home, her children, and her country. She wrote to Robert often, knowing he would answer when he could. To friends she sent letters asking for newspapers, scrounging for any information she could about what was happening in Washington and Richmond.

During the latter part of her stay at Hot Springs, Mary stumbled onto a copy of *Harper's Magazine* that had an illustrated article about Arlington. It was the first news Mary had of her house and property in many weeks. From what she could tell, the house and contents were still intact, though she imagined that the lawns had been trampled by soldiers on maneuvers and the great Arlington Forest decimated to feed countless campfires. She cheerfully showed the drawing of the house to other guests, telling them that it was an accurate likeness and that she hoped to return there someday.

From Hot Springs, Mary went to Shirley. By then, she had not seen her husband in more than six months, since just after he had written his letter of resignation to General Scott. Her world had been turned upside down, and there were times she wondered if she would ever see Robert again.

Her heart leapt with joy, then, when she received a letter from him saying that he planned to come to Shirley and spend a day with his "dear Mim." Capable as she was and accustomed to his absences, Mary missed Robert desperately and prayed that he would be able to make the short trip.

On a lighter note, she was curious to see him in his newly cultivated "beautiful white beard," which, he had written Mildred, "is much admired. At least much remarked on."

But the general could not find a boat going toward the plantation on the day he could travel. He started out on horseback, but when he realized there was not enough daylight left to make the trip, he returned to Richmond. "I will come, however, wherever you are," he wrote Mary on November 5, "either Shirley or the White House, as soon as possible, and if not sooner, Saturday at all events...." But the next day General Lee was ordered to South Carolina, and his reunion with Mary was postponed indefinitely.

There was still the question of where Mary would establish her household for the duration of the war. "There is no prospect of your returning to Arlington," the general told her flatly. "I think you had better select some comfortable place in the Carolinas or Georgia and all board together [with the children].... It is a good opportunity to try a warmer climate for your rheumatism. If I thought our enemies would not make a vigorous move against Richmond, I would recommend to rent a house there."

Mary went to Rooney's White House plantation, where Annie and Agnes had been living between visits to other relatives. Rooney's young son, Robert III, had been seriously ill for some time, and his wife, Charlotte, was five months pregnant with her second. As she had done so often, Mary assumed the role of family nurse, lending the struggling young mother experienced help she could "*depend* upon."

As the school year began, the rest of the family scattered—Rob and Mildred back to their studies, Daughter to Kinloch, and Annie and Agnes on a round of visits, including one to Stratford, their father's birthplace. Daughter also tried to call at Ravensworth, but it was now occupied by Federal troops.

Meanwhile, the Arlington estate was being destroyed piecemeal. The mill at Four Mile Run, of which Custis had been so proud and which Lee had recently spent a large sum restoring, was partially dismantled for firewood and then wrecked beyond repair in a skirmish with Confederate pickets. Fences on the farm were gone for firewood as well; animals were commandeered and crops destroyed. Even the once natty river steamer that had ferried picnickers to Arlington Spring was pressed into service as a platform for launching Federal observation balloons to spy on Confederate positions.

Britannia Peter Kennon, the Lee children's "Aunt Brit," had rescued the curtains and carpets in the house and stored them safely at Tudor Place. But soon, the pace of looting accelerated to the point that the servants were powerless to stop it. The cellar lock had been broken, and numerous Washington relics, including the famous frigate punch bowl, were missing.

In tears, the housekeeper, Selina Grey, presented her key in person to General McDowell, begging him to honor his promise to protect the house and its contents. Lee relatives also asked him to allow them to move what was left to Tudor Place. But the general thought the articles should stay safely in official hands.

Eventually they were put on public display at the Patent Office—the same place Mr. Custis had once suggested that his gifts of Washington memorabilia be shown. The display of Mary's belongings was accompanied by a large sign that crowed, "Captured from Arlington."

CHAPTER NINETEEN

A GRANDDAUGHTER OF
MRS. WASHINGTON

*M*rs. General Lee spent the first Christmas of the war at the White House plantation. Rooney got leave to join his wife and son there for a short while, and Rob arrived as soon as school was out. Annie and Agnes finished their rounds of visits and came back too. Mary was pleased to have so many of her family together again, and the four who were missing were constantly in her thoughts and prayers. Robert was on an extended trip to fortify East Coast defenses; Custis remained on duty through the holidays; daughter Mary was spending Christmas in Richmond with the Caskies, a family she and her mother had met at Hot Springs; and Mildred stayed at school, probably in part because enemy lines were moving closer and it was too dangerous to travel.

Realizing that his sister had never spent Christmas alone before, Rob wrote Mildred a long letter describing the scene at White House: "The farm is lovely, the land lying level near the river & breaking into beautiful hills as you go back inland. The house is small, but very comfortable & very nicely furnished; the grounds around the house are being improved daily."

Though she had a relatively modest bill of fare and none of her elegant silver and china, Mary had a more meaningful Christmas than many of the elaborate celebrations of years past. Rooney was there, representing the thousands of family men in uniform fighting to defend their homes and traditions. Baby Robert, his health improving, slept contentedly by the fire, the first of a new generation that would carry the legacy of Washington into the future. The only sour note was the pain and stiffness in Mary's hands, feet, knees, and hips. That winter her arthritis took another turn for the worse and made walking and climbing stairs even more difficult than usual.

Mary wondered where she would spend next Christmas. Would the war be over by then? Would she still be at White House? Or would she be safely back home at Arlington, with the sad events of the past year fading like the memory of a bad dream? In a letter written from South Carolina on Christmas Day, Robert warned Mary not to expect life to be the same again. Arlington, if not already destroyed by occupying forces, would be unfit to live in.

> Even if the enemy had wished to preserve it, it would almost have been impossible. With the number of troops encamped around it, the change of officers, the want of fuel, shelter, & etc., all the dire necessities of war, it is vain to think of its being in a habitable condition. I fear, too, books, furniture, & the relics of Mt. Vernon will be gone. It is better to make up our minds to a general loss. They cannot take away the remembrances of the spot & the memories of those that to us rendered it sacred. That will remain to us as long as life will last, & that we can preserve.

Another link with the peaceful past was severed when Mildred's school closed abruptly soon after Christmas. Following General "Stonewall" Jackson's withdrawal from Winchester, the school's owners felt that they could no longer guarantee their students' safety and sent the girls home. Resourceful young Mildred got to White House by rail on her own.

But the White House plantation would not give Mary and her family refuge much longer. Just as the Federal soldiers had overrun Arlington and Ravensworth, they would soon march on to White House and secure it for the Union. General George McClellan and his army of more than 100,000 were poised to strike any time, and Rooney's Pamunkey River home was directly in their path.

Newspapers were almost impossible to get now, but whenever Mary got hold of one, she scoured it thoroughly, cutting out articles to send to people she thought might be interested in them. Often her hands were too stiff to work the scissors; then she marked the newspaper and asked one of the girls to cut out the stories for her.

Mary worried about her husband, both because of the crushing burden of leadership he had shouldered and because he was not receiving the respect and recognition she thought he deserved. Reading a Richmond paper on March 8, Mary learned that her husband had returned to the Confederate capital from his extended inspection of coastal defenses and that President Jefferson Davis had placed him in charge of all the armies of the Confederacy. That, she felt, was an honor long overdue.

For years, even when Robert was still an officer in the U.S. Army, Mary had chafed at the way he was treated when it came to promotions. In December 1856, when he was still in Texas, Mary had heard that a new brigadier general was to be commissioned and that prominent Virginians had petitioned the president to appoint Lee. She thought he would be promoted to the position, but he was pessimistic. After James Buchanan was elected, Robert saw new hope. "If anything should turn up in the way of promotion," he wrote Mary, "ask your father, if suitable & proper, to apply in my behalf." But Lee had remained a colonel.

Five and a half years later and another world away, some Confederate leaders and jealous officers considered General Lee "too despondent" for command. In fact, he was only trying to be realistic about how difficult a victory would be, outmatched as the South was in every way: men, weapons, foundries, ships, locomotives, gold reserves, and much more. Still, detractors accused him of trying "to repress the enthusiasm of our people," called him "Granny Lee," and insisted he was too timid to lead an army.

When President Davis put General Lee in command of the Confederate forces, Mary felt vindicated. "I see by the papers that he is put in charge of the armies of the Confederacy," she declared to a friend. "Now they have got into trouble, they send for him to help them out & yet he never gets any credit for what he has done.... He never complains or seems to desire anything than to perform his duty, but I may be excused for wishing him to reap the reward of his labors."

Only a day or two later, she "had the satisfaction of seeing him for one day after a separation of nearly a year." It was the first time she had seen him since he had grown his beard. For his part, General Lee saw his wife weaker and more crippled than ever, walking with two crutches when she walked at all and depending more and more on her rolling chair to get around the house.

During their all too brief reunion, Robert and Mary discussed at length whether, in light of McClellan's threat, it might be better for her to move to Richmond after all. Weary as she was from moving the past ten months, Mary hesitated. She had left Arlington only to see it occupied by destructive enemy troops, and yet she learned later that their orders were to leave her alone if she was in the house when they arrived. She feared that the same fate awaited White House if it were empty and thought that as long as she, Charlotte, and the baby were there, Union soldiers would respect the property.

As Mary pondered her next move, the cold, wet winter gave way suddenly to a lush and beautiful spring. Seeing the trees come into bud and the crocus and daffodils begin to bloom reminded her of Arlington—especially those gardens her mother loved so—now little more than a magnificent ruin.

From his headquarters in Richmond, General Lee knew only too well how powerful General McClellan's army was and how dangerous his wife's position had become. McClellan was preparing a massive assault on Richmond. Should the Federals select one of the river routes that Lee thought they would, "their whole army & etc. will land at the White House," he wrote Mary on April 4, 1862. For her to be "enveloped in it would be extremely annoying & embarrassing.... No one can say what place will be perfectly safe or even quiet, but I think a locality within the route of an invading army will be least so."

In the past, Robert had advised Mary not to move to Richmond. But now that he had established his headquarters there, he changed his mind. "Write me your views," he encouraged her. "If you think it best for you to come to Richmond, I can soon make arrangements for your comfort and shall be very glad of your company and your presence."

By March 11, Mary was considering that course of action, though she expected to see little of her husband if she joined him in Richmond. He was already planning a trip to Norfolk and would be out of town much of the time. She spent two more months in the main White House residence. Looking for a way to keep her family out of danger while still watching over her son's property, Mary moved them to a smaller, less conspicuous house on the estate.

Finally, on May 11, with Union soldiers only a few miles away, Mary packed up and left with Annie and Mildred for Criss Cross, a nearby plantation that was not so directly in the Federals' path. Agnes accompanied Charlotte and her baby to Hickory Hill, the Wickham estate near Ashland. Rooney was back at his post; Rob had finally been allowed to enlist and on March 28 had joined the Rockbridge Artillery as a private.

Before hobbling slowly out to the waiting carriage, Mary—visions of a ruined Arlington in her mind's eye—posted a defiant note on the door of the main residence at the White House:

> Northern soldiers who profess to reverence Washington, forbear to desecrate the home of his first married life, the property of his wife, now owned by her descendants.
> A Granddaughter of Mrs. Washington.

A week later, a Union patrol arrived at Criss Cross and insisted on searching the house and speaking with Mrs. Lee and the other women there. Mary was incensed at the indignity. While soldiers poked and peered into one room after another, she wrote a stinging note addressed to "The General in Command" and handed it to the officer in charge as he left:

> Sir: I have patiently & humbly submitted to the search of my house by men under your command, who are satisfied that there is nothing here which they want. All the plate & other valuables have long since been removed to Richmond & are now beyond the reach of Northern marauders who may wish for their possession.
> Wife of Robert Lee, General C. S. A."

The "General in Command," General Fitz-John Porter, sent a reply assuring Mrs. Lee that she would receive "proper care and protection with as little of constraint to her wishes and movement as might be compatible with her position inside the Federal lines." What General Porter meant was that Mary was essentially under house arrest.

Barely able to walk and preoccupied by signs of new problems with her grandson's health, Mary nonetheless fearlessly challenged the general's messengers, railing against being confined to her house and watched by sentinels. Dr. George Lyman, one of the two officers General Porter sent, later recalled, "Upon arrival our reception was not very gracious." Mrs. Lee "complained bitterly of the indignity…and especially of General Porter's part in the matter, he having been formerly a favored guest at Arlington."

Dr. Lyman and his fellow officer, Captain Kirkland, did their best to explain that General McClellan, who by now had replaced Winfield Scott as the Union general in chief, wanted only to protect Mrs. Lee until she could get safely through to the Confederate lines. She, in turn, insisted that she wanted to go back to White House. Lyman and Kirkland assured her that she was free to do that as well, as long as she had an escort from Criss Cross.

To Mary, the idea of the great-granddaughter of Martha Washington being escorted to her own family property—the plantation where George and Martha Washington had been married—was absolutely out of the question. What she did allow, however, was the posting of a guard at Criss Cross for her protection from Union irregulars, deserters, or other soldiers who might have no respect for her as a woman or as the wife of a general.

After a few days, though, even the guard was too much for Mary, and she, Annie, and Mildred once again moved away from the military front. With General Porter's permission, they traveled a few miles up the Pamunkey River to Marlbourne, the home of agriculturist Edmund Ruffin, the prominent proslavery spokesman for states' rights who had fired the first shot at Fort Sumter.

Mary had only a short time to enjoy her gracious host's company and to discuss their shared interest in plants and flowers. The advancing Union forces caught up with her again, and this time Mary was treated not with deference, but with suspicion. Perhaps because of his prewar friendship with the family, General Porter had extended every courtesy possible to Mary and her retinue. On the other hand, the colonel in charge at Marlbourne suspected her of being an enemy spy, somehow forwarding information about his troop movements to her husband in Richmond.

The emotions swirled inside her—frustration, anger, betrayal, and sadness all compounding her worry over her husband and three sons at war and the ceaseless misery of her poor health. Robert had left the choice about coming to Richmond to her; now it seemed her only remaining option. Mary sent word requesting an escort to Confederate territory.

On June 10, 1862, a wet, unseasonably cold day, Mary, Annie, and Mildred stepped into the coach sent for them and headed for the Confederate lines. They stopped by General McClellan's headquarters, where he himself waited to wish them well and hand them the pass they would need. General Lee had dispatched Major W. Roy Mason to meet Mary at the Union general's office and escort her the rest of the way. Two Union officers on horseback, one of them carrying a white flag of truce, preceded them down the muddy road.

About one o'clock in the afternoon the two riders encountered Confederate sentries. The men explained that they were escorting Mrs. General Lee and wanted to pass her through the lines. The sentry officer, Lieutenant Robert Haile of the 55th Virginia Infantry, sent for the officer in charge, and a Union lieutenant soon joined them. To Lieutenant Haile, all three enemy soldiers seemed to be "men of refinement and sense." One of them offered him a flask. "As I was wet and cold," he wrote that night in his diary, "I thanked him and took a good pull at it. Found it to be nice whiskey."

The Confederate office in charge, Captain Burke, appeared, and "after a good deal of talking and formalities Mrs. Lee was passed to our lines." Major Mason took her on to a farm safely within Confederate territory. And there waiting for her was General Robert E. Lee. Mary had been a fugitive for more than a year. As she embraced her husband, she gave thanks to God that they were safely together again.

In Richmond, Mary accepted the kind hospitality of her friends the Caskies at their house on the corner of Eleventh and Clay Streets until she could arrange for a permanent home. The general returned to his modest lodgings at the Spottswood Hotel, a few blocks away at Eighth and Main. Housing was in short supply. The population of Richmond had quadrupled in a year, and the city was teeming with soldiers in need of quarters, food, fuel, clothing, feed for their horses, and seemingly everything else.

Even writing paper was almost impossible to buy. Ever the correspondent, Mary began tearing pages of note paper in half, using one for one letter and one for another, writing as small as possible in her jagged, arthritic script. She urgently sent for "50 cts. worth of *cheap note* paper" and some stamps. To a former neighbor who remained in Northern territory, she wrote that she would be "much obliged" if her husband would send from Washington "the *cheapest* writing paper of any kind he can procure & a dozen spools [of knitting yarn] of all kinds, 4 very coarse. They are not to be had in these parts."

In spite of her debilitating illness, Mary knit almost every day, sometimes several hours a day. She continued knitting socks for the general and mailing them to him in her letters. As the weather began to turn, she switched from lightweight socks to wool ones. Because his men were so poorly supplied, Lee gave them away. The first four pairs went to the two slaves who traveled with him: his valet Perry, a former dining steward at Arlington, and his cook Meredith, formerly a cook at the White House.

From then on, Mary knit socks faithfully, sending them in batches to the general, who then passed them out to sick soldiers or others in dire need. News that the commanding general gave away new socks—knit by his wife, no less—was one of the countless stories of his kindness that made Lee a matchless inspiration to soldiers and citizens alike in the South.

As Mary sat calmly knitting in the Caskie parlor, the city of Richmond roiled around her with the movement and tension and rumors of war. Refugees and wounded soldiers poured in, while residents by the thousands evacuated, filling the streets day and night with baggage wagons as they left for safer locations farther behind the lines. Though the Confederate government remained in town, President Davis sent his wife, Varina, and children to Raleigh, North Carolina, and loaded government records onto railroad cars so they could be taken to safety at a moment's notice.

By the end of May 1862, McClellan had marched to within nine miles of the city. His soldiers could see the church steeples of Richmond, and the citizens there could hear the blast of the artillery. Confederate resolve, along with mud so deep that wounded soldiers drowned in it, kept the Union away.

When Mary arrived in the capital, wounded soldiers had been coming in from the battlefield for days. The Lee daughters spent long hours comforting the injured at the temporary hospitals set up all over the city, or rolling bandages at the Caskies' house. Mary was appalled at the waste and destruction, not only in Richmond, but also throughout Virginia, including at her beloved home.

> Poor Virginia is being pressed on every side, yet I trust God will yet deliver us. I do not allow myself to think of my dear old home. Would that it had been razed to the ground or submerged in the Potomac rather than have fallen into such hands.... All the beautiful valley of the Shenandoah to be given up to those cow thieves who will plunder & destroy everything. Their whole souls seem bent upon plunder & that is the only thing that induces them to fight.
>
> If I had time to detail to you some of the outrages they have committed in Fairfax County you could scarcely believe such things possible in this enlightened age & by people professing the religion of Christ. I trust the day of retribution is yet to come & oh, our prayer should be that God would haste to help us.

During the hot, humid summer of 1862, Richmond seemed like "one immense hospital," filled with wounded and dying soldiers, the stench of death lingering in the streets. Infection was rampant, and even healthy citizens and soldiers fell ill by the hundreds. Mary wondered if she should try to escape to the hot springs again for part of the summer in spite of the war. Traveling was dangerous, and she was cut off from her sources of income. Her plantations had been confiscated, and her bank was in enemy territory, though a friend in Washington had graciously agreed to act as her "banker," withdrawing money on request and sending it to her by mail or messenger when she could.

Hoping the trip would improve two-year-old Rob's health, Charlotte had decided to go to the mineral baths. Since the Virginia springs were too close to the lines, she took the train south to Warrenton Springs, in Warrenton, North Carolina. Annie, Agnes, and Mildred all went with her, leaving Mary and Daughter behind at the Caskies for the present. Annie wrote her mother that the large resort hotel there was a "nice, clean, comfortable place," and Mary made plans to join the group there as soon as possible.

But another illness in the family kept Mary in Richmond. Custis arrived in the city with a life-threatening fever, and Mary and Daughter nursed him day and night. While Custis's condition was still serious, Mary heard from Warrenton Springs that her only grandchild had died. The doctors said the cause was "gangrene of the lungs"—probably bronchitis or pneumonia. Charlotte returned to Richmond alone on July 5 to bury her son in her parents' plot at Shockoe Cemetery. Because of Custis's condition and her own disability, Mary could not leave the house to attend the funeral.

Later in the month, after Custis had recovered enough to return to duty and the Union army had been driven away from the outskirts of the Confederate capital, Mary went to spend the rest of the summer with the Wickham family at Hickory Hill. But tragic news followed her even to that quiet country setting.

Soon after Mary had left the White House, where she had posted her defiant note signed "A Granddaughter of Mrs. Washington," Union soldiers overran the plantation. One of them, the captain of a gunboat making its way up the Pamunkey, left a note of his own: "Lady—A Northern officer has protected your property in sight of the enemy, and at the request of your overseer." He also collected a small horde of books, paintings, and valuables that had been left in the house for safekeeping.

In spite of General McClellan's order not to destroy the house, the Union soldiers then torched it. It burned to the ground, leaving only blackened chimneys. Eventually, all the sheds and fences on the place were burned, the livestock slaughtered, and the tools and farm equipment stolen or destroyed.

About the same time, Mary received a letter at Hickory Hill from Markie Williams, who had received permission to return to Arlington for the clothing and other personal items she had been unable to retrieve on her earlier trip. With her Aunt Brit, she crossed the Potomac on July 23, taking a baggage wagon in hopes of salvaging some of the Lees' belongings for them while she was there. Because General Whipple, the commanding officer, was out, Markie was not allowed to take anything away except what was hers. "Oh! What a sad, sad visit it was," she reported. Mrs. Whipple was living in Mrs. Lee's downstairs parlor, where Mary had so often sat painting, knitting, reading, and writing.

The garden was overgrown and neglected, but still full of roses, jasmine, and other flowers that pushed up through the weeds. A sentry guarded the area to enforce a rule against picking the flowers. Ignoring him, Markie walked in with the old gardener Ephraim. The garden was still his domain, and he carried garden shears with him to cut her a bouquet. "If you hasn't a claim to some, Miss Martha, I don't know who has," he said. When a sentry on the grounds stopped Aunt Brit, old Ephraim secured a pass for her.

Markie told Mary that, as she walked back to the carriage and the still empty baggage wagon, with sentries patrolling up and down constantly, "Ephraim said in an unusually loud tone, 'Miss Martha, when you write to Miss Mary, please give my best love to her & all the family & tell her we miss them all very much indeed. These people does the best they can for us, but it ain't like those we all been raised with.'"

To her beleaguered Southern kin, the Northerner added in closing, "We have heard with the greatest pleasure of dear cousin R[obert]'s success & of the general appreciation in which he is held.... God bless and keep you all."

Enfolded in the letter was a single leaf from the garden at Arlington.

While thoughts of home were never far away, Mary filled her days with practical work, knitting socks—cotton ones again now that it was summer—writing letters to friends and relations on both sides of the conflict, and keeping up with her children. Only Daughter was with her at Hickory Hill. The other three girls were still at Warrenton Springs, and her sons were absorbed in their military duties.

With the end of summer approaching, Mary wondered where to send sixteen-year-old Mildred to school. The general had wanted her to go to St. Mary's Academy in Raleigh, but Mildred had at first resisted attending a large school where she would be a complete stranger. By the time she agreed to go, Mary had to depend on Annie and Agnes to make arrangements for Mildred's wardrobe and get her to school from Warrenton. She fretted by mail over whether Milly had rubber overshoes, enough clothes, and a proper chaperone for the trip.

Around the end of September, after Mildred stared school, Mary thought she might have time to visit Annie and Agnes at the springs before the weather turned too cold. But she stayed on at Hickory Hill to comfort Charlotte, still grieving the loss of her first child and now seven months pregnant with her second.

Meanwhile, a fresh crisis developed at Warrenton Springs. Annie, always the most delicate member of the family, had battled chills and headaches off and on throughout the summer. When several guests at the hotel came down with typhoid fever, Annie caught it too. Her temperature soared, and she became listless and hard of hearing. Agnes wrote her mother of the illness, and Mary left for Warrenton as quickly as possible. Because of her handicap, she could no longer travel alone, so her cousin Ella Carter went with her.

On October 13, Agnes wrote Mildred: "Annie continues the same, very tired & her fever still unbroken. Ella, Ma & I keep up our nursing." The family sat up around the clock, with Mary usually taking the night shift, sitting alert, attentive, and compassionate through the long evening hours as Annie struggled for her life.

On October 18, Mary reported to daughter Mary that Annie was much worse. "The disease must be at its crisis now...," she wrote. "She has been suffering today with pain in her stomach and bowels.... She is so deaf that she can scarcely hear a word." The doctor gave her morphine for the pain, though it caused her to sleep most of the time.

A day later, as Mary related soon after, Annie "insisted upon being propped up in the bed & cleaning her teeth, changing her gown & sheets, after which she asked to have her favorite hymnbook brought to her." She asked her mother to read "In Extremity," which began, "When I can trust my all with God / In trial's fearful hour...." She ate more than usual—an egg, beef tea, and brandy—and then slept again.

Mary situated herself in the next room, with the door to Annie's room wide open, and started writing letters. "Hearing her stir," she recalled later,

I went to the bed & found the cheek which had been so long scarlet & with fever—cold as marble. Her hands too cold & clammy. I sent for the doctor but he did not seem so alarmed as I was & said it was want of circulation.... *I thought* it was the icy touch of death, but we made all our arrangements for the night & gave her morphine every hour & brandy according to his directions. Her feet were quite warm & we chafed her hands & lay them in my bosom.

After 12 o'clock she seemed not to notice who was around her & never called me, which she was apt to do frequently during the night. Her eyes were raised to the ceiling & her breathing became more laboured. Toward day we found she could not swallow the brandy. The Dr. came & said her pulse was scarcely perceptible & she lay quietly, her life ebbing away, with her hand warm & soft in my bosom, till at 7 o'clock all was still.

Gentle Annie, her father's "Little Raspberry," was dead at twenty-three.

CHAPTER TWENTY

LEE'S MISERABLES

*M*y darling Annie—I never had expected to wreathe a funeral wreath for her," Mary grieved in a letter to Daughter. Bereaved as she was, she still had a difficult decision to make. With travel of every kind so unpredictable and often hazardous, she had to decide where to bury Annie.

Mary thought it best to bury her daughter in Warrenton, but Agnes begged her to try to take Annie back to Richmond, with the hope of eventually reinterring her at Arlington. Mary wrote Robert and telegraphed Custis for advice, but in the end she had to act on her own. William Duke Jones, owner of the hotel where they were staying, was a distant cousin, and when he offered to lay Annie to rest in his family cemetery near the springs, Mary accepted.

From their meager and diminishing supply of yard goods and sewing notions, local ladies made black silk bonnets for Mary and Agnes to wear in mourning, and guests and residents of Warrenton sent flowers to cover Annie's coffin. The afternoon before she left for Richmond, Mary went back to the gravesite alone. It had been "beautifully turfed & planted around with flowers & evergreens by kind hands without my knowledge. I…covered the grave with my flowers & tears & took leave of my sweet gentle child. Oh what an unspeakable comfort to know she was fully prepared for the great change."

Safely back at the Caskies', Mary got a letter from Robert, who had written her from his field headquarters at Winchester to console her in their loss:

I cannot express the anguish I feel at the death of our sweet Annie.... But God, in this as in all things, has mingled mercy with the blow, in selecting that one best prepared to leave us.... I wish I could give you any comfort, but beyond our hope in the great mercy of God, and the belief that He takes her at the time and place where it is best for her to go, there is none.

A second blow followed quickly on the heels of the first. Mary had scarcely settled in and returned to her sock knitting when she got word from Hickory Hill that her daughter-in-law had given birth prematurely to a frail and sickly daughter. Charlotte waited for the tiny girl to grow stronger before having her christened, but the improvement never came. Mary's second grandchild died two weeks before Christmas and was buried in Richmond beside her first.

Mary and Agnes went to Hickory Hill to console Charlotte and stayed there through the Christmas holidays. No one else in the family could join them. All the men were on duty; Mildred spent her school vacation in Raleigh because it was too dangerous to send her home; and daughter Mary—in typical fashion—did not make it home from a visit to Cedar Grove. When her father had warned her to move from there some weeks earlier, she ignored him; when Jeb Stuart sent two of his best scouts to rescue her, she sent them back empty-handed. Now Daughter was stranded behind enemy lines.

The host and patriarch of Hickory Hill, Robert's eighty-year-old uncle, William Wickham, did his best to make Mary and Agnes feel welcome. He was in good spirits, and Wickham cousins came to share in the holiday festivities. Still, Mary had her hands full trying to comfort Charlotte, who had lost both of her children within six months. And what should have been a wonderful diversion for Agnes unexpectedly turned to disappointment when Orton Williams came to court her.

Orton seemed more handsome and mature than Mary remembered him, "tall, blond, erect, scrupulously groomed," wearing a saber and a dashing pair of Wellington boots. But he was acting disturbed. Now a captain, Orton had changed his name from William Orton Williams to Lawrence (his brother's name) William Orton. He had shot a man under his command and had become so unpopular with his troops that he had to be reassigned. Rumor was that he drank heavily.

Sad and vulnerable so soon after Annie's death, Agnes doted on Orton and the attention he gave her. He brought her a Christmas present—lavish in wartime—of a riding whip and gauntlets, and the two of them took long rides together on the plantation. The day he was to leave, Mary expected him to ask for Agnes's hand in marriage, but to everyone's surprise, as young Harry Wickham remembered, "after a long session in the parlor (from which we children had been warned to keep away), he came out, bade the family good-bye, and rode away alone."

Nearly six months later, the Lees would read sad and unbelievable news in the Richmond papers: Orton Williams had been hung as a spy. Wearing a Union major's uniform, he had been stopped and searched by a suspicious duty officer near Franklin, Tennessee. He was carrying a thousand dollars in Confederate money, and his real name and rank were inside his hatband. On orders from General James A. Garfield (the future president), Williams and a companion were tried as spies, convicted, and hung within hours.

From his camp at Fredericksburg on Christmas Day, Robert reflected on the tragic effects of this fratricidal war: "What a cruel thing is war to separate and destroy families and friends, and mar the purest joys and happiness God has granted us in this world; to fill our hearts with hatred instead of love for our neighbors, and to devastate the face of this beautiful world!"

"I pray," he continued, "that on this day when only peace and goodwill are preached to mankind, better thoughts may fill the hearts of our enemies and turn them to peace." The thoughts of many North and South were indeed turning toward peace by Christmas of 1862, but both sides still wanted it on their own terms.

On New Year's Day, 1863, President Abraham Lincoln issued the Emancipation Proclamation, freeing slaves in the states still in rebellion. By then, however, the Arlington slaves were free already. Even as he led an army at war, General Lee faithfully continued to manage the legal affairs his father-in-law had entrusted to him. On December 29, 1862, he had filed a deed of manumission at the courthouse in Spotsylvania County, Virginia, freeing his wife's slaves and all the other Custis plantation slaves in accordance with the terms of Mr. Custis's will. "They are entitled to their freedom," Lee declared, "and I wish to give it to them."

Mary's acceptance of the institution of slavery and the assumption of black inferiority had always been at odds with her lifelong interest in their welfare. As a child she played with the Arlington slaves; later she fed and clothed them; in violation of state law she taught them to read. She often thought they were a burden, and she always thought they should someday be free. The only slaves she had ever owned were the ones she inherited from her father, and by then he had already legally guaranteed them their freedom. Now her father's will and the events of the war had resolved Mary's ambiguous position: The day Lincoln issued his proclamation, the Lees were unaffected by it. They were slaveholders no more.

Although the Emancipation Proclamation had no direct consequences for the Lees, a law put on the books soon afterward went much further in making sure that unrepentant Southerners—Mary Custis Lee most of all—would pay for their attempt to achieve independence from the Union. On February 6 a little-heralded federal law entitled "An Act for the Collection of Direct Taxes in the Insurrectionary Districts within the United States" went into effect. As owner of the Arlington estate, Mary was assessed a special tax of $92.07, payable in Alexandria. If she or the general knew of the assessment at the time, neither had the means or the inclination to pay it.

Against lengthening odds, the Lees kept hoping that someday, somehow they would return to Arlington in peace. In a Christmas letter to Mildred, Robert had expressed what the entire family felt: "Notwithstanding its present desecrated & pillaged condition, I trust that a just & merciful God may yet gather all that He may spare under its beloved roof. How filled with thanks & gratitude will our hearts then be!"

Seen from Washington, Arlington House looked as regal as ever, perched serenely on its Potomac hillside. General McClellan had ordered it burned if the rebels invaded Washington; so far it had been preserved. The commander of troops moved out, and several married officers and their families took his place, filling the halls with the laughter of children and the rooms with dinnertime conversation in an eerie echo of bygone days.

But the surrounding estate was being systematically ruined on the express orders of Lincoln's secretary of war, Edwin M. Stanton, who wanted to make it as difficult and expensive as possible to restore the property once the war was over. Part of the land was taken up with an enormous stable complex for the horses and mules that served military units in and around Washington. Fences and outbuildings went up on the grounds. That winter was unseasonably wet, and the fine lawn was soon churned into a thick froth of knee-deep muck that never dried. Higher up on Arlington Heights a large, rambling convalescent hospital was built for wounded or sick soldiers who had been treated and were resting and recovering before returning to duty.

The most ambitious new development was down by the river around the famous Arlington Spring. Although the Emancipation Proclamation did not apply to slaves in federally held territory, slaves everywhere took it literally. Penniless, hordes of them streamed into Washington looking for food, shelter, and jobs. Some of them settled around the spring, and their presence attracted still more black families to the old Custis picnic grounds. In time, Freedmen's Village was established on the spot, and the U.S. government built housing, roads, a school, a chapel, a hospital, a home for the aged, workshops, and other buildings for the people there. Eventually the permanent population swelled to more than 2,000.

Back at the Caskies' after the Christmas holidays, Mary suffered through what another resident in Richmond called "the dreariest, coldest, wettest, saddest winter...within the memory of man." Snow, sleet, and rain pelted the city, and Mary was confined to the house for months from the effects of the cold and damp weather on her arthritis. For weeks on end she could barely hold a pen or a knife and fork; her knees were swollen and completely immobilized. Yet somehow she could still knit. Day after day, she sat wrapped in a shawl, knitting socks and mittens by the hour to send to the general. Agnes labored alongside her, and whenever friends came to call, Mary encouraged them to take up a pair of knitting needles and join them.

As yarn became scarcer and more expensive in the capital, Mary sent out "yarn scouts" to find supplies of it elsewhere. They accepted donations when they could get them; other times, Mary bought materials with her own money. Inflation was rampant, and even staple items were becoming rare. When someone sent her a jar of molasses—sugar was all but impossible to find, and molasses was the standard substitute—she thoughtfully sent the jar back when it was empty, knowing they were "very scarce." Mary once had anything she could have wanted; now she learned to do with very little.

To Mrs. General Lee, no task was too small or unimportant if it promoted the Confederate cause or boosted morale. In February 1863 she answered a letter requesting locks of hair from all the Confederate generals to make a wreath of honor:

> I have only been able to procure a few specimens & will not wait any longer to send them to you. Genl. Lee's stock of hair is so small that I fear the small lock I send will be of little use. You will have to supply all deficiencies from the flowing locks of our very youthful Brigadiers.

Near winter's end, Mary expectantly unwrapped a small package from her husband. In it she found a new painting of him. The accompanying note made her smile to imagine him sitting in a damp tent, surrounded by mud and showered with sleet, and writing to her in his jovial old way. "I send you, Mrs. Lee, a likeness of your husband that has come from beyond the big water. He is a hard favoured man & has a very rickety position on his pins. I hope his beard will please you for the artist seems to have laid himself out on that."

As winter turned to spring, Mary continued housebound, knitting with a determination that others found remarkable. Scarcely able to stand or walk across the room, she seemed to knit with nearly supernatural stamina. "Almost unable to move," noted one visitor, Mrs. Lee was "busily engaged in knitting socks for sockless soldiers." A neighbor recalled that while some women came to help with the knitting, others came just for the comfort of visiting with Mary, who "listened, and strengthened, and smiled even when her own heart ached…. The brightness of her nature, amidst uncertainty and pain, was wonderful." Mary knew that because she was General Lee's wife, her attitude was tremendously influential; being upbeat was something else she could do for the good of the cause. She gave her cares over to God and pressed on.

Through the newspapers and conversations with her husband, Mary knew the Confederacy was struggling to survive and that its future as a nation was very much in doubt. After the first victory at Manassas in 1861, many Southerners had thought the Union would sue for peace. Now almost two years later, a Federal blockade, the depletion of the South's relatively meager resources, and the lack of formal recognition by a single foreign country all hurt the Confederates' chances for independence.

On May 11, from her chair in the parlor, Mary could hear church bells tolling all over the city in mourning for her husband's most brilliant field commander, General Thomas "Stonewall" Jackson, who had died the day before. Shot accidentally by one of his own men at the Battle of Chancellorsville, he had survived the amputation of his left arm only to contract a fatal case of pneumonia.

So far, Mary's own family was safe, despite some illness, accidents, and close calls. The previous summer, a Yankee sharpshooter had missed General Lee's face by a fraction of an inch; the bullet left a scratch along his cheek. Two days later he was holding his horse when the animal reared, tripping the general and breaking his hand. Custis had been seriously ill that same summer, and the following year Lee himself battled "a good deal of pain in my chest, back, & arms" that "came on in paroxysm"—angina pectoris from which he never fully recovered. At Kelly's Ford in March of 1863, Rooney had his horse shot out from under him but got through the battle unhurt.

On June 9—the same day Orton Williams was hung—Rooney, now General William Henry Fitzhugh Lee, C.S.A., became the Lee family's first serious casualty of the war. During the Battle of Brandy Station, he was shot in the upper leg with a particularly dangerous new type of Union ammunition, one that fired a zinc cap designed to separate from the bullet and cause the wound to fester. Fortunately, he was hit at such close range that both the bullet and cap passed cleanly through his body.

Lee ordered Rooney to Hickory Hill to recuperate and sent Rob, who was serving as an aide on his brother's staff, to escort him there. Though in constant pain, Mary made her way slowly by carriage to meet them at the plantation. There, despite her condition, she assumed her role as the family nurse. Rooney was a big bear of a man and healthy until he was shot; his mother anticipated a quick and complete recovery. Mildred, safely home from school, joined her in the country, as did Agnes and Charlotte.

Mary took the lead in supervising the care of both Rooney and Charlotte, who was more despondent than ever after her husband was wounded. When she was not tending to her patients or writing letters, Mary was knitting. Hickory Hill seemed a welcome refuge from all the tension and bustle of wartime Richmond.

Then on the morning of June 26, when the family had just finished breakfast and was gathering on the front porch to enjoy the cool of the morning, Mary heard gunshots in the distance. Suddenly and without warning, a posse of Federal officers rode up the drive and toward the house. Rob ran across the yard to the plantation office where Rooney was recuperating and warned him about the raiders. Too weak to escape, Rooney told his brother to hide himself, and Rob ran out the back of the building and into the woods.

The Federals had come specifically to capture Rooney Lee: If one General Lee was the cause of all their trouble, they could take another General Lee prisoner to help even the score. Helpless, Mary watched as the raiders swept through the house. They returned to the porch empty-handed but soon found their prey in the office and, with a ragged yell of triumph, carried Rooney out into the yard on his mattress. After roughing up old Mr. Wickham, they appropriated his horses and carriage, bundled Rooney aboard, and drove him away to the nearby landing for a river voyage behind the lines, passing by the blackened ruins of his White House home along the way.

A few soldiers remained behind for a little while and then left as suddenly as they had come. As soon as the coast was clear and he could avoid immediate capture, Rob came back to the house before leaving to report the kidnapping. Old Mr. Wickham's beating could have been worse; he would recover. But as soon as the raiding party rode out of sight, Charlotte broke down completely.

Mary's delicate daughter-in-law was a physical and emotional wreck. All of Mary's patience, nursing skill, and personal experience with pain and disappointment could not bring Charlotte around. Without knowing how she would be able to do it, Mary offered to take her anywhere she wanted that summer to try to recuperate. Charlotte asked to go to Hot Springs, which Mary had described to her in the past as a very pleasant, relaxing place.

The hotel at Hot Springs was one of the few resorts that had somehow remained open despite the impact of war: a shortage of food and fuel, serious inflation, a drastic falloff in business, and the constant threat of invasion. Though the operation was reduced in size and scope, it still welcomed anyone who could get there. For Mary, getting there presented a whole other range of challenges. Scarcely able to shuffle between her bed and her chair, she couldn't manage the overnight train trip to the mountains.

With a little ingenuity, what would otherwise have been an excruciating experience turned into quite an enjoyable one. A boxcar was fitted up with a bed, chairs, and other furniture as a combination bedroom/sitting room for Mary, Charlotte, Agnes, and daughter Mary, who had been able to leave Cedar Grove when the Federals withdrew in anticipation of an assault on Washington. The weather for the journey was clear and temperate. With the big sliding doors open on either side of the car, Mary enjoyed the cool mountain breezes and took in breathtaking vistas along the way.

During more than a month at Hot Springs, Mary faithfully swam in the mineral baths but "without any visible improvement except a slight relaxation in one knee," as she wrote Mildred, who was back in school at St. Mary's. Charlotte was not getting any better either, and so in mid-August, Mary decided to move to nearby Warm Springs for a month.

There she rented "a delightful cottage with a meadow full of haycocks & a clear stream running thro' it & very near to the bath, which is one of the finest in the world." They were, she thought, very "comfortably fixed. Mary & Agnes each have a room opening into mine; mountains all around. The fare is tolerable—corn, tomatoes & plenty of nice vegetables.... I do hope I may get better here for I have suffered greatly of late, especially at night."

Mary read, visited with old friends at the springs, including the Caskies, and sewed clothes for herself. She had become experienced at remaking old clothes to keep them in fashion, and she still kept up with the latest styles. After Annie's funeral, she had upgraded her black silk mourning bonnet with "an English crepe veil, as the one I got in Warrenton is so indifferent." Now at Warm Springs, she made a garibaldi-style blouse—loose fitting and "very comfortable"—and showed Agnes how to make one of her own.

The weather continued cool and pleasant that summer, the mountain wind whistling through the dense stands of fir. Agnes and Daughter went walking every day, gathering blackberries and other little treats along the way. The only real reminders of the war were the large numbers of soldiers, both healthy men and war casualties, prominent among the "few old ladies & children" that made up the rest of the guest list.

Mary and her friends took what comfort they could in the war news. As always, Mary relished letters from her husband, and she heard from Custis—now a general serving in Richmond on President Davis's staff—that Rooney was mending well, walking on crutches, and hoping to be exchanged soon. But much of the news these days was bad.

Many people in the South were just beginning to understand the consequences of two events that had unfolded on different battlefronts July 4. In the West, the city of Vicksburg, Mississippi, had surrendered to General Ulysses S. Grant after a forty-seven-day siege, thus giving the Union complete control of the Mississippi River from New Orleans to St. Louis and splitting the Confederacy in two. In the East, General Lee had retreated in a downpour after failing to defeat the Federal forces at Gettysburg, Pennsylvania, halting the deepest significant penetration ever into Northern territory. On July 16 the Charleston *Mercury* was still insisting that "Lee is master of the situation," but by the thirtieth the editors had changed their tune: "It is impossible for an invasion to have been more foolish and disastrous."

On the trip back toward Richmond at the end of the summer, Charlotte became too ill to go on, and Mary had to leave her with a doctor in Charlottesville. Then she and her two daughters stopped for a while near the little town of Liberty at a farm that took in boarders. Ever eager for word from her husband, Mary wrote him from there, taking every opportunity to send letters to him with people she knew were traveling his way and encouraging him to write often.

Absorbed in his duties and with the tide of the war clearly turned against him, from time to time the general felt obliged to remind his "Mim" of the reality of his situation. "You forget how much writing, talking & thinking I have to do when you complain of the interval between my letters," he had told her in the spring. "You lose sight also of the letters you receive." Later, he accused her of "relapsing into your old error, supposing that I have a superabundance of time & have only my own pleasures to attend to."

In October, Mary, Agnes, and Daughter arrived back in Richmond at last, most likely having traveled from Liberty by riverboat. Instead of returning to the Caskies', Mary rented a small house at 210 East Leigh Street, between Second and Third. Unfortunately, there was not enough room for Charlotte. Sick as she was, she had to board down the street.

Mary Custis Lee, mistress of Arlington, had not so much as a chair or a spoon to call her own in the Confederate capital, so she borrowed everything she needed to set up housekeeping: odd pieces of furniture, tableware, linens, a few pictures and mirrors for the walls. But she and her daughters made do, entertaining visitors with what few dishes they collected, reading to each other from a copy of Les Misérables, which they and their friends rechristened Lee's Miserables, and knitting away on mittens and socks. Agnes and Daughter joined everybody else in the city in trying to find enough food for their household. Coffee and sugar were all but unobtainable, and potatoes were twelve dollars a bushel.

The Confederate government got wind of Mrs. Lee's cramped quarters and proposed to provide her with a house and support, but the general declined the offer, thinking it would set the wrong example to accept such a generous gift while his men suffered with so little. "I'm glad you have some socks for the army," he wrote his wife in Richmond. "Send them to me.... Tell the girls to send all they can. I wish they could make some shoes too." In one command alone there were 400 men without shoes and 1,000 without blankets.

Early in December, one of Mary's most frequent and fervent prayers was answered when Robert arrived at Richmond on army business and came to see her at the little house on East Leigh. The last time he had been in the city, she was at the springs, so it had been nearly half a year since they had seen each other. Each was distressed by the other's look. Robert saw that his wife's disability was worse than ever. Mary saw her husband much changed for the worse: his once-slim figure now heavyset by comparison (he had had to order bigger uniform jackets), his beard nearly snow white, his energy and mobility hampered by the pain of angina, his spirit burdened by the sacrifices of an unwinnable war.

The couple had not spent Christmas together since 1859, and this season Mary longed to have him with her to reawaken something of the warm homey spark of Christmases past. Custis, Daughter, Agnes, and Charlotte were all there, as was Mildred, who was home from school, this time for good. Gentle Annie was in her grave, but Rooney was recovering well, the rest of the family was safe, and there was much to be thankful for. To Mary's disappointment, the general returned to the field on December 21. He considered it his duty to spend Christmas with his men.

Within a day or two of the general's departure, Charlotte became gravely ill. Imprisoned first at Fortress Monroe, Rooney had been moved to a cell at Fort Lafayette, two installations his father had helped design and build. At Fort Lafayette, he got word that his wife was dying. Custis, a brigadier general like his brother, proposed to Union authorities that he take his brother's place in prison for forty-eight hours so Rooney could see his wife again before she died. The Northern officers in charge refused.

At news that her husband could not be with her, Charlotte lost interest in living any longer. She died on Christmas Eve and was buried beside her children. From his headquarters on the banks of the Rapidan, General Lee sadly observed that she had "joined her little cherubs & our angel Annie in heaven." Whatever her medical problems had been, the general was convinced his daughter-in-law had died of a broken heart.

CHAPTER TWENTY-ONE

FIVE YEARS AND
A LIFETIME

*I*n January 1864, Mary moved a few blocks down the street from the little house at 210 East Leigh Street to an elegant brick house at 707 East Franklin Street, joining Custis and several other bachelor officers already living there. General Lee was afraid that she and the men would be in each other's way, but the new arrangement turned out better for everyone. Mary and her daughters had more room; the officers enjoyed the company of the ladies and the domestic order they brought to a house they had nicknamed "The Mess"; and Mary had the company of Custis, who always had the latest war news, including the whereabouts of Robert and updates on Rooney.

Mary and Custis entertained visitors almost constantly, and friends and relatives often spent the night. In a scene reminiscent of Arlington days, Custis ended up sleeping on the floor at least once because of all the overnight company. Even though it was often crowded and she had to do all her visiting from her rolling chair, Mary enjoyed the company. With tea at $25 a pound and flour $12 a barrel, friends pooled their larders and shared what they could get.

Unlike some of the well-to-do families, however, Mary never tried to forget the war with parties and dances. Not long after she moved, she received a social call from Mary Chesnut, wife of James Chesnut, advisor to

President Davis and former senator from South Carolina. Mrs. Chesnut, a well-known socialite in wartime Richmond, was impressed with Mrs. Lee's industry in spite of her arthritis. In her diary entry for February 26, 1864, Mrs. Chesnut recorded:

> We paid our respects to Mrs. Lee. Her room was like an industrial school: everybody so busy. Her daughters were all there plying their needles, with several other ladies. Mrs. Lee showed us a beautiful sword, recently sent to the General by some Marylanders, now in Paris. On the blade was engraved, *"aide toi et Dieu t'aidera"* [help yourself and God will help you]. When we came out someone said, "Did you see how the Lees spend their time? What a rebuke to the taffy parties!"

Sometimes, in writing to thank his wife for the socks and mittens she sent, Robert playfully chided her for miscounting them. Even when he was at the battlefront, the general's precise and practical engineering mind could not let the mistake pass unnoticed. "Get one of the girls to count them accurately & set down the number," he teased. Responding to another shipment, he noted: "Here are sixty-seven pairs...instead of sixty-four." And, with obvious pleasure and a spark of the wit that remained undiminished by the burdens of command, "The number...stated by you was correct. 30 prs. good & true. I am glad to find there is arithmetic enough in my family to count 30. I thought if you placed your daughter at work all would go right."

As fast as he received them, the general saw to it that the socks were distributed to the neediest soldiers. He only wished that his wife's industriousness would inspire more women at home. "I have sent two hundred and sixty-three pairs [to the Stonewall Brigade]" he reported. "Still...about one hundred and forty...are without socks. If two or three hundred would send an equal number, we should have a sufficiency."

Finding herself in Richmond without a single pet cat, Mildred befriended a squirrel. She named him Custis Morgan—after her brother and, because he would not stay in his cage, after General John Hunt Morgan, who had escaped Federal captors and returned to safety in the South. Watching the little creature's antics was a welcome diversion and gave the family something to write about in letters besides the war. To a friend, Mary wrote that the new addition to the family "runs all over the house, jumps on my head & pulls off my cap & shawl & is in all kinds of mischief."

Hearing of Custis Morgan's escapades, the general recommended "squirrel soup thickened with peanuts. In such an exit from the stage, Custis Morgan would cover himself with glory." To break him of the habit of biting, the general prescribed "[immersing] his head under water for five minutes in one of his daily baths." Before the family had a chance to try any of Lee's suggestions, Custis Morgan escaped out a window and disappeared for good.

In March, Rooney was exchanged at last, and his brothers and sisters waited eagerly for him at the train station. Even the general managed to get away long enough to welcome his son home. Mary could only wait at home in her chair for the sound of footsteps on the front stairs and the sight of her second son, pale yet completely healed after nine months as a prisoner of war. With his wife and children dead, Rooney was restless and unsure of what to do with himself, and after resting and recovering his strength at Franklin Street, he rejoined his old unit in the field.

During the summer of 1864, the oppressive temperature sent Mary to her sickbed once more. She lay propped up on her bed in the stifling heat, stricken with "typhoid diarrhea," knees and ankles swollen once again, hands painful and twisted, unable to take a single step unassisted. But both her frailty and the increasing difficulty of travel made it unlikely that she would be able to escape the miserable conditions in the city to spend her customary season at the springs.

Hospitals were filled with wounded, whose suffering was all the worse because of the heat. Rats were everywhere, infection was rampant, and volunteers who nursed the sick and dying—including the Lee girls—had to endure the patients' short tempers as well as the sight and stench of their injuries. Cloth for bandages was scarce; thread to stitch slings or repair torn uniforms cost $4 a spool. Three spools was a month's salary for a Confederate private.

Mary's recovery was hampered by continuing hot weather, lack of medicine (anything available went to the military hospitals), and, according to the doctor, a shortage of fresh fruit. The general did his best to supply the diet she needed, but all he could send were a few apples, one pear, and two lemons a woman had given him from her own tree, plus a dried up one he found in his valise. "This," he explained, "is all the fruit I can get." Nevertheless, Mary slowly improved.

On June 30, Mrs. Lee received a touching letter from her husband that stirred tender memories of another time long ago:

> I was very glad to receive your letter yesterday, and to hear that you were better. I trust that you will continue to improve and soon be as well as usual. God grant that you may be entirely restored in His own good time. Do you recollect what a happy day thirty-three years ago this was? How many hopes and pleasures it gave birth to!

In her imagination, Mary saw once again the Arlington parlor hung with garlands, the Mount Vernon sideboard covered with Martha Washington's china and the most sumptuous feast money could buy; the famous punch bowl filled to the top of the mast with her father's favorite recipe. The room shimmered with silver and crystal in defiance of the rain outside, and Robert stood impossibly straight and handsome in his uniform jacket and crisp white trousers ordered from New York just for the occasion. And outside—the rose garden, the lawn, the forest the Marquis de Lafayette had praised so highly, and beyond it all, the unparalleled view of Washington City.

Mary read on:

> God has been very merciful and kind to us and how thankless and sinful I have been. I pray that He may continue His mercies and blessings to us, and give us a little peace and rest together in this world, and finally gather us and all He has given us around His throne in the world to come.

Then Robert had to close; President Davis had just arrived.

Even as Mary recalled that "happy day thirty-three years ago" at Arlington, her husband's bitterest enemies were making sure that the Lees would never return to it. By the time that Mary sent her cousin, Phillip R. Fendall, to Alexandria to pay the $92.07 tax that had been assessed on her estate, the total due, including penalties, was $138.10. Even then, the tax commissioner refused the payment, saying the law required the owner to pay the tax in person.

Federal officials knew full well that Mary's status as the wife of the Confederate commander-in-chief—not to mention her handicap—made it impossible for her to pay the tax personally. The requirement was consistent with the overall intent of the law: Few owners would come forward in person, and the Federal government could then confiscate their properties for delinquent taxes.

On the icy cold and blustery day of January 11, 1864, delinquent properties went on the block at the Alexandria courthouse. Arlington was the first property up for sale. Despite the weather, a large crowd was on hand; even so, the highest bidder for Arlington was the United States Government. Valued at $34,100, the famous house and 1,100 acres went for $26,800.

One possible explanation for the low bid was that some prospective buyers believed the wartime tax law would be declared unconstitutional after the war and that the property would revert back to Mrs. General Lee. There were other questions: What if postwar courts overruled the tax commissioners for having refused to take Mrs. Lee's payment from Phillip Fendall? What if they invalidated the sale because the government did not pay Mrs. Lee the proceeds from the sale over and above what it took to satisfy the tax liability?

In May 1864, by order of Secretary of War Stanton, the Arlington estate was designated a national cemetery. The *National Republican* hailed the news as "a happy thought." It was, the *Morning Chronicle* proudly proclaimed, "the righteous use of the estate of the rebel General Lee.… The people of the entire nation will one day, not very distant, heartily thank the creators of this movement."

The mechanics of the operation fell to Montgomery C. Meigs, Stanton's Quartermaster General, who as a young lieutenant fresh from West Point had assisted Captain Robert E. Lee on his first trip to St. Louis in the summer of 1837. After Jefferson Davis had resigned his Senate seat, Meigs had taken over the rebuilding of the Capitol, including replacing the old wooden dome with a taller and more elegant iron-framed one—a project that continued throughout the war. Now Meigs was put in charge of turning one of the most storied estates in the country into a graveyard.

Meigs approached his duty with relish. He considered Confederates to be traitors of the vilest sort and General Lee the worst of the lot. Though he had 1,100 acres to work with, the Quartermaster General ordered the first graves to be dug "encircling" the great white mansion as close to it as possible. He was angry to discover that the first burials, on May 13, 1864, were half a mile from the house near the old slave graveyard. The officers living in the house, seeing the burial detail preparing to dig in the garden, had ordered them down there instead. Hundreds more soldiers who died in local hospitals and prison camps were buried beside them in the weeks that followed.

Meigs again sent orders for soldiers to be interred beside the mansion. Again the resident officers sent the burial details off to another distant corner of the property. Furious, Meigs wrote a letter on June 15 specifying his intention that "the land immediately surrounding the Arlington Mansion be used as a national cemetery and that the bodies buried in the northeast section be moved to it." This time he went over the ground himself with a surveyor, marked out plots, and stepped off a long row of graves overlooking the Potomac along the border of Mary's flower garden.

A British visitor later that year caught something of the sadness of it all as he looked out the dining room window of the mansion "at the glorious view of the distant city":

> It is a queer, old-fashioned place, with heavy columns and flights of steps, strangely like what it is being now turned into—a mausoleum. The doors were all wide open, and we walked in unquestioned by the soldiers who were lounging about the entrance.... To see the home of Robert Lee sacked and made into a cemetery, and to fancy the thoughts that would fill that great heart...were so strange to me, and in their strangeness so painful, that I doubt whether I ever had a sadder walk than that visit to the heights of Arlington.

At the same time solders' graves were being dug across her lawn, Mary got a chance to get away from Richmond for a while. A family friend, Dr. Charles Cocke, extended a gracious invitation for her to visit Bremo, his elegant 1,500-acre estate on the James River. It was eighty miles from Richmond, but she could make the trip in comfort by canal boat. Tempting though the offer was, Mary had reservations about leaving. Visiting at Shirley in May, Mildred had been caught when Union troops arrived. After reminiscing with her about serving under Lee in Mexico and Texas, the soldiers had freed her to go back to Richmond. But Mary feared she too might become stranded behind enemy lines and separated from her husband.

With food in town becoming ever more scarce and expensive, Robert encouraged his wife to leave. "I do not see how you will be able to live in Richmond," he told her. "You had better be looking out for some part of the country where there are provisions. How Custis, yourself, 3 girls, Billy, and Sally [servants] can live long on 1/4 lb. of bacon and 1-1/2 pt. of meal [the daily soldier ration] I cannot see.

As Mary considered what to do, the war came closer. Off and on for months she had heard the sounds of artillery in the distance, and like the rest of the population, she knew well the sound of the tocsin—the warning bell. On May 12, General J. E. B. Stuart, a long-time family friend (and a particular favorite of Daughter), died in a house nearby after being wounded at Yellow Tavern the day before. Jeb's summons at Arlington had sent Lee to Harper's Ferry in defense of the Union arsenal there, five years and a lifetime ago.

In August, Mary left for Bremo with Mildred and Agnes; daughter Mary stayed behind with the same "typhoid diarrhea" her mother had had. Bremo seemed like paradise after the heat and endless shortages in Richmond. The weather was more agreeable, the pantry was well stocked, and Mary soon gained strength from the quiet nights, calm days, and plentiful table. Nevertheless, she suffered a setback, which she described in a letter dated August 11:

> Thro' the mercy of a kind Providence, while suffering with the fever, my rheumatic pains left me & I only suffered from debility when I came here. I do not know how I could have endured both at once. Unfortunately, a few days after my arrival I had a severe fall from my crutches slipping on the polished floor. Tho' my health has been restored with the change into the country, my pains have returned and the prospect of walking seems as far off as ever.

After three mercifully quiet months, Mary returned to Richmond and her accustomed routine: knitting socks and mittens with whatever yarn she could get, writing letters on whatever scraps of paper she could find, and eating whatever humble fare was available. Usually that meant Confederate coffee—made with chickory, nuts, parched corn, or (sometimes) coffee—with no cream or sugar; cornbread without butter; and eggs, either bartered or bought for ten Confederate dollars a dozen.

For all the shortages she endured, Mary had a grateful heart at Christmas. The general was absent from Richmond on Christmas Day, but his wife gave thanks for the fact that their children were alive and safe and that they were blessed with a simple but ample holiday meal. Daughter, Agnes, and Mildred decorated the rooms of their house on Franklin Street with cedar boughs and holly branches.

Early in the new year, Mary received a letter from Robert telling her about some generous visitors who came to call:

Yesterday afternoon three little girls walked into my room, each with a small basket. The eldest carried some fresh eggs, laid by her own hens; the second, some pickles made by her mother; the third, some popcorn grown in her garden.... I have not had so pleasant a visit for a long time. I fortunately was able to fill their baskets with apples, which distressed poor Bryan [his steward], and I begged them to bring me nothing but kisses and to keep the eggs, corn, etc. for themselves.

As soon as she found someone trustworthy going toward the girls' house, Mrs. Lee sent the oldest of them a small package of sewing notions along with a note:

My dear little friend:
General Lee gives me such a fine account of your industry that I am tempted to send you this little basket of working materials, which I hope you will find useful in these hard times. I have put in it a handkerchief for your Mamma, which she must use for my sake & I must thank you both for your kind attention to my husband.
Yrs. most truly,
M. C. Lee

As another year of war began, Mary and whatever daughters and friends cared to join her gathered every morning to knit. They worked in her room on the second floor at the back of the house, overlooking a small garden, now frozen and still in midwinter. With fuel so scarce, it was often the only room in the house with a fire. Between Christmas 1864 and the following spring, Mary and her fellow laborers produced 859 pairs of socks and 190 pairs of mittens.

In January 1865, Mary and her family received a lavish gift of food from friends and relations in the country, where provisions were still relatively plentiful. It was a testament to General Lee's place in the hearts of Virginians that, under such dire circumstances, his family was so well provided for. There was enough to share and enough that they could barter what they didn't need for other supplies.

Mary carefully recorded the names of her benefactors in order to thank them later: five hams from Julia Stuart at Cedar Grove; a barrel of apples from the Randolphs; staples from Hickory Hill. She received ten barrels of flour, thirty pounds of butter, and similar quantities of other scarce commodities.

However much food there was in the larder on Franklin Street, it was clear to General Lee that the South could not fight on much longer. He encouraged his wife to start thinking about how she would get out when the Confederate capital was evacuated.

"I received from the express office a bag of socks," he wrote her on Washington's Birthday, 1865. Then came a warning:

> You will have to send down your offerings as soon as you can, and bring your work to a close, for I think General Grant will move against us soon....but trusting to a merciful God, who does not always give the battle to the strong, I pray we may not be overwhelmed. I shall, however, endeavor to do my duty and fight to the last. Should it be necessary to abandon our position to prevent being surrounded, what will you do?

Echoing the advice he had given his wife about leaving Arlington, he continued, "You must consider the question, and make up your mind. It is a fearful condition, and we must rely for guidance and protection upon a kind Providence...."

An Irishman then touring the South painted a vivid picture of Mrs. Lee's wartime surroundings in his diary entries for March 8 and 9, 1865:

The aspect of Richmond at this time is wretched—shops with nothing in them except enough to show how miserably they are run out, stores with open doors and empty bales and broken up packing cases and dirty straw. The streets full of all manner, description, character and phases of the human species, knots of rowdies, rustic and urbane, in all habiliments, interspersed with those in every image of semi-dubious, dull, sparkling, moody, furious, wise, mad, raving, or stupid intoxication.

Pickets of mud-stained, slough-hatted, rawboned cavalry. Every species of grey, brown, fresh, threadbare, jaunty, and ragged uniform—or rather multiform. Here and there smart officers and grisly, hard-lined, determined veterans, always neat among their rough and uncouth comrades (as yet untutored in the ways of war). Mud, mud, mud everywhere, even through the halls and corridors of the hotel....

The hotel, of vast size, is now miserably furnished, scarcely anything in the bedrooms except the beds and a few broken chairs, all the carpets having been sent (and this is also the case of private houses) to the military stores to be cut up for army blankets. There are even coats made out of odds and ends of the same carpets, which have saved many a poor fellow's life on picket and outpost duty.... Almost all the crockery in the hotel is cracked and broken, and we had to buy 3 tumblers for our room at 25 dollars each—60 dollars for a bottle of brandy and so on....

The Virginians still, in its forlorn condition, exult in the beauty of their unconquered city and say, 'Oh! But you should see it in the summer!' God knows if it will ever see another summer! Sherman threatening on the North, Thomas coming from Tennessee and threatening Bristol, and Grant with 150,000 men investing the city on the South. Yet these earnest people talk of seeing their favourite city when the leaves are out!

On March 29, Agnes left Richmond by train for a long-planned visit to Petersburg, even though her father warned her not to go because General

Grant's enormous army, stretching its front wider and wider outside Richmond, was poised to attack the city any day. Two nights later, when Grant commenced a bombardment of the Confederate lines at Five Forks, only sixteen miles from Petersburg, General Lee sent an escort to get his daughter on one of the last trains out of town.

Agnes made it home about 2 o'clock the next morning, Sunday, April 2. With all the commotion of her absence and late return, plus the ringing of the tocsin that started before daybreak, the girls might have been tempted to stay home from church. But Mary had invited two students from the Virginia Military Institute—relations of their friends the Cockes—to visit "sometime on Sunday, being the only day when we dine sufficiently early for them to return in time to the institute." V.M.I. had relocated temporarily to Richmond after the Federals torched their campus in Lexington. "I will take care that they attend church," Mary had promised.

True to her word, she had the girls and houseguests up in time to walk over to St. Paul's Episcopal Church, just off Capitol Square. She could no longer go to church herself, but whoever went always shared the sermon with her at Sunday dinner, along with whatever tidbits of news and gossip they picked up.

The members of St. Paul's included some of the Confederacy's most important figures, among them President Jefferson Davis and his family. Davis was already in his seat when the girls and their guests entered the church and sat down. The service began, and at the appropriate time the rector began serving communion. At that moment the sexton walked quietly down the aisle to President Davis and whispered something to him. Davis rose at once and walked quickly out of the service. One by one, other politicians and military leaders left, until the murmur of the remaining congregation threatened to disrupt the service completely. After the minister appealed for quiet, the communicants returned to their worship.

By the end of the service, townspeople had gathered in animated knots up and down the street. Before they reached home, the girls heard the news: Grant had snapped Lee's thin and exhausted line of defense around the city. Confederate records and gold bullion were being transported to Danville. The only way to save what was left of the South's brave and long-suffering army was to retreat.

Richmond was to be evacuated immediately.

CHAPTER TWENTY-TWO

HOW VAIN
THAT HOPE

*F*rom the front windows of her rented house, Mary watched as hordes of citizens took to the streets of Richmond. The Confederate army had withdrawn, and Union troops were expected within hours. Desperate to escape, residents packed up whatever they could carry and headed for the relative safety of the countryside. Everyone knew what General Sherman had done at Atlanta; now there was nothing to stop General Grant from doing the same to the Confederate capital.

The girls had told their mother the news as soon as they returned from church. Most people in the city had long since decided where they would go when this moment came, and Mary had made her decision too: She was staying put.

For one thing, the wife of General Lee could not appear to be running from the enemy. That to her was unimaginable. For another, at this time of crisis she wanted to be in the capital, where she had the best chance of being with her husband. And from a practical standpoint, she could scarcely take a step unaided, completely dependent as she was on her crutches or wheelchair. Even with help from her daughters or someone else, being evacuated in the midst of an increasingly militant, frightened, and desperate crowd of thousands was itself a life-threatening risk.

Insisting that Richmond was bound to fall, neighbors and well-wishers implored Mary to leave. Calmly and steadfastly, she held her ground. She had moved all she was moving. Arlington was gone, and the White House plantation was reduced to a pair of blackened chimneys. She was not giving up another home to the Northern invaders. She would make her stand here at 707 East Franklin.

Rich and poor jostled together in the street. Wagons piled high with furniture and provisions threaded their way among other refugees on foot. Mary listened to the commotion outside—mothers screaming for their children, drivers swearing at their horses, wheels and footfalls growing in number by the minute, building toward a massive crescendo of sound.

After a time, the cacophony ceased, and the quiet was almost more unnerving that the racket had been. The streets were virtually deserted, with only a stray bridle or odd bundle of clothing, dropped in flight, to mark the recent exodus.

Then Mary and her girls heard the shattering of glass and the grating sound of rough voices shouting in the distance. Most of the able-bodied men had been on the battlefield for weeks or months; the rest had left earlier in the day to help Lee's men make an orderly withdrawal. Now the only men in the capital were prisoners (released by their guards as they abandoned their posts), stragglers, deserters, and other misfits.

Authorities had emptied all the liquor stores in town to keep them away from invading bluecoats. The roaming mobs discovered this and dropped to their knees and bellies to drink it out of the gutters. Unchallenged, knots of drunken criminals then lurched up one street and down another, smashing windows and looting as they went. The women and children who remained in Richmond were at their mercy.

Like other women in the now lawless city, Mary and the girls bolted their doors and windows and spent a sleepless night listening to the ruckus: coarse oaths, gunshots, fighting, drunken laughter, the sound of splintering wood and grating metal. Through the closed and barred windows a spring breeze carried the strong smell of burning tobacco. The warehouses on the riverbank were on fire, torched either by careless looters, fleeing citizens, or the arriving Federals.

Soon afterward, a series of explosions rocked the city as Confederate ships in the river caught fire and their ammunition stores exploded. Toward dawn the Lee women were jolted from a fitful sleep by a blast that sounded like "a hundred cannon at one time." The Richmond powder magazine had blown up, adding more heat and flame to a fire already burning out of control.

During the day, fire crept nearer as sparks jumped from one roof to the next, spreading the destruction building by building, block by block. One eyewitness called the scene "one vast livid flame [that] roared and screamed before the wind." A friend and admirer of Mrs. Lee made an appeal to the Union commander, General Godfrey Weitzel, for an ambulance to take her to safety, pleading that she "was an invalid, unable to walk, and that her house…was in danger of fire." The request was granted, but Mary declined the offer. "Richmond is not the Confederacy," she said, confident that her house would be spared and that somewhere, somehow, her husband would fight on.

An east wind whipped the flames ever closer to the room where Mary sat knitting—defiant, confident, at peace. The house next door and the church across the street both caught fire. Neighbors who remained formed a bucket brigade to wet down the roof of 707 East Franklin, and daughter Mary stationed herself on the front porch with a bucket of water to douse any stray sparks.

Just when it seemed inevitable that the Lee's rented house would burst into flames, the wind shifted, driving the fire back over the blackened remains of its previous path. Having no new fuel to consume, the flames began to die down.

At last the windows were unbarred, and the Lee women looked out upon a city in shambles. Broken glass and stolen goods littered the streets. Mary saw smoke and fire to the east and south along the river. And there in the distance, snapping in the breeze atop the Confederate Capitol, waved the stars and stripes of the United States of America.

Well-disciplined Union soldiers took control of the city, clearing the streets of looters and rabble-rousers, and General Weitzel posted a sentry at the entrance to Mrs. Lee's house to make sure she was not disturbed. Watching the young men who took turns standing guard on her porch, Mary saw them not as ruthless enemies, but as weary, homesick soldiers no older than her twenty-one-year-old son Rob. And so she did what she hoped another mother would do for her own son if she had the chance: She sent breakfast out to the sentry on a tray every morning.

Days passed with no word from General Lee. After the retreat of April 2, all communication had been cut off. A week later, Sunday the ninth, Mary heard the sound of distant cannon fire. Had a counteroffensive begun? Would the Confederates retake their capital? Then the news reached her: General Lee had surrendered. The cannon shot had officially marked the occasion.

"Was it to this end," the wife of a Confederate officer asked, "that the wives and children of many a dear and gallant friend were husbandless and fatherless...that our homes were in ruins, our State devastated?" Mary Chesnut was more plainspoken in her diary: "Now we belong to negroes and Yankees. I do not believe it. They are everywhere, these Yankees, like red ants, like the locusts and frogs which were the plagues of Egypt."

Mary Chesnut was one of many who expected other Confederate generals to retreat to positions of strength and keep on fighting. "They say Johnston will not be caught as Lee was," she wrote. When told that her husband had surrendered, Mrs. General Lee replied, "General Lee is not the Confederacy. There is life in the old land yet."

But the war was over. Custis, captured by Federals but quickly released, arrived midweek from the field with news that the fighting had stopped for good. His father was encouraging soldiers—passionate followers not yet ready to let their dream die—to put aside all thoughts of guerrilla warfare, turn in their weapons, and go home.

Saturday morning, April 15, the day before Easter, Mary heard a commotion outside on the front stoop. The door opened, and there stood her husband and Rooney, surrounded by curious bystanders. The two soldiers walked forward into the front hall and closed the door behind them. When Rob returned safely in the middle of May, Mary's family would be fully accounted for at last.

Robert was home for good; Mary's prayer for his safety had been answered. Her prayers for victory had also been answered, but not in the way she had expected. The old life had been transformed forever. The same morning the general came home, the Lees heard the shocking news that President Lincoln had died at the hands of an assassin. In the midst of so much uncertainly, this clouded the future even more. Was a new insurrection beginning? Would retribution against the South be harsher than ever?

The immediate question for Mary now was: What would they do?

Though Arlington was still in government hands, the White House, Romancoke, and other properties remained in the family, and General Lee retained some investments from the days before the war. Soon job offers, some of them very lucrative, flooded in to the general, but they invariably revolved around using his name and reputation to promote various business interests. Robert politely refused them all.

Mary lost no time in applying for the return of Arlington. But despite the tenuous legality of the government's wartime confiscation, popular opinion in Washington was dead set against returning it. On May 25, 1865, under the headline "Arlington and Mrs. General Lee," the Washington *Daily Morning Chronicle* declared:

> Mrs. Lee, the wife of the rebel leader, Robert E. Lee, has formally announced her determination to lay claim to Arlington Heights, and is in a very ill humor because that baronial estate has not been sufficiently cared for by the vile Yankees.... There is in the vicinity of Arlington House, indeed on a part of the property, a romantic spot in which some hundreds of Union heroes *murdered by the orders of Mrs. Lee's husband, or by her husband's troops, are buried.* These sacred remains shall not be profaned by the unhallowed touch, much less outraged by the usurping demands, of this race of savages and traitors. Heaven save the nation from the humiliation!

While Mary was pondering how to pursue her claim, she and Robert received a letter from Mrs. Elizabeth Cocke, a relative of the Cockes at Bremo, offering them a small house near Oakland, her Cumberland County plantation home. There they could escape the summer heat of Richmond and get away from the crowds of veterans, well-wishers, friends, and curious strangers who followed the general constantly and milled around the house at all hours. There they could consider in quiet how best to build their future. The house had the additional advantage of being near the James River, which allowed Mary to make the fifty-mile trip in relative comfort by canal boat.

With the decision made to accept the offer, Mary began receiving farewell calls from many of the townspeople she had grown to know and love during her time in Richmond. Those she could not see in person, she wrote to, sending what small mementos she could collect in the aftermath of war and looking ahead to a brighter future.

In a note to the mother of Mildred's friend Charlotte Haxall, Mary succinctly conveyed her feelings about the friends who had endured the final months of the war with her:

I cannot leave Richmond, my dear Mrs. Haxall, without expressing my deep appreciation of your many kindnesses since I first knew you here, & my regret that I cannot tell you so in person. I have nothing to leave you by way of memento save this little bunch of sweets I send you, which you must lay among your handkerchiefs. I trust we shall meet yet in brighter times when our poor unhappy South may have a name & a place in the world. Now she seems well nigh annihilated. Yet God can raise her from the dust—to Him alone can we look for aid & succor.

On June 30, Mary boarded a canal boat at the Richmond wharf; she arrived at the landing near Oakland the next morning. Custis, who had ridden his father's horse, Traveller, from Richmond to meet them, was there with Mrs. Cocke's son Edmund to escort them to the house. Union soldiers had raided several times, but without serious damage; the fifty huge oaks that lent their name to the place still stood guard on the front lawn. After a warm welcome, the Lee family sat down to a bountiful breakfast reminiscent of the old days at Arlington: ham, sausage, broiled tomatoes, and four kinds of bread.

Derwent, the house Mrs. Cocke had so generously offered, was on a quiet part of the 3,000-acre estate just over the line in Powhatan County. Compared to Oakland, or even to 707 East Franklin, it was a modest affair: a simple frame house with two rooms and a hallway downstairs, topped by two rooms and a hallway upstairs. Though the general relished the solitude and the relative comfort of four walls and a roof after years of nights in a tent, the others soon wished they were elsewhere. Mildred later remembered her time at Derwent as a series of "petty trials of wretched service, cooking, marketing" while living in "an ugly, meanly built little house."

As soon as their mother was comfortable, Rooney and Rob left for the

White House to begin rebuilding it from the ashes. Every structure there had been destroyed and every fence post for eight miles around pulled up and burned. The two slept on the ground under an open sky for a week until they could build a simple shelter. "They are young & hearty," Mary decided, "and able to struggle with their destiny."

Daughter Mary, restless as she so often was, departed for an extended visit to friends in Staunton, leaving Mary to set up housekeeping with Robert, Custis, Agnes, and Mildred. During the war, Agnes had settled into the role of caretaker for her mother, helping her get dressed in the morning, make her way around the house during the day, and get ready for bed at night. Continuing that pattern at Derwent, she became more and more her mother's caregiver, while Mildred—the general's "Precious Life"—spent long hours walking in the woods with her father and talking about the future.

Three weeks into her stay, Mary described her new home in a letter to her cousin Caroline Peters as "a retired little place with a straight up house." The setting, Mary noted, produced "a quiet so profound that I could even number the acorns falling from the splendid oaks that overshadowed the cottage." Its only beauty, she said, "is a fine grove of oaks which surround it. Thro' the kindness of a friend who has given us the use of it, it has been rendered habitable, but all the outbuildings are dilapidated & the garden is a mass of weeds." Fortunately, "the kindness of our neighbors supplies us with vegetables, meat & ice so that we want for nothing." And the isolation was a welcome change from the tumult of wartime Richmond and the crowds the general attracted after peace came.

As for the future, she could only speculate, though even in the midst of utter defeat, there were praises to lift up and hope to embrace:

> How I should love to welcome you all once more at my dear old home, but will that ever be? God only knows.... Our future will be guided by circumstances; I dare not look into it. All seems so dark now that we are almost tempted to think God has forsaken us. Yet we have many blessings, one of the first that all my children have been spared to me from this cruel war. God took my precious Annie to Himself & for that I bless His holy name. Oh how much agony she was spared which her tender spirit could ill have borne.

Mary was scarcely settled at Derwent when Agnes came down with typhoid fever, the same disease that had killed Annie. Mildred shouldered the responsibility for nursing her; Mrs. Lee helped as she could and kept a prayerful vigil over her daughter as her temperature climbed to life-threatening heights. Isolated as they were, doctors were unavailable and medicine was in short supply. Nonetheless, Agnes' fever broke at last, and the danger passed. Mary lifted up her praises to God that, unlike her dear Annie, Agnes would be with her a while longer.

During the summer, Rob stayed at Derwent to recover from malaria and a severe case of poison ivy. Of that quiet season with his mother, he later remembered:

> She was a great invalid from rheumatism, and had to be lifted wherever she moved. When put in her wheel-chair, she could propel herself on a level floor, or could move about her room very slowly and with great difficulty on her crutches, but she was always bright, sunny-tempered, and uncomplaining, constantly occupied with her books, letters, knitting, and painting, for the last of which she had great talent.

In August, General Lee accepted the presidency of Washington College in Lexington, Virginia. The school, founded in 1749, was a legacy of George Washington, who had given stock valued at $20,000 to the struggling college in 1796. Now it was struggling yet again to recover from a war that had left it short of teachers, students, and money. Its trustees were convinced that General Lee was the man to restore its fortunes.

In September, Robert left Derwent for the four-day horseback ride to the campus to take up his duties and prepare a house for Mary and the family. Custis secured a teaching job at Virginia Military Institute, whose campus adjoined Washington College; Rooney and Rob continued rebuilding the old Custis properties they had inherited; Agnes and Mildred stayed with their mother; and daughter Mary continued her series of visits to friends and relations.

Mary chafed at being "deprived of the benefit of a mail," which she guessed was "too great an indulgence for such 'Rebels,'" and at the trouble she had sending and receiving letters at her country hideaway. It was, she told a friend, one of many indications that it would be a long time before the country was restored to its former state. "Indeed," she said, "I do not think it ever can be as it was before… even should we be able to exercise the true Christian spirit of charity & forgiveness."

The loss of her home and property sorely taxed Mary's own spirit of charity and forgiveness. The more she read and heard about its abuse at the hands of the Union authorities, the more incensed she became. She remained steadfastly cheerful and uncomplaining to her friends and family, but there was a spark of anger and resentment that glowed undimmed at the thought of thousands of graves around the great mansion on Arlington Heights.

As Mary waited for her new house in Lexington to be readied, the thought of returning to Arlington burned inside her with newfound strength. As long as it stood and she lived, there was still a chance that she might get it back. In a letter of September 21, 1865, five months after the Confederate surrender, she struck a defiant tone: "My heart yearns to the home of my youth, the most beloved spot on earth to me, and the knowledge of how it is occupied & desecrated is a bitter grief to me. Yet I shall never rest until it is restored, nor will I *ever* relinquish my claim to it."

Sitting in the small, unadorned living room of the cottage at Derwent, she recalled the spacious, elegant rooms of her ancestral home and the unequaled view of Washington City that unfolded at the foot of its famous hillside. "The whole Yankee Nation could not offer a compensation meet for it," she went on. "Independent of its great natural advantages, it has been the scene of every memory of my life either for joy or sorrow. The graves of my beloved parents rest there. There my children were born & there I was married. Every tree they have felled had been cherished with the tenderest care."

That summer she expanded on the topic in an essay recording the "exciting events of the past four years," which she hoped might "at least be interesting to my friends & rescue from oblivion incidents which would not be included in the regular histories of the war."

A reader looking for her unguarded view of the Civil War needed go no further than the title: "My Reminiscences of the War Waged Against the South by the United States Abolitionists Immediately After the Election of Lincoln." Laying blame for the hostilities squarely upon the abolitionists,

Mary nonetheless acknowledged that God ordained everything that had happened according to His perfect will.

> The infamous attempt of John Brown & his accomplices to incite our negroes to murder and insurrection, though thro' the mercy of God a signal failure, should have opened our eyes to the machinations of the party of fanatical abolitionists, unprincipled & evil, who exalted this vile assassin into a hero & martyr.
>
> Even after the election of Lincoln by this faction, peace might have been maintained if they had not predetermined to provoke the South to hostilities, or if their chosen President had possessed the moral courage to resist the evil influences that were brought to bear upon him. He has gone to render an account to the Judge of all the earth for the misery he has wrought in an unhappy country, and we know it would not have befallen us without His permission who overruleth all things. We must do our duty as best we can and believe that the inscrutable Providence who permitted our present situation may be preparing us for a more useful and higher destiny, which without this lesson we might neither have retained or appreciated.

Mary had been a faithful patron of the Colonization Society for many years, and long before the war she had expected eventually to see the end of the institution of slavery. However, it appeared to her that lawless radicals had taken matters into their own hands, eradicating it at a single stroke without considering the social or economic cost, particularly the sudden necessity for blacks to find employment and take up the responsibilities of citizenship. And she saw absolutely nothing about the issue that justified commandeering her house and estate.

She wrote of Orton's visit and of her preparations to leave the house:

> I hoped to return in a short time & having known so many of the army officers, I had some reliance on their chivalry, honesty, & courtesy. I could not then conceive of the numbers in that army who adopted the new code of morals that designated the defense of our rights & liberties a crime, but theft, murder, & arson military virtues....

Now, she concluded sadly, the garden was a ruin, the "splendid forest leveled to the ground," and even her parents' graves "curtailed & penned up by a railing & surrounded closely by the graves of those who aided to bring all this ruin on their children & country." Even as she was leaving, she had hoped that the invasion of Arlington Heights "might be abandoned & that in a few weeks I should return."

"How vain that hope."

As she worked on her essay and her ever-present correspondence during the general's absence, Mary received numerous invitations to visit. But she kindly declined them all, explaining, "I am so helpless I can only get across the room with great difficulty & with the aid of crutches & I can only move from one place to another thro' *necessity*. If it pleases God ever to restore to me the use of my limbs it would afford me great pleasure to visit the many kind friends who have invited us to their homes since the war."

The school year began at Washington College, and still the Lees' home was not ready. Robert was living in a hotel in Lexington, and he encouraged his wife to come join him. Though his lodgings there were on the third floor, he assured Agnes in a letter that her mother's meals could be sent up on a tray. Fortunately, Mary received two generous offers that combined to give her a much more enjoyable place to pass the time until the house on campus was repainted and furnished for its new occupants.

The first offer was from Dr. and Mrs. Charles Cocke, inviting her back to Bremo. The second was from the president of the James River and Kanawah Canal Company to loan Mrs. Lee his private boat for the trip. On her way from Richmond to Derwent by canal boat, Mary had shared a small, stuffy compartment with the girls while Robert slept on deck wrapped in a blanket. This trip, she enjoyed the relative luxury of a spacious private stateroom, a private dining room, and a cook. Pulled by mules walking the towpaths on either side of the canal, the vessel made four miles an hour. Agnes, Mildred, and Rob traveled with Mary. They journeyed by day and tied up for the night—often near farmhouses where they could buy fresh eggs, butter, and other provisions. "It was slow but sure," Rob observed, "and no mode of travel…could have suited my mother better."

Arriving at Bremo, Mary took the same room she had slept in the previous spring. In it was a bed Dr. Cocke had designed, which she could get in and out of more easily. Agnes left for a wedding in Richmond, leaving Rob and Mildred as Mary's traveling companions.

Winter was approaching, and the house at Washington College was ready at last, but the furnishings had not yet arrived. Their long-time furniture builder in Alexandria was just getting back into business after restoring his war-ravaged factory, so Robert ordered a few pieces from Baltimore. He was still waiting for them on December 2, when he rode Traveller the mile and a half from town to the river landing to meet his wife and escort her to their new home after her river voyage—the last stage of a journey that had lasted four and a half wearying and dispiriting years.

The president's house at Washington College was just down the hill from the main block of classroom buildings. It was a fine, though not large, two-story brick home with white columns framing the porch. Reverend George Junkin, who had been president of the college before the war, had lived there when his daughter married a young V.M.I. professor named Thomas Jonathan Jackson, and the couple had once lived in an apartment added to the house. Later immortalized as "Stonewall," Lee's great commander and friend now lay buried scarcely a mile away.

The front parlor of the house was empty except for an elaborately carved and inlaid new piano, presented to the general by the instrument maker. Upstairs another touching surprise awaited Mary. Her rooms were already completely furnished through the courtesy of friends from Baltimore. A one-armed Confederate veteran had made the furniture in Mrs. Lee's honor.

The family silver, sent by train to Lexington only days before the war began, had been buried in two large chests on the grounds of the Virginia Military Institute and had escaped discovery. However, it was too tarnished and moldy to use right away. So the family sat down to their first meal—a hot breakfast waiting for them when they arrived, courtesy of the mathematics teacher's wife—with utensils from General Lee's well-worn camp chest. The same chest provided campstools to serve in place of the dining room chairs that had not yet arrived.

More surprises, both bad and good, awaited Mary. Along with the silver, Mary had sent her most precious Washington and Custis documents to be buried for safekeeping. When the container holding them was retrieved and opened, she found many of the irreplaceable letters and papers rotted and mildewed beyond saving. Mary burned them herself, remembering later, "I almost wept as I had to commit to the flames papers that had been cherished for nearly a century. Those that remained were all defaced and stained." Another legacy gone.

It was all the more a pleasure, then, to see the floors covered with carpets rescued years before from Arlington, now folded under at the edges to fit in these far smaller rooms. Their rich, elegant patterns were a reminder of days that seemed so long ago: elegant rooms ablaze with candles, silver shining on every table, the laughter and conversation of dear friends and cousins ringing throughout the house, her father presiding at the Washington punch bowl in his old-fashioned knee breeches and ruffled cuffs, Robert standing tall and strong and handsome in the parlor encircled by smiling young ladies, and the children and their friends mingling with the crowd.

Ten years ago, it had all seemed part of a life that would go on forever. Now it was forever gone.

CHAPTER TWENTY-THREE

YET HOW RICH

C ompared with the bustle and excitement of Washington City or
Richmond, the town of Lexington, Virginia, was a small, quiet,
isolated place. The same Blue Ridge Mountains that made the
countryside so beautiful and the summer air so pleasant also cut Lexington
off from the outside world. In 1865, the closest railroad station was
Goshen, twenty-three miles and eight bone-rattling hours away by stagecoach along what one traveler described as "the worst and rockiest roads I
ever saw." There was also a stage once a day from Staunton and a river
packet three times a week. The general advised a visitor that no matter
which way he decided to come, "you will wish you had taken the other."

Because it was so much trouble to get to Lexington, Mary no longer
enjoyed the steady stream of visitors to which she had long been accustomed. Nor was she any longer able to travel as she had done for years,
even during the war. Without the railroad, she was a prisoner of sorts,
unable to endure a stagecoach journey or—except in extreme situations—
the slow and cramped canal boat, which she had to be carried on and off
of like a helpless child.

Mary considered her new neighbors "very kind & well *educated* but not
fashionable." The descendants of the city's Scotch-Irish founders were taci-
turn Presbyterians, hard working, intensely religious, and generous at

heart, although to some outsiders they could appear severe and narrow-minded. During her first two months in Lexington, Mary received more generous gifts of food, the first from the wives of her husband's new colleagues at Washington College. With supplies still spotty in the South, faculty wives had filled the Lee larder with pickles, preserves, butter, jelly, apples, lard, root vegetables, and more. As she always did, Mary carefully recorded the names of all the donors and listed their gifts so she could acknowledge them properly.

As a New Year's gift, a group of Confederate veterans sent General Lee's family an enormous store of food to enjoy and to share with the students and official college visitors who were so often in the house: nine hams, two pork shoulders, salt pork, a turkey, thirty pounds of buckwheat flour, a barrel of white flour, twenty-two bushels of corn, two bushels of cornmeal, dried peaches, molasses, and other treats.

Yet another addition to the larder came three weeks later. The accompanying letter explained that it had been intended as a Christmas present, but that it might be even more useful in January "in view of the late burglary committed on your premises."

Newly arrived groups of freed slaves had been drifting idly around Lexington during the day and then returning under cover of darkness to steal what they wanted. Some of the booty, many locals were convinced, turned up in "a Yankee store set up here which is strongly suspected of receiving these stolen goods." Later after another theft, Mary vented her frustration to a friend: "We are all here dreadfully plundered by the lazy idle negroes who are lounging about the streets doing nothing but looking at what they may plunder during the night. We have been raided on twice already, but fortunately they did not get a great deal either time."

Mary blamed the situation on the Freedmen's Bureau, which had been established by an act of Congress in the closing weeks of the war. The original intent of the Bureau had been to help freed slaves make the transition to freedom by providing them with land that had been abandoned by Southern owners and confiscated by the Union. But Andrew Johnson, who became president after Lincoln's assassination, considered the policy unconstitutional and granted pardons restoring the land to its former owners. The Bureau then set out to provide free public education for blacks, building hundreds of schools across the country. Southerners, however, roundly despised the agency. They considered it nothing more than a radical arm of the Republican Party and believed that its teachers and administrators fanned the flames of racial animosity.

Thinking about it brought Mary's anger and sadness and helplessness bubbling to the surface:

> But all thro' the country the people are robbed nearly as much as they were during the war & they can ill afford to lose any thing now. When we get rid of the Freedmen's Bureau & can take the law in our hands we may perhaps do better. If they would only take all their pets north it would be a happy riddance.

Other political situations also rankled the South. Senator Thaddeus Stevens was demanding that the former Confederate states be treated as "conquered provinces," not as prodigal sons to be welcomed back into the fold. In the fall of 1865, several Southern states had sent their wartime leaders back to Washington to represent them in the reunited United States Congress. But rather than seat dozens of rebel leaders, including the former vice-president of the Confederacy and four Confederate generals, Congress sent them all home and set up the Joint Committee on Reconstruction to decide the conditions under which rebellious states could recover their congressional representation and civil rights. Mary reflected the Southern view of the committee when she called it "the Reconstruction Committee *so-called,* for in reality they seem to be aiming at the *destruction* of all that is sacred & true."

In February, the general—who had been pardoned and yet also indicted (but not arrested) for treason—was summoned to testify before the Reconstruction Committee. While he was away in Washington, Mary decided to try to revive interest in her *Recollections.* The publisher still owed her money from the prewar sales of the book, and she hoped that more copies could now be printed. At the same time, she feared that "the teaching & principles of Washington are as much ignored as if he had never existed."

"Still," she continued, "I do not wish that the publication should be *lost,* tho' this may not be the *propitious* time for it to appear before the world. The South is too entirely ravaged to allow even the luxury of books."

Reflecting her view of the times in an unguarded moment, Mary wondered how her book could sell in the South, broken and poor as it was, because the little that Southerners were able to scrape together "by hard labor for the base support of their families [has been] *stolen* by a set of *lazy idle* negroes who roam about by day *marking* what they may steal by night & are kept attending political harangues of which they understand about as much as the African gorilla."

"Still," she concluded, "I wish them no greater evil than a safe landing in their fatherland." Like many people North and South, Mary assumed that freed slaves would have the greatest opportunity for happiness and self-sufficiency in Africa, and she believed they would want to go there. Her opinion, affirmed by the Colonization Society and other organizations in both regions, was that the social assimilation of blacks into American culture would be a difficult, unsettling process that could take decades. Or centuries.

Mary's publisher offered to sell her the copyright of her book and all the plates for $1,000, and her sales agent agreed to relinquish his interest for $500. However, as she admitted, she was "entirely unable to purchase it" at that price. Friends offered to buy the rights for her, but she was not willing to "incur any debts I [am] not *certain* of being able to repay." She also continued to doubt the public's interest in her book in the aftermath of the war. "Though the book I know contains much that is valuable & interesting, I know it does not at *all* suit the tastes of the present day." In the end, the publisher agreed to print a new edition on the same terms as the first, and it went on sale in 1867.

Mary was very pleased with the new *Recollections,* though she still wondered about its public reception, "for I fear it may not find much favor in the eyes of the masses in this radical age." And should the publisher decide to reprint again, Mary promised to "endeavor to furnish him with a better picture of myself & correct a few errors that have crept into the work."

Mary herself read whatever books she had at hand. Her own library, once magnificent, was scattered and gone, and many of the college books had been stolen or ruined. She devoured the newspapers that came her way—Mildred described her mother as "up to her eyes in news"—and gratefully read from cover to cover any magazines her friends mailed her.

Reading, needlework, and painting took up most of Mary's time. She had, she explained, "been undergoing a severe attack of rheumatism which has now prevented my moving without crutches for 3 years." In spite of this disability, "I have the privilege of using my hands & eyes, which is a great comfort to me."

Mary considered it a blessing that her first winter and spring in Lexington were relatively free of the excruciating pain that so often tormented her. She felt well enough to take an occasional carriage ride around the town and out into the countryside, which was beginning to bloom with spring. She kept up her steady schedule of correspondence, and—the new buds on the trees of the campus reminding her of her lost estate—frequently interrupted her own thoughts on paper to insert yet one more reference to Arlington and her hope of returning there one day.

"My heart will never know rest or peace while my dear home is so used," she declared to her friend Emily Mason in a letter on April 20, 1866. "I am almost *maddened* daily by the accounts I read in the papers of the number of interments continually placed there. My faith & patience on that subject is nearly exhausted.... If *justice & law* are not entirely extinct in the U.S. I *will have* it back."

Yet after nearly every outburst came her humble acceptance of the will of God. Speaking of the estate's "desecration" in another letter, Mary reminded herself, "There is but little enjoyment, & I fear I am unthankful for the many blessings that are still spared me above others who have lost all.... I am troubling you with my own sorrows when every heart has its own bitterness."

Mary was also concerned and saddened at the fate of the former president of the Confederacy, Jefferson Davis. Near nervous collapse from overwork, he had been captured in Georgia little more than a week after the invasion of Richmond. Charged with treason and helping plan the assassination of President Lincoln, he was sent to prison at Fort Monroe, where Mary had lived as a young bride and which held such conflicting memories for her: Her first son had been born and her second son imprisoned there.

On June 6, 1866, Mary wrote to him:

My heart has prompted me, my dear friend, ever since I knew of the failure of our glorious cause to write to you and express my deep sympathy. How much more since I learned of your captivity, your separation from your beloved family and your incarceration in a solitary dungeon…. We did so long to hear that you could reach in safety some foreign clime where you could enjoy the repose and consideration which seems to be denied you in your own country….

The only consolation Mary could offer Davis, "besides our deep attachment and remembrance of you," were the words of her favorite hymn, "Jesus, I My Cross Have Taken," a poem by Henry F. Lyte set to a melody by Mozart:

> Jesus, I my cross have taken,
>   All to leave and follow Thee;
> Destitute, despised, forsaken,
>   Thou from hence my all shalt be;
> Perish every fond ambition,
>   All I've sought, and hoped and known;
> Yet how rich is my condition,
>   God and heav'n are still my own!

By mid-July, Mary's friend Emily Mason had visited Davis in prison and written her about it. For a time, Davis was shackled in leg irons in a dank stone cell with a light burning day and night. Mary was enjoying a round of mineral treatments at Rockbridge Baths when she got the letter. "Poor Mr. Davis," Mary replied, "I had no idea he was still kept as a *caged* lion."

Rockbridge afforded Mary the first true recreation she had had in years. Mildred, Agnes, and the general were all with her, and the trip had been mercifully short—only eleven miles from Lexington. "This is a very quiet place," she reported. "The bathing is splendid. I enjoy it exceedingly & it agrees with me perfectly, tho' I do not see that it has made much impression on my disease."

One reason she enjoyed her stay so much was that she could get in and out of the bathing pool without having to walk or be carried up and down the steps leading to the water. As she explained, "The Genl. has had a windlass fixed *outside* [the bathhouse] & a chair attached to it inside in which I seat myself & am immediately let down into the midst of the water & drawn up again in the same manner."

The treatment seemed to completely cure the swelling in her feet and ankles, and the general thought she walked on her crutches "oftener and longer than heretofore, and probably with more confidence." The only dark moment of her stay came when she had another bad fall. Rob thought that the accident "seriously impeded" her improvement; the general, back in Lexington, wrote of his concern that she had "received such a fall, and fear it must have been a heavy shock to you. I am, however, very thankful that you escaped greater injury."

Her fall notwithstanding, Mary returned to Lexington feeling better than she had in years. There, she and the general established a household routine that lent a much-needed sense of order and predictability to their lives. It was an indirect yet comforting reminder of family life at Arlington, which in turn had derived from General Washington's daily regimen at Mount Vernon. In this way, in an unpretentious house on the campus of a college he had helped endow, George Washington made his presence felt once again in the lives of his foster son's descendants.

Each day the whole household, including any guests, sat down at the table promptly at 7 A.M. The general led morning prayers, and then break-fast was served. After the meal, Robert left for chapel services and his day at the college. Mary spent the morning reading, sewing, writing letters, and receiving callers. At two in the afternoon, Robert returned for dinner, which the cook took out of the oven when she saw him coming up the walk. After dinner, Robert took a nap and then returned to his office, while Mary picked up her needlework or correspondence. At the end of the day, the general usually took a ride on Traveller before returning for tea or a light supper in the early evening.

Beginning at 8:15 P.M., students and friends were welcome to call. Each student received at least one personal invitation to the house during the school year, and many of them came far more often. Whatever daughters were at home welcomed guests to the front parlor, while Robert and Mary sat in the dining room—she sewing by the fire and he reading aloud to her as he had done in their courting days.

At ten o'clock sharp the general came in to the parlor and began closing the shutters. Frequent guests knew he was giving them the signal to leave. Once all the shutters were closed, visitors who remained suddenly discovered that their charming hostesses had retired for the night and that the only person left in the room was General Lee. It was a hint too broad for anyone to miss.

Mrs. Lee met every student who was visiting for the first time, and she had opportunities to speak with them at length when they were invited to dinner or a reception. She also enjoyed the company of professors from the college and V.M.I., and their wives and children. They in turn were invariably impressed by Mary's cheerful spirit. One young V.M.I. professor observed that Mrs. Lee "suffers a great deal, but bears it all patiently and is always planning for the comfort and happiness of others."

A young faculty wife remembered her at a reception, "seated in her wheel chair, immaculate in her attire, her silver hair almost covered with a dainty lace-trimmed organdy cap, her face framed with silver curls. A bright word of greeting was on her lips for all who came." In Mrs. Lee she saw "one in whose footsteps the women of the South should follow," displaying "the true heroism of life; for Mrs. Lee had accepted her fate and met it bravely, had cherished her affections, had performed her duties, and had shown that duties faithfully discharged bring a dearer recompense than any circumstance of ease and luxury can supply."

For all the attention she received, Mary was far from relatives and old friends, and at times she felt sharp pangs of loneliness. "With the exception of my immediate family I am entirely cut off from all I have ever known & loved," she wrote, and in a moment of weariness she characterized herself as "often very sad and lonely." "There are so many students," she noted. "I suppose they are studying very hard, as they never seem to find time to visit me." Callers came often to see her husband or daughters, but it seemed there were few for her. Housebound as she was, some loneliness was inevitable. Just to get outside, she had to be carried in her chair down the steps of the front porch.

By the end of the Lees' first year at Washington College, the school was in better financial condition than its trustees ever could have imagined. Cyrus McCormick, inventor of the mechanical reaper, had donated $15,000 to the school since the general's arrival; another benefactor endowed ten scholarships. All told, the school had received more than $100,000 in less than a year. In return, the trustees doubled the general's salary to $3,000 per year plus a percentage of tuition, agreed to build a chapel, and approved plans to build a spacious new home for him and his family.

While Washington College prospered, the United States sank deeper into the charges, countercharges, retributions, and recriminations of Reconstruction. On January 7, 1867, Congress requested an investigation into President Johnson's conduct in the aftermath of the war to see if there were grounds for impeachment. On March 13, the Federal government suspended the state government of Virginia, and the Commonwealth of Virginia officially became Military District Number One. Every other former Confederate state, except President Johnson's home state of Tennessee, was likewise occupied.

Mary was both horrified and enraged. With political action imminent against her beloved Virginia, she wrote on March 10:

> It is bad enough to be the victims of tyranny, but when it is wielded by such *cowards & base* men…it is indeed *intolerable*. The country that allows such *scum* to rule them must be fast going to destruction & we shall care little if we are not involved in the crash. God only knows what our future may be. It is dark enough now, but He can cause the light to shine out of the darkness.

That winter, Mary also wrote to Varina Davis, wife of the imprisoned ex-president. "I need not tell you how often we think of you all," she began, "& how much we are rejoiced at even the slight amelioration in your condition." But her thoughts soon turned, as they so often did, to the continuing quest to reclaim her old home.

> I am still confined mostly to my chair & through the kindness of friends have many comforts. But my heart yearns for the home & scenes of my past life. I feel as a stranger & exile, always looking forward to some change in my condition. It may be only the *last* change I shall ever experience. Much as I long to go there, I dread to witness the plunder & desecration of my once cherished & beautiful home. I only wish I had set the torch to it when I left, or that it was sunk in the bottom of the Potomac, than used as it now is.

As the prospects of recovering Arlington grew increasingly remote, Mary looked back with longing, wondering if she could have done anything differently. "Had I been able to go to Washington myself," she mused, "I might, I believe, have gotten it long since. But, alas, I cannot travel. President Johnson has so much to contend with I do not like to trouble him with applications by letter, though I fear this delicacy of feeling is wasted & will delay the restoration of my property. It is so hard to be patient."

Ever present though it was, the hope of regaining Arlington never consumed Mary to the exclusion of other interests and concerns. In a letter peppered with stern observations about Reconstruction and her old home, she also lavished encouragement on a friend whose son had recently been baptized:

> May he soon unite himself to the people of God & be a Christian not in name only but in deed & truth. The Savior in whom he trusts will guard & shield him from the allurements of the world & the temptations of the Devil, while he leans upon *Him* for support & guidance. May nothing ever tempt him to wander from that blessed influence.

For all the changes in her life, these thoughts were entirely consistent with the private prayer journal she had begun during the first sweet days of her religious conversion in the summer of 1830. Upstairs in her room overlooking the rose garden, with the night breeze rustling the lace curtains at the window, when the tender shoots of Christianity were still fresh around her heart, she had written:

> I would not exchange the hope I have now in my Savior for all that the world could give. I now solemnly dedicate myself & all that I have or may possess to His service. Have I not the sweetest promise for the days of temptation & darkness? Why should I fear? Oh doubting soul, trust entirely to thy God for He will yet glorify thee! My prayer is for a stronger faith, though I sometimes shrink at the tribulation I may be called to endure for this purpose. But Jesus is all sufficient.

Mary's faith was the one thing that had never changed since she had given her life to Christ in 1830. Like every other Christian, she sometimes displayed her faults and shortcomings; even so, in every season and circumstance of life, good or bad, she thanked God for His mercy and looked to Him for strength.

In 1867, Mary and Robert joined Grace Episcopal Church in Lexington. The general became a member of the vestry, valued for his spiritual strength, his celebrity, and the fact that he was a trained engineer who could expertly oversee the various repairs and improvements the little church needed. Though she got out to church only at Christmas or on other signal occasions, Mary directed the church sewing group, which held its regular meetings in her parlor at the president's house.

Mrs. Lee's industriousness inspired the other ladies. To raise money for various causes in the parish, she worked day after day on items to sell at fairs or other fund-raising events. Her output would have been enormous even for a healthy woman; its quality and beauty made it all the more remarkable. Mary had always had an artistic flair, and now she funneled it into producing goods to advance the kingdom of God.

She knit socks, mittens, and caps; braided reins; cut and sewed exquisite doll clothes, lovingly fashioned from her old evening gowns; made and decorated beautiful yet practical muslin aprons; pieced quilts; and made and stocked "housewives," sewing kits packaged in cloth pouches that the students bought to mend their clothes. This was all in addition to the everyday darning and mending she did for her husband and children. God had graciously spared her the use of her eyes and hands, she said, and she planned to make the most of His gifts.

Another of Mary's projects during the spring of 1867 was helping a family interested in adopting Confederate war orphans. The difficulty was in finding guardians who would give up the children. On April 8 she explained to a mutual friend:

> I am so much isolated here that I do not have an opportunity of knowing many such cases. And the two that could possibly have answered her requirements, the friends, tho' exceedingly poor & working for their daily bread, were still unwilling to give up the children.

In one case they were two fine little boys whose father died in a Northern prison camp & their uncle had taken them to share his pittance with his own family. The other was a little girl…whose house having been burned was carried along with Sherman's army, & at last fell into the hands of a kind family in North Carolina who also, though very poor, were still unwilling to relinquish her.

Knowing how the South was struggling made reports of Northern prosperity especially galling to Mary. When Rooney returned from a business trip to Philadelphia, he "gave such an account of the splendor and prosperity of everything as makes my heart sick."

> Not that I would *envy* them if it had been fairly acquired. But I know how much has been gained from the *ruin* of the South & they still desire to grind her to dust…. I wonder how our people, helpless & disarmed as they are, can bear it. Oh God, how long? He seems indeed to have hidden His face from us & yet what hope can we have but in His mercy?

By her own admission, Mary dwelt too much on war matters, and she attributed it to the fact that she was confined to the house. Bidding goodbye to some friends leaving town for a visit, she admitted, "I only wish I could have been along too, but the greatest feat I can expect to accomplish will be to walk across my room without crutches & even that I have no hope of accomplishing."

Still, she was encouraged by the improvement that had come from her visit to Rockbridge Baths the previous summer. There was much less pain and swelling in her legs and feet. Since then, she had tried several medicines and treatments of various sorts. After years of disability, Mary was a seasoned hand at assessing the potential for rheumatic treatments. In June she was "trying a new remedy suggested by Dr. Jackson of Philadelphia & after my return from the springs, if I am no better, shall be willing to try Dr. Faville's. I have seen the pamphlet, but think the whole thing savors of quackery."

In the summer of 1867, Mary at first expected to return to Rockbridge Baths or to go to Hot Springs, which she had visited several times in the past—once by boxcar. Instead, she and the general made plans to go to White Sulphur Springs, one of the oldest and most popular of all the mineral resorts, in the hope that it would be even more effective. "I would prefer the [Rockbridge] Baths greatly," she explained, "as being nearer & more pleasant, but feel it a *duty* to try a more powerful remedy."

The first week in July, as soon as commencement exercises at V.M.I. and Washington College were over, Mary set off on the fifty-mile journey westward through the mountains by stagecoach and railroad. The general rode Traveller, meeting his wife at an inn every evening. A young professor traveled with the general; Agnes went with her mother, accompanied by her friend Mary Pendleton, whose father was rector at Grace Episcopal Church. Custis came as well: It was his responsibility to carry his mother on and off the stagecoach or rail car and to make sure she was safely and comfortably situated in her wheelchair during stops.

White Sulphur Springs was in Greenbrier County, which since 1863 had been part of the new state of West Virginia. The resort had welcomed wealthy citizens and public figures for many years, including President Martin Van Buren, who had spent the summer there during his administration. A large, elegant new hotel had been built in 1854 and was now open for the first time since the war. Visitors luxuriated in the mineral baths, took in the beautiful views of the Allegheny Mountains, and spent their days visiting with other wealthy or prominent Southerners who gathered there in season—friends they seldom had the chance to visit any other time.

The Lees settled into the Harrison Cottage, a quiet, vine-draped building with a covered porch on exclusive Baltimore Row. Of course General Lee was the center of attention from the moment he arrived until the moment he left. While he and the rest of the party spent their days riding, walking, and visiting and their evenings dining and dancing, Mary divided her time between the mineral baths, her front porch, and her cottage. Meals were delivered to her in her room and served by her personal maid, Milly Howard. Rob considered Milly a "faithful and capable servant" who was most eager for Mrs. Lee "to appear at her best, and took great pride in dressing her up, so far as she was allowed, in becoming caps, etc., to receive her numerous visitors."

Every afternoon the general returned to his wife and sat with her on the porch, enjoying a few private moments when they were able, but more often greeting the guests that sometimes walked boldly up to them—and this at a time when social introductions were expected—to engage in conversation.

Mary had long since grown accustomed to these intrusions and to the attention lavished upon her famous husband. According to one account, as she and the general sat enjoying the afternoon air one day, a stranger approached and launched into an effusive monologue: "Do I behold the honored roof that pales into a shadow? Do I see the walls within which sits the most adored of men?" Then, looking at Mary, "Dare I tread the floor which she who is a scion of the patriotic house of the revered Washington condescends to hallow with her presence? Is this the portico that trails its vines over the noble pair—"

Mrs. Lee had heard enough. "Yes," she cut in, "this is our cabin. Will you take a seat?"

Later in the summer, Robert and Mary traveled to Sweet Springs. There, one of the public parlors that opened onto a wide verandah was converted into a bedroom so Mary could move around more freely. Rather than being confined to a cottage as she had been at White Sulphur Springs, she could roll her chair out through the French windows to the verandah and on into the dining room, where she could take her meals with the other guests and watch the dancing afterward.

During the summer, Mary received the exciting news from Rooney that he was engaged to Mary Tabb Bolling. He had rebuilt his ruined plantation and harvested bumper crops of wheat and corn. Now he was marrying a beautiful girl from Petersburg and, after losing his first wife and both children during the war, bringing his bride home to start a new life.

Mary wished that her other children would consider marriage, but she realized that Rooney might be the only one ever to wed. She referred to the subject from time to time in her letters. On one occasion: "My children seem not to be disposed for matrimony." Acknowledging the receipt of some lace caps as a gift, she wrote back, "The white one I must keep for the first wedding in my family, of which there seems to be no present prospect." And another time: "The girls…seem to be in the position of 'poor Betty Martin' who, you know the song said, could never 'find a husband to suit her mind.' I am not in the least anxious to part with them; yet I think it quite time, if they intend to change their condition."

Daughter Mary was already thirty-two (one student described her as "right old and ugly," though "one of the most pleasant ladies I ever saw"), and Custis, still living and taking meals with his parents, appeared to be a confirmed old bachelor at thirty-five. But Agnes, Rob, and Mildred had relatively bright matrimonial prospects, especially twenty-one-year-old Mildred, who was lively, pretty, and surrounded by admiring college men.

Robert and Custis went to Petersburg for Rooney's wedding by way of Richmond, where they were summoned to give testimony in the trial of Jefferson Davis. Mary was relieved to hear from her husband that Davis looked "astonishingly well, and is quite cheerful. He inquired particularly after you all."

A few days later, another note from the general read, "Our son was married last night and shone in his happiness. The bride looked lovely and was, in every way, captivating. The church was crowded to its utmost capacity, and the streets thronged." Mildred was one of ten bridesmaids, "all life," her father reported, "in white and curls."

Christmas that year was a truly wonderful time. Except for the newlyweds, who remained at the White House, Mary had her whole family around her for the first time since Arlington days. The house was decorated with holiday greenery; the day was crisp and fine. The general had presents for everyone, which they opened by tradition at the breakfast table, set once more with the recovered Arlington silver and covered with steaming hot delicacies of the season.

After breakfast was cleared and before the family went to church, Lee mounted Traveller to deliver gifts to the neighborhood children. Sitting in her wheelchair by the fire through the last weeks of autumn, Mary had made them all: doll clothes for the girls and mittens or braided reins for the boys.

But more and more frequently in the new year, Mary's arthritis kept her from the work she enjoyed. For months at a time she was unable to do any "nice work"—fine embroidery or other artistic sewing—and had to content herself with darning and simple mending. Accustomed to making clothes for her friends' children or grandchildren, she apologized when she could not send them a little gift along with a letter.

Though her hands had been idled, Mary's eager curiosity about current events was as strong as ever. "I am the only person in the house—except the girls occasionally—who reads the papers," she wrote. "The General & Custis will not look at them. Better perhaps for their tempers & peace of mind, but I always like to know the worst & never desire any evil to be hidden from me."

In 1868, Mary would have plenty to read about.

CHAPTER TWENTY-FOUR

A MEMORY CHERISHED

*I*n February 1868, President Andrew Johnson, who opposed martial law in the South and other Reconstruction policies he considered vindictive and unconstitutional, dismissed Secretary of War Edward M. Stanton in order to reassert control over the army as commander-in-chief. Stanton, however, refused to give up his office, and days later, the House of Representatives voted articles of impeachment against the president. The Senate trial lasted from March until May.

Mary followed the news eagerly to see if a man she considered sympathetic to the plight of the devastated South would be turned out of office. In the end, President Johnson's opponents failed by a single vote to remove him, but the experience convinced him to let Reconstruction run its course.

This all came exactly a year after a far greater figure in the Southern mind and heart had been vindicated in court. On May 13, 1867, after two years in prison, Jefferson Davis was released without ever being brought to trial. Writing to her cousin shortly after the former president's release, Mary exclaimed:

> I am sure you have all rejoiced in the release of our President, whose misfortunes & heroic endurance of them has endeared him so strongly to every Southern heart & must command the love &

respect of Christendom. Those evil spirits who, like their Father the Devil, can rejoice in nothing that is pure or lovely will continue to *howl* even after their hold upon him has been wrenched away.

By the time President Johnson's impeachment trial ended, the war had been over for three years, and the South was emerging at last from the ashes of defeat. Cities and railroads were being rebuilt, plantations worked again (now with paid laborers or sharecroppers), businesses reopened, and credit reestablished.

Mary felt a surge of hope and optimism when, on April 23, Smith's Island, part of the old Custis estate, was restored to the family by court action. To her, it was a hint that Arlington might yet be wrested from the government. Its recovery was also a great boost to the family's financial fortunes. Rooney and Rob bought the land from their grandfather's estate for $9,000. That money was then divided equally among Washington Custis's surviving granddaughters in partial fulfillment of their original $10,000 legacies: Daughter Mary, Agnes, and Mildred each received $3,000. Soon afterward, the brothers sold the island for $16,000, pocketing a profit of $3,500 each.

With memories of her earlier life stirring inside, Mary wrote longingly from Lexington on June 27:

All that I ever knew & loved seems passing away & I long for old scenes & old haunts. I feel caged here in every sense of the word. My infirmity confines me almost entirely to my chair & to the house & I cannot even see out of any window any thing but the few trees in the yard. Tho' this is a picturesque country I cannot take root in a new soil. I am too old for that.

Not a moment too soon, Mary left the confinement of the president's house for her annual trip to the mineral springs. Traveling the extra distance to White Sulphur Springs had not seemed to bring her any additional benefit, so she returned to Warm Springs, leaving Lexington by stagecoach on July 14. With Agnes, Mildred, Custis, the general, and her maid, she took the stage to the railroad station at Goshen and the train from there to the springs, making the trip in a single day.

The family had been in the Brockenborough Cottage on the grounds of the resort only a few days when Mildred became ill. To Mary's horror, the doctor diagnosed typhoid fever, which had already killed one daughter and almost taken another. Mary grieved even more over the fact that her own room was on the ground floor, while Mildred's sickroom was upstairs. Not only could she not nurse her youngest child to whatever extent her strength would allow, she could not even see her. The general became Mildred's nurse; his "Precious Life" could not fall asleep at night unless she was holding his hand.

By the first of August, the crisis was past, though Mildred remained bedridden for weeks. Seeing that her daughter would recover, Mary resumed her customary mineral baths and visiting with acquaintances from Alabama, Maryland, Kentucky, Iowa, and other places, who were constantly arriving and departing —"an ever-changing sea of faces," as the general said. To Rooney, he reported that his "dear Mim" was in fine spirits: She "bathes freely, eats generously, and sleeps sweetly."

As in years past, the mineral baths made Mary more comfortable but did nothing to help her mobility. "I am better in health," she noted, "but see no improvement in my facility of walking. Nor do I have hope of any, hard as it is to resign myself to such a state of helplessness. I dread another long, cold winter, but that with all other troubles must soon pass away & it will matter little how much I have suffered, but how I have borne it." Later she added, "While I try to bow in resignation to the will of God, it is very hard to relinquish all hope for this life, even when that of a future is not withdrawn."

By the end of August, Mildred was still too weak to speak or walk, and her hair had fallen out. Even so, the doctors assured Mary that she would get well. Late in the summer the family moved on a short distance to Hot Springs, with both Mary and Mildred being carried to and from the stage. Lee traveled on to White Sulphur Springs by himself for a time, and then in September the whole family returned to Lexington for the beginning of the school term.

Christmas that year was a special time of thanksgiving that Mildred had been spared. She had long been her father's favorite, and the general remained especially attentive to her during her extended period of recovery. "Not long before Christmas," Rob later recalled, Mildred "enumerated, just in fun, all the presents she wished—a long list. To her great surprise, when Christmas morning came she found each article at her place at the breakfast table—not one omitted."

Washington College continued to thrive under General Lee's care. Enrollment was up fourfold; endowment funds had multiplied fantastically; the grounds had been restored and new buildings built. The general's favorite project was a college chapel, heartily approved by the trustees and built just down the hill from the Lee home. The general watched it going up; when it was completed, he moved his office into the basement.

At the same time there were reminders of the tension and discord of Reconstruction. For the Lees, 1869 was a year marked both by hope for the future and sad legacies of the past.

On February 15, the United States government formally abandoned its indictment for treason against General Lee. That same month Rooney and his new wife, Tabb, welcomed their first child, a son. They named him Robert Edward Lee III, the same name he and Charlotte had given the son who died.

Also in February, President Johnson authorized the return of the personal property that had been confiscated from Arlington. The move was initiated by James May, a friendly Illinois congressman, and approved by the president and his cabinet as a small recompense for all that Mrs. Lee had lost.

Three years earlier, daughter Mary had visited Arlington and had been allowed to make an inventory of family belongings still there. Her list included Washington's campaign tent and tent poles, a suit of his clothes, a framed Washington coat of arms, two old-fashioned glass chandeliers, various pieces of furniture and decorative items, and more than sixty pieces of the famous Cincinnati china. Mary thought the items had been removed for safekeeping at that time, but instead, the government had added them to what had been on display at the Patent Office since the outbreak of the war.

Johnson had only days left in his presidential term. General Ulysses S. Grant would be sworn in as president on March 4, and Johnson felt there was no hope that Mrs. Lee would recover any of her property after that time. Having received the Cabinet's assent, Johnson instructed Secretary of the Interior Orville Browning—a Lincoln supporter who had nevertheless opposed emancipation—to turn over the confiscated furniture, china, and other items to anyone Mrs. Lee designated. Overjoyed at the prospect, Mrs. Lee sent Beverly Kennon, a cousin who lived in Washington, to receive the property.

On February 26 a brief notice appeared in the Washington *Evening Express* announcing the return of the articles. Immediately, John A. Logan, a member of the House of Representatives, former Union general, and advocate of harsh Reconstruction policies, introduced a resolution "to ascertain by what right the Secretary of the Interior surrenders these articles so cherished as once the property of the Father of his country to the rebel general-in-chief." To turn them over was "an insult to the loyal people of the United States."

A second story in the *Evening Express* on February 29 was filled with inaccuracies: It was the *general* who had come calling for these priceless mementos, and they would be taken from *Arlington,* a hallowed national cemetery. The night of March 3, with less than twenty-four hours remaining of the Johnson administration, a congressional report concluded that Mrs. Lee's belongings were in fact "the property of the Father of his country, and as such are the property of the whole people and should not be committed to the custody of any one person, much less a rebel like General Lee." The President's order to Secretary Browning was countermanded; Mrs. Lee's request was denied.

Even as she lost hope of recovering the treasured heirlooms that had brought her joy in the past, Mary took pleasure in new circumstances that made her disability more bearable in the present. On May 31 the trustees of Washington College presented General Lee with the keys to a new house. Though architecturally plain, it was nearly twice the size of the old residence. Best of all, the general had designed it with a large verandah on three sides to accommodate Mary's wheelchair. Long windows on the ground floor had sills low enough to be fitted with ramps so that she could get directly in or out through a choice of rooms. She was out of her "cage" at last, able to enjoy the air and the scenery, to receive guests on the porch, and to come and go as she pleased for the first time in years.

The general counted it his special privilege to push her in her rolling chair. Students lingered as they walked by during the day, hoping to catch a glimpse of the college president pushing his wife tenderly to and fro on the grand porch, leaning down from time to time to speak to her or to stroke her tenderly on the cheek.

The new house had the latest innovations, including running water and central heat. There was also a fine stable for Traveller and Grace Darling, a cowshed, greenhouse, woodshed, and even a little house for Mildred's beloved cats. Mary's own favorite, Mrs. Ruffner, claimed a special place of honor in the new surroundings. On almost every pleasant day, passersby could see Mrs. Lee on her porch in her chair, sewing or reading, a shawl draped around her shoulders and Mrs. Ruffner fast asleep on her lap.

Houseguests for commencement that year were admonished to be at the breakfast table for prayers at seven o'clock sharp. What Mary saw when she rolled her chair into the dining room that morning unleashed a flood of memories: On each lady's plate was a freshly picked rose bud, still wet with dew.

That summer Mary went to nearby Rockbridge Baths, where she had so enjoyed the waters three years earlier. There she received the sad news that Robert's brother Smith had died. "For him," she mused, "the toils of life are ended & for the last 8 years they have no doubt weighed heavily upon him as indeed they have upon us all."

Her mood brightened dramatically with a visit from Rooney's wife, Tabb, and her new grandson, neither of whom she had ever met. Mary had a grandmother's unbounded pride in little Robbie. He was, she observed, "a large, splendid fellow exactly like his Mother & the Bollings. No Custis or Lee about him. He is just 6 months old & already knows his grandma, to whom he is a great source of pleasure. He is so good too—always laughing & crowing & looks at each person as if he was determined to know them again."

While Mary visited with her new relations, Robert, Agnes, and Mildred went on to White Sulphur Springs, whose waters Lee thought were more beneficial to him. The number of people in attendance there proved that the nation was recovering well from the war, at least financially. There were twice as many guests as the year before, some having traveled on the newly completed transcontinental railroad from as far off as California. Ladies appeared at dinner in Paris gowns and breathtaking jewelry. There were dances day and night, and the young people gathered on the lawn to play the newest rage, croquet. "The girls are well," Lee wrote to Mary at

Rockbridge. They "would send love if I could find them." They were "always busy at something," he wrote, "but never ready."

At the end of the season, to Mary's delight, Tabb and Robbie traveled with her back to Lexington for a visit in her spacious new home. When the two left for the White House, Mary resolved to visit them there at the earliest opportunity. There was a new railroad from Richmond to a station not far from Rooney's plantation, where he and Tabb could pick her up.

The next spring Mary had her chance when General Lee left on what started out as a quiet vacation but ended up a triumphal grand tour. Fearing that he was no longer up to the rigors of serving as a college president, Robert had told the trustees he thought he should resign. He worried that if he died in office, his wife, "who is helpless," would have to vacate the president's house to make way for his successor and would have no place to live. The trustees had begged the general to stay on as president and to take a two-month vacation to regain his strength.

On March 24, 1870, the general and Agnes left on a vacation slated to carry them all the way to Florida and back. During the trip, Robert faithfully sent letters to Mary, sharing as much of it as he could with his housebound wife: an uncomfortable reunion with General George Pickett in Richmond; a visit to Annie's grave—his first—where the ladies of Warrenton had built a beautiful twelve-foot grave marker; his first experience on a Pullman car; the crowds that grew exponentially as word got around that General Lee was on the way; Columbia, where the city declared a holiday; Augusta, where Lee met a curious but quiet thirteen-year-old boy named Woodrow Wilson; on to Savannah aboard a private car; Cumberland Island, Georgia, where he paid his respects to his father's grave; by steamer to Jacksonville.

While he was away, Mary organized her own vacation. She had talked for months about traveling on her own to the White House, but her husband had never expected her to follow through. "She says she will go down in the spring," the general told Rooney at Christmas," but you know what an exertion it is for her to leave home, and the inconvenience, if not the suffering, is great. The anticipation, however, is pleasing to her and encourages hope, and I like her to enjoy it, though I am not sanguine that she will realize it."

Accompanied by Markie Williams—her dear cousin whose father had died in Mexico and whose brother Orton was hung as a rebel spy—Mary made the leisurely trip from Lexington to Richmond by canal boat. From there she took the new train the rest of the way.

"The road was fine," she said of the last part of her trip, by carriage from the rail stop through New Kent County. The land was in bloom, and the artist and gardener in Mary blossomed as well as she described a countryside "lovely with wild flowers and dogwood blossoms, and all the fragrance of early spring—the dark holly and pine intermingling with the delicate leaves just brought out by the genial season, daisies, wild violets, and heart's-ease"—one of her mother's favorites. "I have not seen so many wild flowers since I left Arlington."

Mary arrived brimming with newfound self-confidence: It was the first trip she had taken on her own initiative in more than a decade. At the White House she reveled in the attentions of Tabb, Rooney, Rob—who came up from Romancoke regularly to see her—and, most important of all, little Robbie, who interrupted her in the middle of a letter to Mildred. "*He has just come in my room looking like a rose with mouth wide open to kiss me & is now quietly eating a cracker.*" His grandmother, she admitted, "does not accomplish much but play with him."

From her idyllic country retreat, Mary regularly sent inquiries and instructions to Mildred about housekeeping, maintenance, hiring and discharging servants, the results of the church fair, grocery shopping, looking for a lost breast pin, and other domestic concerns. As happy as she was to be away from home for a while, she still kept a close watch on how the household was run.

On May 13, the general and Agnes joined Mary at the White House after their incredible odyssey through the South. As she welcomed them back to Virginia, Mary thought that neither of them looked particularly healthy. "Your papa...looks fatter, but I do not like his complexion, and he still seems stiff," she informed Mildred in Lexington. "As for Agnes, she looks thin, but I think it was partly owing to the *immense chignon* which seems to weigh her down and absorb everything."

When General Lee went back to Lexington on May 28, Mary stayed behind for a time and then spent a week at Bremo. When she arrived home at last, she learned that in the general's absence the trustees had voted her free lodging in the president's house and an annual stipend for the rest of her life in the event of Lee's death. The general had protested, writing, "I am unwilling that my family should be a tax to the college, but desire that all of its funds should be devoted to the purposes of education. I know that my wishes on this subject are equally shared by my wife." The trustees, though, knew how concerned Lee was about what would happen to Mary after his death, and they quietly ignored his directive.

"Robert is not well," Mary confided to her brother-in-law Carter on August 1. She explained that the general had caught a cold in the intensely hot weather and that his angina pains had returned. "But he is now under medical treatments," she continued, "& I hope will soon be better." She wrote these words slowly and painfully: Her hands were so stiff that at times her handwriting was all but illegible. But if she felt tired and sore, Robert seemed even worse. Anyone who knew him well could see how weary and sallow he was. One old acquaintance thought he had aged twenty years in the last five.

Later in the summer, accompanied only by James White, a former Confederate captain and professor at the college, Lee went to Hot Springs in search of relief. While he was away, Mary received the wonderful news, which she had been secretly anticipating for a while, that Rob was engaged to Mildred's friend Charlotte Haxall, whom she and the general called "Lottie."

When her husband returned for the start of the new school year, Mary noticed a marked decline in his general health. At the doctors' suggestion, he asked her for the first time ever, arthritic hands and all, to help him with his correspondence.

On a raw, chilly, late September day, after awaking from his customary afternoon nap, Lee left home for a meeting of the vestry at Grace Church, which he served as chairman. The meeting was a long one, and Mary waited for him to return before serving tea. October 12, 1870, Mary recounted the subsequent events in a letter to her friend and cousin Mary Meade:

My Dear Cousin Mary,

I have been thinking of writing to you for a long time, but this day of my great sorrow I feel that I can do nothing else & must do something. I have prayed & wept till my fountain of tears seems dried up & all my prayers to spare my husband's life have been unanswered so that I can only now pray "Thy will oh God be done for me & mine." This morning at 10 o'clock he expired.....

On the evening of the 29th, the same time when that terrible storm commenced, was our regular church evening & after it was over a very protracted vestry meeting of a rather exciting nature.... When I went in to tea at 7 he had not returned & I sat down to my sewing waiting for him.

About half past 7 we heard him come in, put his hat & coat as usual in his room & then as he entered the dining room, I said, "You have kept us waiting a long time. What have you been doing?" He stood up at the foot of the table to say grace but did not utter a sound & sank back on a chair. I said, "You look very tired. Let me pour you a cup of tea." But finding he made no reply & seeing an expression on his face that alarmed me, I called Custis who asked him if he wanted anything & on his failing to make any reply we sent off immediately for the Dr. who had been at the same vestry meeting & he sent for the other one too.

In the course of 15 minutes we had both here, & they applied cold cloths to his head & hot applications to his feet & got him undressed & put in bed. While undressing he seemed perfectly conscious & helped to pull off his things but didn't speak & slept almost continuously for 2 days & nights.

In early October, Mary gave her cousin Edward Carter a prognosis of the general's condition: cautious but hopeful. She left a blank at the top of the page for the day of the month; the days and nights had run together, and by then she had no idea what day it was. Her sixty-second birthday had gone by unnoticed on October 1.

A veteran of so many sickbed vigils, Mary sat at her husband's bedside hour after hour. The doctors' first diagnosis had been "overstrained nerves," which would pass with sufficient rest, Mrs. Lee told her cousin Mary, "but finding he did not improve as they had hoped, they cupped him & gave him medicine which roused him somewhat & they confidently expected his recovery. He did not speak except a few words occasionally, but always greeted me with an outstretched hand & kindly pressure, took his food with some pleasure & we vainly thought was getting on comfortably." But the next Sunday, Lee became suddenly worse, "almost insensible & lay in that condition until Tuesday night when *all* hope was relinquished...."

On October 10, Mary sent a note to General Francis Smith, superintendent of V.M.I. asking for a pound of beef, "lean & juicy if possible," to make some beef tea as the doctors had suggested. She needed it at once, she explained apologetically, "as I cannot get it at market before tonight." She vacillated between fear that the general would die and fear that he would live and be confined upstairs in his bedroom where she could not get to him unassisted.

We *all* sat up all night every moment almost expecting to be his last. He lay breathing most heavily & the Dr. said entirely unconscious of pain. I sat with his hand in mine all moist with heavy perspiration & early in the morning went into my room to change my clothes & get a cup of tea.

When I went back he lay in much the same condition, only there were some more severe struggles for breath—these became more frequent and intense & after 2 very severe ones, his breath seemed to pass away gently, & he so loved & admired now lies cold & insensible.

We all prayed God so fervently to prolong a life so important to his family & country, but *He* in His mysterious Providence thought best to call him to those mansions of rest which He has prepared for those who love & serve Him—& oh, what a rest to his toilsome & eventful life.

So humble was he as a Christian that he said not long ago to me he wished he felt sure of his acceptance. I said all who love & trust in the Savior need not fear. He did not reply, but a more upright & conscientious Christian never lived.

He has been for the last two years fully impressed with the belief that he should not live long, but I thought it was only because he did not feel well & I did not feel as if *he could die,* at least *before me,* & was selfish enough to wish that I might be spared what I now endure, thinking too my life was of so little importance compared to his.

Assured of her husband's spiritual victory, Mary had still hoped that one day the general would lead the old Confederacy's return to its rightful place in public affairs.

Nothing could add to his estimation in the hearts of his country-men & yet I was ambitious enough to hope the day might come when in a political sense at least he might again be its deliverer from the thralldom which now oppresses it. By our country I mean the South....

Oh cousin Mary, life seems to me so aimless now, so blank. Everything in the house was always done with a reference to his comfort, *his wishes* & now there seems to be no object in having anything done.

Custis, Agnes, and Mildred were at home. Mary had telegraphed Rooney and Rob to come as soon as they could. Daughter Mary was on an extended visit in the Midwest and would not make it to Lexington in time for the funeral.

"I know...all will mourn with me," Mary concluded, "for we have a common sorrow."

I pray that his noble example may stimulate our youth to a course of uprightness which never wavered from the path of duty at any sacrifice of ease or pleasure, & so long too has the will of God been the guiding star of his actions.

I have never so truly felt the purity of his character as now when I have nothing left me but its memory, a memory which I know will be cherished in many hearts besides my own.

Even as Mary wrote her letter in the next room, Agnes prepared her father's body, dressing it in the dark broadcloth suit the general had bought in Richmond to attend Rooney's wedding. The funeral, three days later on October 15, was attended, one eyewitness said, "by everybody who could get to Lexington in time." The service was held in the campus chapel Lee had built and where his basement office lay untouched since he last walked out of it. The day was beautiful and clear and the chapel windows were raised to admit the unseasonably warm autumn air. Across the quadrangle the tall white columns of the main building were wrapped in mourning black.

Mary did not attend the service. She stayed at home alone reading old letters—witty missives full of life from the young adventurer in the mosquito-infested swamps of Cockspur Island, the brave explorer writing of Indians that wore nothing but beads and body paint, the victorious warrior on the streets of Mexico City. From the chapel, the temperate breeze carried the triumphant sound of the congregation singing her husband's favorite hymn:

> How firm a foundation, ye saints of the Lord,
>   Is laid for your faith in His excellent Word!
> What more can He say than to you He hath said,
>   To you who for refuge to Jesus have fled?

> "The soul that on Jesus hath leaned for repose
>   I will not, I will not desert to its foes;
> That soul, though all hell should endeavor to shake,
>   I'll never, no, never, no, never forsake!"

To a well-meaning correspondent who spoke of the general's "untimely" death, Mary replied:

> We must not deem that untimely which God ordains. He knows the best time to take us from this world; and can we question either His love or wisdom? How often are we taken from the evil to come.
>   How much of care and sorrows are those spared who die young. Even the heathen considers such the favorites of the gods; and to the Christian what is death but a translation to eternal life. Pray that we may all live so that death will have no terrors for us.

Robert E. Lee's body was placed in a crypt beneath the chapel. The trustees promised Mary that they would have it moved anywhere she wished, but she could think of no better place than there—beneath the building he loved most at the institution he had hoped would be instrumental in raising up a new generation of leaders for the South.

CHAPTER TWENTY-FIVE

RIPENING FOR HEAVEN

*B*eginning within days after her husband's funeral, Mary was bedridden for more than a month, first with what she described as a "bilious attack" and then with a painful and debilitating swelling of one leg and foot. The pain was so intense that she had to be lifted in and out of bed and could scarcely turn over on her own.

As letters of condolence poured in from around the country, Mary kept up with them as much as she was able, though trying to sit up and write prolonged her suffering. Gifts were offered large and small. Custis was elected his father's successor, which meant that Mary could stay in the president's house without feeling that she was a financial drain on the college.

A former Confederate general wrote proposing to raise $100,000 from other Confederate veterans for her support. "I fear they will tax themselves too severely," she replied, "and I could never consent to receive aught from them but a small portion of the love & veneration they bear to the memory of their Chieftain. Should I ever need anything beyond the provision he has made for me, I will accept some of the generous offers made me by the College."

Mary was just as courteous and attentive to neighbors who brought little gifts or treats to her, and, in keeping with local custom, she returned their gift baskets with a small gift of her own. To one neighbor she wrote:

I have long intended, my dear Mrs. Smith, to return your little basket, but have delayed with the hope of filling it with something that would be acceptable to you.... I have nothing but a few poor flowers; yet I will send them & hope to get a rose bud, the last on a bush planted and cherished by Gen'l Lee, which you might value.

And later, incapacitated but never inconsiderate, Mary wrote: "I can only write you a few lines, as I can scarcely mark with my pen, to offer you some Richmond oysters which I hope you will all enjoy & some ginger which the young ones too may enjoy. The weather prevents our meeting, but my heart is with you & yours."

By mid-November, the pain in her foot and leg were better, she wrote to her friend Virginia Long, yet still "I am obliged to keep my foot propped up and cannot bear any weight on it at all. I trust now it is to be restored to its usual condition, which is helpless enough but better than the present."

As Mary wrote, her thoughts drifted back to her recent loss. Had the general "been successful instead of the Hero of a Lost Cause, he could not have been more beloved and honored. I am content and would not have him back if I could, tho' I must continue my weary pilgrimage alone without the support on which I have leaned with perfect confidence for more than 30 years."

Even as Mary adjusted to this dramatic change in her life, she reached out generously to others. In February 1871 she responded to news that her brother-in-law Carter was in financial trouble by offering to send him her profits on the sale of the new printing of the *Recollections*. "I was in hopes to have sent it 'ere this," she informed him in an encouraging letter on February 6, "that it might have served to provide you some comforts and paid some debts, but we have to be patient in all things & bide our time, remembering it is God the omniscient & all merciful who ordains our trials as well as our enjoyments."

God had been with his brother until the last, she reminded him, even though Robert was unable to express his conviction in those final hours; in the end, his mighty trials had been the crucible of his spiritual victory: "The sublime resignation apparent in his whole being assured us that God was with him. He had been for many years the most humble Christian I ever knew & for the last few years, ripening for Heaven."

The storm that had begun the night Robert was stricken had continued for days, causing floods that wiped out bridges and wrecked canal locks. In the spring of 1871, as soon as the storm-damaged canal had been repaired, Mary journeyed again to the White House. She enjoyed visiting with Robbie and his new baby sister, Mary Tabb Lee. She also cheerfully assisted with plans for Rob's wedding to Lottie Haxall, which had been postponed in the wake of the general's death.

Little Robbie captivated his doting grandmother, who pronounced him "sweet & good" and "the sunbeam of my life." But regarding discipline, she spoke with the voice of experience: "Don't spoil him," she admonished Rooney and Tabb. "I fear he will have too many indulgences to make a great & self-controlled spirit essential to a great & good man; but we must pray that God will direct him in all his ways & teach him early to love & serve Him."

After a rejuvenating visit to the White House, Mary returned to her home—now officially Custis's home—on the campus of Washington College, a name changed that year to Washington and Lee. "I think Custis will accept the Presidency of the College," she had written earlier, "and we shall still continue to make this our home if he does. I could not bear to move into a new home, and my own Arlington is not yet open to me."

It was sad returning from Rooney's without the general there to welcome her. As much as Lee had been away during their thirty-nine years of marriage, the last five had been spent in relative quiet and close companionship. Mary's great rock, her great friend, was gone. Neither Custis nor Daughter was particularly affectionate by nature, though they respected and dutifully served their mother. Custis chafed at a job for which he felt ill suited and which he thought he had only because his name attracted contributions to the school. Daughter considered Lexington a dreary backwater and was impatient to travel again.

One bright note in the fall of 1871 was Rob's marriage. Mildred and Agnes went to the White House for the wedding—it was considered a more suitable site for the festivities than Rob's relatively spartan "bachelor hall" at Romancoke—and left their mother in the care of Custis and daughter Mary.

The two girls stayed on through Christmas for what should have been a happy time. But tragedy intervened: Mary Tabb Lee, just a year old, died of whooping cough during the holidays. Mary had seen her granddaughter only once. "I can scarcely bear it," she confided to a friend, writing of baby Mary's death, "but God is good. I cannot write more."

With General Lee gone and her influential friends in government replaced for the most part by the next generation, Mary at last came to grips with the fact that Arlington would never be hers again. Before leaving on his triumphal tour of the South, the general had gone over the prospects of recovering it with his lawyers one last time. Restoration of the property to the Custis estate seemed impossible. Now as a widow whose life revolved around friends, church, and campus activities in an isolated mountain town, Mary came to the settled conclusion that she had lost her "dear old home" forever. At last she sent for the Arlington furnishings stored at Ravensworth.

This was the load of household goods she had sent on ahead to her Aunt Maria Fitzhugh that spring ten years earlier, when she expected to visit for a few weeks until the invaders left her home. The furniture and other items had been there all this time, a half day's wagon ride or less from Arlington, ready to be restored to their former places any time. Now Mary asked Aunt Maria to ship them to Lexington by canal boat. The boat carrying them foundered and sank, but the lot was eventually recovered and restored, even the waterlogged paintings.

Mary also petitioned the government, not for return of the estate, but for compensation. Whether the confiscation of her plantation during the war had been legal or not, it was an irrefutable fact that neither she nor the Custis estate had received a penny of the sales price beyond what was due to the government for delinquent taxes. Though she had failed so many times before, Mary renewed her campaign to expose the occupation of Arlington as unconscionable and illegal.

On January 22, 1872, a petition was referred to the Judiciary Committee of the United States Congress "praying an appropriation of three hundred thousand dollars for the purchase of the property known as 'Arlington,' in the county of Alexandria, State of Virginia." Mr. Custis's will, leaving his only child the estate, was entered into the record, along with the tax sale certificate showing that the government had sold it for "the sum of twenty-six thousand eight hundred dollars, no portion of which sum has ever been paid to the owners of said property, or to any other person, so far as your petitioner is informed."

The petition then listed a number of reasons why "said certificate is wholly insufficient in law to pass any legal or valid title to said property to the United States." In summary, the reasons were: the United States could not under the Constitution "exercise exclusive legislation" over the property unless Virginia ceded its own right to do so; the government was obliged to sell only enough property to pay the tax due, "the tract being clearly divisible;" the amount of the tax was tendered in full before the sale, but refused by the tax commissioners; and that for these and other reasons, "it cannot be doubted but that a serious cloud rests upon the title."

The petition failed. But Mary had the option of filing a new petition, as did Custis as "owner of the reversion"—the person the estate would revert to upon his mother's death.

While considering her next steps, Mary threw herself wholeheartedly into another project. Grace Church was a small Episcopal congregation of meager means in a town where most churchgoers were Presbyterian. The vestry had approved a plan to build a new church building as a memorial to General Lee, but donations had fallen short of what the project required.

With the old church demolished and a fine new stone building going up in its place, Mary turned her artistic talents more eagerly than ever to the service of God. Her arthritis was so severe now that she could seldom sew, but she could still hold a paintbrush. For some time she had been coloring photographs of paintings of George and Martha Washington, General Lee, and herself to raise money for the church. By 1872 she was systematically producing them to support the building fund.

That summer season, Mary took her pictures and her paints with her to the springs, where she painted and sold tinted photos to friends and visitors. The card-sized images were snapped up as fast as she could produce them. She asked her fellow guests to tell their friends back home about the church being built in honor of General Lee and to encourage them to send contributions. At summer's end she returned home with nearly a thousand dollars for the fund.

Mary contacted other friends near and far to garner support. When a New York acquaintance wrote requesting an autograph of Washington on behalf of someone else, she sent her one, taking advantage of the opportunity to suggest a favor in return:

He will be able to repay the obligation if he considers it such by uniting with you or any other friends who may be interested in the South in aiding me in efforts I have been making…to raise funds to build a Church in memory of General Lee…. So I thought in writing to some of our friends I would mention our great need of help & even a small sum from many of them would aid us materially. A memorial church for Gen'l. Lee should not be left unfinished for want of a few thousand dollars.

With her friend she also shared the sad news that her son Rob "lost his sweet young wife last autumn." Charlotte Haxall had died only a year after her marriage.

In 1870, General Lee had made a valedictory tour, greeting old friends, visiting places dear to him, and making his peace with the world. In the spring of 1873, Mary Custis Lee set out on a valedictory tour of her own.

With Rob as her traveling companion, she journeyed to Alexandria for a tearful reunion with her dear Aunt Maria —a widow herself now for more than forty years—whose husband's death had been the catalyst for Mary's spiritual awakening so many decades earlier. It was her first visit to the region since the war, and Mary received a deluge of visitors at the Fitzhugh townhouse where her mother had been married. Vast numbers of friends and admirers from Virginia and Washington called, unable to imagine they would ever have the chance to see Mrs. General Lee again. Mary later wrote of her visit:

> I was so constantly occupied in seeing my many old friends that I had scarcely a moment to myself. It was a great satisfaction to me to be so warmly received by them, & not the less so that I know I am united in their hearts with the love & veneration they have borne to Gen'l. Lee.

The newspaper reported Mary's visit in detail. According to conventions of the day, women of breeding were virtually never mentioned in the press, and yet on June 12, 1873, the *Alexandria Gazette and Virginia Advertiser* carried a front-page story that was as close to a celebrity interview as decorum would allow:

Mrs. Lee is about sixty years of age.... She is a lady whose noble character and Christian graces render her an object of reverence to all who meet her. Her mind is richly stored with the recollections of the patriotic, cultivated and distinguished persons who will ever be prominent in our national history....

Mrs. General Lee has for many years been a great sufferer from inflammatory rheumatism, and quite unable to move without assistance; but in her age and affliction she had a noble and dignified countenance. Her features much resemble those of Martha Washington. With her sad yet firm expression of face and eyes, beautiful and sparkling with the uncommon intelligence which marks her conversation; with her almost snowy white hair, fine, soft and in waves and curls, framing her full forehead, and covered by her plain widow's cap, she sits before one a grand and lovely picture, combining within itself much of the history and glory of the immortal past with the modern events of our history.

The paper boldly supported Mary's position that Arlington had been taken illegally and that she should receive fair compensation for it:

No one can see this much-suffering lady and hear her accounts of her old home and not feel convinced that on the day our Government shall have remunerated the mistress of Arlington for its loss, and made that settlement with her which is esteemed just and legal by all who fully understand the circumstances of her absolute ownership of the estate, it will add to its repute for just and honorable dealing.... Mrs. Lee does not ask to have the estate restored to her. It has become a national cemetery, and as such she presumes with other citizens it will ever remain, but she does expect a reasonable remuneration for the ground.

The fury of earlier years over the loss of her home seemed to the writer to have entirely dissipated:

The pure and lofty womanhood and the true nature of Mrs. Lee's character was revealed in the farther fact that she conversed upon

333

the whole matter without one single expression or shade of bitterness. Of the President [Grant] and his administration she spoke in the sincerest terms of respect, and seemed entirely calm and patient in the reflection that at the proper time the right would prevail. Like her great husband, she "recognizes no necessity for the state of things" that existed when the late war commenced, and now she recognizes no necessity for any other state of things than that of profound peace, amity and concord between the North and the South.

Yet when Mary perused a copy of the new edition of her *Recollections,* the constant references in it to Arlington brought her ever-present thoughts of the place boiling to the surface. Describing the book, she wrote,

> [There is] no allusion to the *present* state of that home...or of the agony endured by the *sole survivor* of that family once beloved & honored.... It seems to me almost like a terrible dream— the present occupation & condition of that place. It is rarely out of my thoughts either waking or sleeping & the longing I have to revisit it is almost more than I can endure.

Mary's wait was about to end.

On a sunny late spring morning in June of 1873, Mary left Aunt Maria's by carriage with some of the "young friends" who were there to visit with her. The group passed along a pleasant, tree-lined road that Mary had last traveled going the other way, away from the only home she had ever known, on an equally beautiful spring day twelve years earlier.

As they approached the familiar driveway, Mary's stomach fluttered and her heart raced. This was the moment she had thought of, "either waking or sleeping," almost every day since the same drive had disappeared from her sight around a bend in the road. Her flight that May morning had made her a refugee; to this hour she had never had another house to call her own. Even this one—"dear old Arlington"—was not hers anymore. She knew now what she had never even suspected the last time she saw it: She would never spend another night under its roof.

The carriage turned up the drive. Mary stared out the window at the stumps of once magnificent trees that now dotted the desolate grounds.

Down toward Arlington Spring, she saw the humble buildings of the Freedman's Village stretching along block after block of dirt roads. Two thousand former slaves lived there now, awaiting an undetermined future. Then she saw the graves—row upon row upon row of them with simple marble tombstones, their ranks extending out of sight.

"I rode out to my dear old home," she wrote to her friend Elizabeth Cocke on June 20, "so changed it seemed but as a dream of the past. I could not have realized that it was Arlington but for the few old oaks they had spared, & the trees planted on the lawn by the Gen'l. & myself which are raising their tall branches to the Heaven which seems to smile on the desecration around them."

The carriage crested the hill, and there it was—Arlington House. The massive columns she had watched being built. The great classical pediment pointing to the sky. The welcoming windows though which she and her parents had watched as Washington City burned and later as it was transformed over decades from a malarial tidal marsh into a capital worthy of its namesake.

Over one of the doorways was a plain wooden sign: Cemetery Office.

Across the Potomac the Capitol shimmered in the sun, its new dome commanding a view forever etched on Mary's mind and heart. Mary spied the Washington Monument, still unfinished, mimicking on a giant scale the stumps that had once been Arlington Forest.

A semblance of her mother's flower garden remained—thanks no doubt to Ephraim and whatever children he could get to help him these days. Just out of sight, over the hill to the south, Mary's parents rested in the spot she had picked for them and under the monuments Robert had designed. In her mind's eye she saw the graves as they once were, alone together, far from the strangers whose headstones now crowded up to within a few paces of them.

Old servants ran to meet Mary, tears streaming unchecked down their cheeks. Their familiar faces recalled a bond from another era—a bond of mutual trust, respect, and love that had outlasted any bond recognized by law.

The other passengers climbed out for a walk around, but Mary remained seated in the carriage, talking with the old servants, looking at the house, taking in the view that General Lafayette had once pronounced so spectacular. How well she remembered General Lafayette. And his son—named George Washington, just like her father.

Mary's mind drifted to the Arlington of long ago, filled with laughter and running children, slaves to manage, parties to plan, clothes to sew; her parents sitting beside the fire at night, Mother at her sewing and Father scratching out old Revolutionary War tunes on his violin; letters from Robert in Florida or Michigan or Texas or Mexico; Robert holding her in his arms and her feeling his warm breath on her cheek and running her fingers through his luxurious black sidewhiskers.

Someone handed Mary a cup of water from the well. Holding out two stiff and misshapen hands, she took it carefully. The water was cool and inviting. She knew the spacious entrance hall would be refreshing too, with the spring breeze blowing through it soothingly front to back, wafting up to the ceiling where the massive wrought iron lantern from Mount Vernon once hung.

Mary savored every swallow, every drop, the taste and smell bringing to mind her earliest memories: the cozy room in the north wing where she learned her first letters, her first Bible verse; the big flat playground between the wings where the "middle house" later appeared; the huge unfinished ballroom where she and her playmates scrambled through Washington's campaign tent and gleefully pounded the keys of his old harpsichord; the legendary flower garden where she had played as a child, courted as a maiden, where Mildred buried her cats, where one last rose had been her final living link with everything.

Had Mary wanted to get out of the carriage, it would have been difficult but possible. Yet she expressed no interest in leaving her seat. She had what she had come for, and it was time to go. She returned the water cup, collected her traveling companions, bid her old servants farewell, and gave the driver his signal. The coachman snapped his reins, the wheels turned, and Mary began the trip back to Alexandria. As Arlington disappeared from view, she did not need to look back.

Returning to Lexington after her triumphal tour, Mary busied herself with a variety of projects. She worked tirelessly raising money for the new church building, and she had another major fund-raising interest as well: helping solicit and compile contributions for a memorial volume about the general, to be sold in order to construct a public monument in Lexington.

She was, she admitted, "quite in despair of its ever being completed" after two years of work and somewhat lackluster response, "but we must hope on."

Correspondents often sent her articles about the general for her comment. One she received earned special praise: "The extract you sent me was most just & true. But how few can penetrate the inner life revealed more especially to the wife who for so many years, even from childhood, knew him…I know how far they are from revealing all the nobleness of his character."

As another school year began, Custis went about his duties as president of the college, and Mildred prepared the house for several cousins who were coming for an extended visit. Daughter Mary was in Europe, and Rooney and Rob were in the midst of another growing season at their plantations. Rooney and Tabb were now the parents of another healthy son, George Bolling Lee, born the previous year.

But Mildred was worried about her sister Agnes. Ever since her illness during her student days at "Staunton Jail," Agnes had suffered from time to time with mysterious digestive and intestinal ailments and with painful neuralgia in her face as well. After her bout with typhoid fever, she was sick even more often. By the time their mother returned from her trip to the springs in the fall of 1873, Agnes was seriously ill. Her sister noticed her "tired eyes" and "white hands." Mildred had to support Agnes in order for her to walk through the house.

Agnes's condition worsened rapidly. Mildred moved her out of the bedroom they shared to daughter Mary's empty room, for whatever benefit the eastern sun and freer ventilation on that side of the house might give. On October 12, the third anniversary of the general's death, Mary had herself carried up the stairs to Agnes's bed. One look told her that her daughter was dying.

Mildred captured the moment. "In the afternoon my poor suffering mother was brought up in her chair & sat close to her bedside holding her hand, the tears streaming down her face." The grief-stricken old woman kept her tragically familiar vigil. Agnes was in and out of delirium. "I never cared to live long," she murmured. "I am tired of life." She asked Mildred to give Markie Williams her Bible. "You know Orton gave it to me."

Mary Custis Lee did not have the stamina to wait out the death of another child. Physically and emotionally spent, she had herself carried back downstairs, hoping to get a little rest and be with her daughter again before the end. But when the end came, the staircase prevented Mary from saying good-bye to Agnes.

At dawn on October 15, Agnes's breathing became steadily slower until, in Mildred's words, "one gasp & all was over for ever!... I rushed down stairs to tell Mama.... When I told her Agnes was dead, [she] cried, 'My poor child, that I should have outlived her! Oh, that I could have seen her again!'"

A week after Agnes's funeral, Mary still seemed stunned by the loss. She sat for hours with a favorite cat in her lap, listless, unresponsive, crying at the mention of Agnes's name. Mildred thought that she sometimes smiled in her "sweet old way" but that her mother was drifting slowly and irrevocably into darkness. "The end was drawing near," she feared, the end of a life of "unselfish love, of daily sacrifice, of high poetic tastes, & simple faith in Christ" and "of total self abnegation."

Mildred sent for Rooney and Rob and telegraphed daughter Mary. By the time the men arrived, their mother had slipped into unconsciousness. On a table beside the sickbed the children placed fresh-cut roses from one of the bushes the general had planted in the garden outside.

On Wednesday, November 5, 1873, Mary Anna Randolph Custis Lee died in her sleep. Two days later, as she had requested, she was entombed in the basement of the college chapel beside the husband she had loved so faithfully and so long. All the businesses in Lexington were closed during the funeral service, which began at noon.

Though notice of her death appeared in the *New York World* and other national publications, the *Southern Collegian* paid what was perhaps the most fitting tribute. Penetrating the Victorian prose, readers of a later generation would still sense the awe inspired by the spiritual and emotional strength of a life and heritage that spanned nearly every seminal event in American history.

"Tempting as the theme is," the paper editorialized, "we forbear to offer any eulogy on the character of this woman so venerated and loved by the entire community in which she resided," linked to America's history and destiny "by so many strong and tender ties, and around whom there has gathered for years past a degree of public interest and affectionate solicitude that has never attached to any other woman in the history of our country."

Mrs. Lee was worthy both of her "illustrious husband" and her "illustrious ancestry" in every way, "in intelligence and in refinement of taste, in kindness of heart and attractiveness of manners, in cheerfulness under the heaviest reversals of fortune and the agonies of bodily pain, in sympathy and in benefactions toward the impoverished and suffering people of her country" and "in her manifold and ceaseless self-denials and labors on behalf of religion and the Church."

In many ways, Mary's life had been one of contrasts and seeming contradictions—of joy and suffering, of plenty and want, of companionship and loneliness, of contentment and longing. Once spoiled, she came to be humble. Once bitter, she came to renounce bitterness. She was materially rich, yet she became poor. She was spiritually poor, yet she became rich beyond measure.

Mary Custis Lee believed that whatever life brought her way, good or bad, came from the hand of God to ready her for a better world. What she believed, she lived. And what she lived, she proved—and leaves us all.

EPILOGUE

 ary's death left Custis and Mildred alone in the president's house at Washington and Lee College. It fell to Mildred to go through her mother's and Agnes's things and respond to the stacks of condolence letters that came in during the fall of 1873. Since June her sister Mary had been overseas, enjoying herself in Rome while Mildred sorted old clothes, letters, and personal belongings and established a routine as housekeeper for Custis. "Custis and I have to bear our sorrow alone—and together—in a home once so happy but now so desolate," she wrote her cousin Harry Lee.

When his great aunt Maria Fitzhugh died in 1874, Rooney inherited Ravensworth and moved there from the White House with his family. Rob remained a widower at Romancoke, and Mildred eventually settled into the rhythm of spending autumn and winter in the country with Rob and then returning to Custis's house in the spring to serve as hostess during graduation.

According to his grandfather's will, Custis was to inherit Arlington and all the Washington artifacts. In 1874 he took up his mother's battle for the return of Arlington to the family, or at least an acknowledgment that it had been wrongfully taken and that some sort of restitution was due. In 1882 the case finally came before the Supreme Court, which ruled that Arlington had been improperly confiscated and ordered it returned to its rightful owner, George Washington Custis Lee.

And so, twenty-two years after she abandoned her home to invaders, nineteen years after it was commandeered as a cemetery, and nine years after her poignant final visit, Mary Custis Lee was completely vindicated in her claim that the estate had been hers all along. The government action responsible for her years of rootlessness and longing, her loss of financial independence, and the destruction of a priceless and irreplaceable family legacy had been an act of unjustifiable retribution against her husband and entirely outside the law.

Custis had no interest in living in the middle of a cemetery and immediately sold the estate to the United States Government for $150,000, half of what his mother had thought it was worth a decade earlier. He gave his sisters Mary and Mildred $7,000 each, the balance of the $10,000 legacies their Grandpa Custis had left them.

Whatever could be located of the Washington artifacts that were in government hands—in the Patent Office, the Smithsonian Institution, and elsewhere—were eventually gathered up and returned to the Lee family by executive order of President William McKinley in 1901. Some were subsequently given or loaned to various museums and institutions, and others, including the Mount Vernon porch lantern and the harpsichord, were claimed by the Mount Vernon Ladies' Association, which had acquired Mount Vernon in 1858.

Daughter Mary continued living abroad much of the time, eventually visiting more than twenty countries and traveling completely around the world. She dined with American dignitaries along the way, met an Indian maharaja, climbed the pyramids of Egypt, and attended a special audience with Pope Leo XIII at the Vatican. American newspapers described her as "brilliant, original, and cultivated," though the daughter of an American diplomat in Cairo remembered her as "a horribly ugly old maid, and very *queer.*"

Unlike Mary, who had no emotional attachment to Arlington, Mildred pined at times for her old home like her mother had, remembering it as the "Kingdom of my childhood." Even so, later in life she also traveled, journeying through Europe and elsewhere. On their sojourns abroad, the sisters occasionally crossed paths, and in 1884 they met in New Orleans for the unveiling of a statue of their father.

Rooney went into politics and, after a successful turn as a state senator, was elected to the U.S. House of Representatives. Taken ill soon after his reelection to the House, he died at Ravensworth in 1891 and was buried there beside his Grandmother Lee and his three children who had died in infancy.

In 1894, after more than twenty years as a widower, Rob married his cousin Juliet Carter. Following his marriage, Mildred resumed her old custom of spending long periods of time with Rob at Romancoke, enjoying her visits even more after his two daughters, Mary Custis and Anne Carter, were born. "One must have *something* to love in this world," she said of her nieces. "They are the most fascinating, sweetest little beings I ever saw."

In 1896, Custis Lee was in his twenty-sixth year as president of Washington and Lee College. Convinced that he was in the job only on account of his name, he had submitted his resignation five times during that period, yet he had always been persuaded to withdraw it. This time, hearing from Custis that he considered himself "utterly useless" as president, the board of trustees accepted his decision to retire.

Following the action of the board, Mildred spent four months cleaning out the house where she and her brother had lived for more than thirty years. In 1897 they vacated the home for Custis's successor. While Mildred took off on another series of overseas journeys, Custis moved to Ravensworth at the invitation of Rooney's widow. He lived there in seclusion until his death in 1912.

Mildred met Mary in Paris, where they soon realized that they were more different in personality and interests than they had ever been. Mildred returned to the United States and became a popular guest at meetings of Civil War veterans' groups. She died in 1905 in New Orleans, where she had gone to attend a week of Mardi Gras festivities. Flags flew at half-staff in the South, and her body was returned to Lexington on a special train. She was placed in a vault beside her parents and Agnes in an annex to the Lee Chapel that had been added in 1883.

Daughter Mary, always the most independent of Mary Lee's children, lived abroad most of the time until 1914, when, with the threat of world war hovering over Europe, she returned to America and moved into the Shoreham Hotel in Washington. She dined with President and Mrs. Woodrow Wilson at the White House and, even into her eighties, visited with old friends in Richmond and Savannah.

Though she had never been sentimental, Mary strenuously defended her father's memory against an incendiary account of her sister Annie's death by Susan B. Anthony and Elizabeth Cady Stanton in their book, *The Official History of Woman Suffrage,* which read in part:

> A young girl scarcely beyond her teens when the war broke out, [Annie Lee] remained firm in her devotion to the national cause, though for this adherence she was banished by her father as an out-cast from that elegant home once graced by her presence. She did not live to see the triumph of the cause she loved so well, dying the third year of the war...homeless because of her love for the Union, with no relatives near her, dependent for care and consolation in her last hours upon the kindly services of an old colored woman.

Incensed at what she called an "infamous lie," Mary claimed in a letter to one of her cousins that the statement "was too absurd, one would think, to be printed in any decent newspaper or book." She concluded that she could not see how Stanton's views *"can* be accepted by Christian God-fearing women, which all women ought to be...."

The last of the Lee children, daughter Mary died at the Homestead in Hot Springs, Virginia, on November 22, 1918, four days after Armistice Day. Singular to the end, she left orders that her body be cremated, the first person in the history of Rockbridge County to do so. Her ashes were placed in the family vault in Lexington.

Over the years, the rest of the family came to rest at Lee Chapel. Rooney's body was moved from Ravensworth in 1922, the general's parents came in time, and finally, in 1994, Annie's body was moved from the cemetery in Warrenton Springs, which had fallen into disrepair.

Of the plantations that were such important places in Mary's life, some have survived almost untouched, while others are gone without a trace. The shining example of the former is Shirley, the Carter plantation where Mary's in-laws were married and where Mary often visited. Today it thrives as a family home and working plantation, owned and operated by the tenth and eleventh generations of the Hill-Carter family. It may be the oldest plantation in American still owned by descendants of the original Crown grant holders.

On the opposite end of the scale is Ravensworth, Mary's haven at so many signal moments in her life. The house caught fire in 1926 and burned to the ground. The land was subdivided for residential development in the 1960s, and today no trace of the house or the estate remains.

Slowly over the years, Arlington House was transformed from a symbol of loss, death, and retribution into a symbol of reconciliation. In 1874, President Rutherford B. Hayes opened the cemetery to Confederate groups who wanted to hold memorial services there. The same year, headstones of Confederate dead, which were inscribed "Rebel," were replaced with new stones similar to the ones on Union graves. In 1900 the Confederate graves were relocated to a special section of the cemetery, where a Confederate monument was erected in 1914.

For many years, the cemetery superintendent and his family lived in Arlington House, which also housed the cemetery office. In 1925 the property was designated the Lee Mansion National Memorial by an act of Congress, and renovations to the interior were begun. Ownership of the house was transferred to the National Park Service in 1933. In 1955, the house was officially named the Robert E. Lee Memorial.

Today thousands of tourists visit the estate every year. Though Arlington Spring is long gone, filled in and paved over years ago to build a freeway along the Potomac, the breathtaking view of the capital that Marquis de Lafayette so admired is still there. The sun still rises behind the bustle of Washington City. And Mary's beloved rose garden still flourishes just off the south wing, where her bedroom windows look out upon the flowers in all their splendor, and the fragrance of the blossoms rises up on the river breeze.

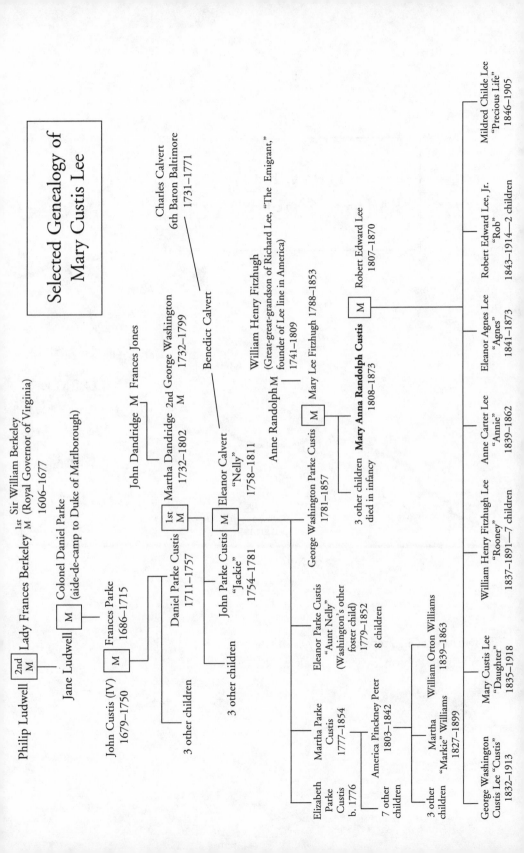

Selected Genealogy of Mary Custis Lee

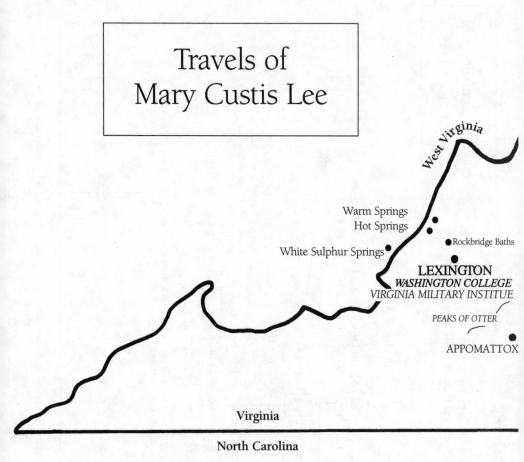

Travels of
Mary Custis Lee

West Virginia

Warm Springs
Hot Springs

White Sulphur Springs•   •Rockbridge Baths

LEXINGTON
WASHINGTON COLLEGE
VIRGINIA MILITARY INSTITUE

PEAKS OF OTTER

APPOMATTOX

Virginia

North Carolina

Audley ■

■ Tudor Place

ARLINGTON ● **WASHINGTON**

Kinloch ■

Ravensworth ■ ● **ALEXANDRIA**
Mount Vernon ■

Richland

■ Cedar Grove

Chatham ■ Clydale Stratford

Rappahannock River ■

Chantilly

Pamunkey River

Hickory Hill ■ Romancoke ■

RICHMOND ●

■ Shirley White
House

Oakland ■ ■ Belmead *James River*

Bremo ■

Derwent

Potomac River

● WARRENTON
Jones Springs

● RALEIGH
ST.MARY'S COLLEGE

The publisher and author would love to hear your
comments about this book. *Please contact us at:*
www.multnomah.net/ladyofarlington

NOTES

CHAPTER 1: THE ROSE OF ARLINGTON

15. Numerous sources have Mary painting in the parlor at Arlington. On September 21, 1865, Mary recorded her memory of Orton's visits and described the room as her "chamber," which was the contemporary term for the sitting room that adjoined a bedroom. Orton was easily familiar enough with the family to have come into Mary's room under the circumstances.

18. In her own description of her departure from Arlington, written the summer after the war, Mary mentions many details, though not specifically picking flowers on that day. However, the fact that she often cut flowers from the garden is well documented in her letters.

18. The unfinished iron framework of a new Capitol dome is visible in many photographs of Washington in the Civil War era. The new dome was completed in 1863.

CHAPTER 2: LITTLE WASHINGTON

19. Much of the information on Mary's ancestors is taken from *Old Arlington: The Story of the Lee Mansion*, an unpublished manuscript by Murray H. Nelligan in the Arlington House archives.

21. Details of the stormy marriage between John Custis IV and Frances Parke are found in an article by Lenora W. Wood in the *Norfolk Virginia-Pilot* for June 3, 1951 (see bibliography).

22. John Custis, insisting on having the last word, ordered the following to be "handsomely engraved" on his tombstone: Beneath this Marble Tomb Lies the Body of the HONORABLE JOHN CUSTIS, ESQ....Aged 71 years yet he lived but Seven Years which was the Space of Time he kept a Bachelor's House at Arlington on the Eastern Shore of Virginia.

25. Some sources cite a rumor that a lazy and irresponsible Jackie Custis had at first connived to get out of military duty but then felt guilty and joined Washington in the field. Though that may be somewhat plausible, so is the argument that his pregnant young wife needed him. We have facts for the "pregnancy" argument; there is little if anything concrete for the "lazy and irresponsible" thesis.

27. Details of G.W.P. Custis's life come from Custis's own speeches and writings and from news coverage in the *National Intelligencer* quoted in *Old Arlington*.

CHAPTER 3: A WORLD IN BALANCE
33. Mary's second name is also sometimes written "Anne" or "Ann." The spelling "Anna" comes from the entry of her birth in the Custis family Bible at the Virginia Historical Society. Some sources list Mary's birthplace as Arlington, but most, including the family Bible, list it as Annefield.

35. Dower rights are legal rights or titles the widow of an estate owner retains after his death.

36. George and Martha Washington still rest today at Mount Vernon despite various attempts over the years to have them moved. Their crypts under the Capitol dome remain empty.

41. Some present-day analysts suggest that a successful plantation economy could have been maintained with hired labor or sharecroppers.

However, Custis and his contemporaries felt that it was "essential," despite their simultaneous claims that hiring freedmen would be more efficient. Such was the convoluted logic of slavery.

CHAPTER 4: CHARMS AND GRACES

48. Some sources list the founding date of the American Colonization Society as 1816. The first meeting was on January 1, 1817, though the society was formally organized three days earlier. The group was founded by a Presbyterian minister from New Jersey named Robert Finley, with the support of President James Madison. The land the society bought and settled in Africa eventually became the nation of Liberia. The society remained active in the country's affairs until 1912.

52. The two school notebooks are in the Library of Congress. One has a notation on the cover that a Union soldier stole it from the attic at Arlington during the war.

56. Lafayette had owned slaves on his Caribbean sugar plantation.

57. Houston was elected governor of Tennessee in 1827 and finally wed in 1829, but the marriage lasted only three months. Later that year, he resigned his office, moved to Oklahoma Territory, and lived among the Cherokees with a "magnificent specimen of Indian womanhood" named Tiana Rogers, an ancestor of entertainer Will Rogers. Houston married again in 1840, just before beginning his second term as president of the Republic of Texas. Houston biographies sometimes incorrectly identify Mary as "Mary Parke Custis" and "Martha Washington's granddaughter."

CHAPTER 5: LIEUTENANT LEE

60. Supreme Court Justice John Marshall became Chief Justice in 1801.

60. The observation that "there was nobody else to marry" comes from Mary Coulling's book *The Lee Girls*.

61. Sources disagree on the nature and severity of Lee's disfigurement. Some fail to mention the nose injury.

65. There were apparently three steamboats used in succession by visitors to Arlington Spring over the years. This name was given to at least one of them.

68. Several sources mention a purported eyewitness who insisted that Lee's proposal took place at Arlington Spring, but none lends any credence to this version.

CHAPTER 6: BORN AGAIN

72. This and other entries from Mary's journal are taken directly from the original document in the archives of the Virginia Historical Society. None of it has been published previously. There is almost no punctuation in the manuscript; sentences run on line after line. In order to preserve the spontaneity and intimacy of the original, editorial corrections have been limited to what is essential to avoid misreading. Those changes are unannotated; any significant edit is annotated with ellipses or brackets.

CHAPTER 7: TWO ROOMS AND A DIRT FLOOR

81. The date of Mary's wedding has also been given as June 13—and, in one source, as June 31! The June 30 date comes from the Custis family Bible.

86. The floor in the Lee quarters would have been of packed earth, neither as primitive nor as uncommon as modern readers might expect.

CHAPTER 8: A TEST OF FAITH

97. This comment about Mary's "laziness" in a letter from Lieutenant Lee to Captain Talcott, dated April 10, 1834, is often quoted to support the view that Mary was a lazy and careless housekeeper. Certainly she did not meet Lee's standards, but the popular depiction of her as a hopeless case in household management is unjustified. As his letters show when taken as a group, Lee was a great tease when writing to his friends. Furthermore, Mary was running a household by herself for the first time, had suffered severe bouts of illness in the past, and was the mother of a boisterous young son.

101. Preparations for the birth of Mary's children are described in a visitor presentation by the National Park Service at Arlington House.

CHAPTER 9: OUT WEST

115. This passage inviting Mrs. Custis to Baltimore is frequently misread as meaning that Mary is telling her mother that she should come to have her portrait painted and that the painting will cost only $500. The handwriting of the numeral admits to either "$5.00" or "$500," but one can scarcely imagine the Lees hailing a $500 portrait as a bargain, or the portraitist painting "Mammy" for free even in the unlikely event Mrs. Custis wanted her included in the picture. It was, however, accepted practice for slaves accompanying their masters to ride on the train for free. In context, the amount is clearly $5.00 for the price of a train ticket, not $500 for the price of a portrait.

118. The Lees probably never had a chance to meet the famous William Clark. He died on September 1, four months to the day after Mary's arrival in St. Louis.

CHAPTER 10: HOME AND AWAY AGAIN

127. According to Thomas in *Lee: A Biography,* Captain Lee's army salary in 1841 was $1,817.

130. The Narrows is where the Verrazano Narrows Bridge now stands, with one end in Brooklyn and the other on Staten Island.

CHAPTER 11: NEW YORK YEARS

134. Completed in 1837, the *Great Western* was the first steamship designed to carry passengers and freight across the Atlantic Ocean. It was engineered by Isambard Brunel, who also designed the more famous *Great Eastern,* launched in 1858, which was four times the size of any other ship afloat but, though it laid the first transatlantic telegraph cable, a financial failure.

136. Castle Island, where Castle Garden was located, has long since been connected to Manhattan Island by landfill.

139. The writer of the Arlington memoir, whose name does not appear on the original document, was almost certainly a Lee cousin and Arlington houseguest. Mr. Custis's own interesting account of a day at Arlington Spring is quoted in *Old Arlington,* page 285.

142. Annie's accident is described in detail in *The Lee Girls*. Most sources have only a general description along the lines of "an accident...received in one of her eyes," as Lee characterized her infirmity in his will.

146. Based on a complicated formula of allotments, Captain Lee's military compensation had actually been cut at least twice over the previous five years.

CHAPTER 12: MEXICAN VIGIL
158. The Lee's house in Baltimore is no longer standing.

CHAPTER 13: EARTH IS NOT OUR HOME
161. This passage noting the epaulettes, frequently quoted in biographies of Lee, is from Robert Jr.'s memoirs, published in 1904.

162. The Missouri Compromise had provided for the admission of Maine as a free state to balance the admission of Missouri as a slave state and had included legislation that smoothed over political and tariff conflicts between North and South for a generation.

164. Cadet Oliver Otis Howard served as a Union general in the Civil War, lost his right arm in battle, and was awarded the Congressional Medal of Honor. In 1869 he founded Howard University in Washington, D.C, and later was appointed superintendent at West Point.

165. There was a delay in picking up the tiles for the new portico from Washington because one of Custis's draft oxen had died and the other had been sold, and he could not afford to replace them right away.

CHAPTER 14: BLESSINGS AND BURDENS
177. Various sources downplay the importance of Robert's confirmation at this time, suggesting that it was a mere formality he hadn't had time to attend to before. From her letters and journal, there is no doubt that Mary had been deeply concerned about Robert's spiritual state since before they were engaged and that his confirmation was extremely important and significant in her eyes.

182. Custis later insisted on repaying his son-in-law for these improvements to the house.

189. This letter from Mary brings into question whether, as some of Lee's biographers suggest, he was taken completely by surprise at her condition when he returned from Texas. He may have been shocked at the extent of her disability, but he obviously had fair warning that his wife walked "very unsteadily & not often without a crutch."

CHAPTER 15: SEASONS OF CHANGE
198. Mary never mentioned the fact that her father had never taken communion. Agnes recorded his regret over the matter in her diary.

CHAPTER 16: TOWARD THE ABYSS
207. In 1854, construction of the Washington Monument was taken over by the controversial American Party, also called the Know-Nothings. The party was opposed to immigrants and Roman Catholics and believed that only native-born Americans should hold public office. Stones for the Washington Monument were donated by various groups, states, and countries. The Know-Nothings had the stone given by the Vatican thrown into the Potomac. Political bickering halted construction, which finally resumed under the Army Corps of Engineers in 1878.

209. Based on her symptoms, Agnes's illness was probably neuralgia, a nerve disorder. Mineral baths would likely have made her feel better, though they would not have cured her.

215. Ever discreet, Mary requested that her inquiries about money be kept private.

CHAPTER 17: A DEATHLIKE STILLNESS
226. The date of Mary's departure from Arlington has never been precisely fixed. These letters to her husband and General Scott were written from there on May 9; she also wrote Lee from Arlington on May 12.

CHAPTER 18: HOMELESS

244. The name of the Potomac steamer is given sometimes as the *G. W. P. Custis*.

244. Some sources describe the sign as reading "Captured at Arlington."

CHAPTER 19: A GRANDDAUGHTER OF MRS. WASHINGTON

247. Many sources claim that Mary and the general did not see each other between the time he left Arlington before the war and the day she was passed through to Confederate lines in June 1862. In the letter quoted here, written from the White House plantation on March 8 to "My dear friend" in Savannah, Mary indicates that she had seen the General "last Sunday."

249. Sources consistently quote the closing of the White House note as "A Granddaughter" or "A Grand-Daughter." Mary may have been using it as a generic term, as she and her relatives used "cousin" to mean a variety of relationships.

251. Lieutenant Haile's pocket diary, now at the Museum of the Confederacy, includes this eyewitness account. The first hundred pages of the tiny volume are numbered in pencil. Some of them are filled with Haile's minuscule, precise handwriting. He died in battle, leaving the last of them blank.

251. The Spottswood Hotel was also the general's headquarters.

253. When Mary made her first trip to the mineral springs in 1836, during her long convalescence after daughter Mary's birth, she had also gone to Warrenton.

256. At that time, no effort was made to isolate patients with typhoid fever, which is spread by water-borne bacteria. Infected guests probably swam and shared drinking dippers with the others.

CHAPTER 20: LEE'S MISERABLES

260. The owner of Hickory Hill was the same William Wickham who owned the townhouse where the Lees had lived in Baltimore.

263. The temporary convalescent hospital may account for persistent rumors that Arlington was used as a hospital, though the mansion itself was never used as one.

266. Some sources have Union troops carrying Rooney down the stairs inside the main house. However, contemporary accounts agree that Rooney was recuperating in the plantation office, which was in a separate building nearby.

269. In keeping with the social standards of the time, it was impossible for any of the Lee daughters, as single women, to live by themselves, and so Charlotte had to be the one to live alone.

CHAPTER 21: FIVE YEARS AND A LIFETIME

271. The men's nickname for the house comes from the military word for a dining hall or a group of soldiers who eat together, though no doubt the place was messy as well.

276. There were probably a few temporary graves on the grounds at Arlington before the first official burials. It was common to bury the dead on or near the battlefield where they fell and reinter them in cemeteries later. Several sources report that soldiers were buried at Arlington in the opening months of the war when there was fighting nearby, but they were reburied elsewhere before the site was designated a military cemetery.

CHAPTER 22: HOW VAIN THAT HOPE

283. Accounts of the evacuation from Richmond and its occupation by the Union vary slightly in the order of events.

292. There is a file in the Manuscript Division of the Library of Congress with a title similar to "My Reminiscences..." and designated "Permanently Restricted," meaning, this writer was told, that "nobody can see it for any

reason ever." The text quoted here is from a typescript at the Virginia Historical Society that is presumably of the same document.

CHAPTER 23: YET HOW RICH

298. The Freedmen's Bureau was headed by her son Custis's old West Point classmate Otis Howard.

299. On October 2, 1865, the same day Lee signed an oath to uphold the standards of his office as president of Washington College, he also signed a loyalty oath to the Union, required of all citizens in the rebellious states for restoration of their civil rights. Secretary Stanton put the document in a desk drawer, intending to keep it as a souvenir, and it was eventually lost unprocessed. The paper was rediscovered in 1970, and Lee's citizenship rights were finally restored by President Gerald Ford on August 5, 1975.

300. This chain of events regarding the sale of copyright is inferred from an incomplete series of letters on the subject of reprinting Mary's book.

309. The quotation describing Milly Howard, from Robert Jr.'s 1904 memoirs, has often been used out of context to imply that Mary was some sort of addle-headed invalid her maid dressed up for display. In fact, Mary was a pleasant and popular hostess at the Springs, her graciousness and intelligence undimmed.

CHAPTER 24: A MEMORY CHERISHED

321. In the days immediately following the general's death, Mary wrote a number of long letters giving details of his last illness to various friends and relatives. None of them mentions the general's supposed last words, "Strike the tent!" No other eyewitnesses mentioned them either. They are legendary, but almost certainly fictional.

CHAPTER 25: RIPENING FOR HEAVEN

332. The time of Mary's visit to Alexandria is sometimes set later in the summer. The exact date is unknown, but obviously must have preceded the newspaper feature. Furthermore, Mary refers to her visit in a letter written from Hot Springs on June 13, 1873, to General Robert H. Chilton, who

had been a member of her husband's personal staff. She apparently went directly from Washington to the White House, which she also mentions in her letter from the springs, and then to Bath County.

336. Mary drinking from the Arlington well appears in *The Lee Girls*.

338. The New York *Herald* and other major newspapers across the country, both North and South, also carried articles about Mary's death that lauded her life and faith.

BIBLIOGRAPHY

Because women of Mary Custis Lee's station in the nineteenth century were very seldom written about during their lifetimes, most of the information for this book came from letters Mrs. Lee sent and received over the years. The principal sources for the letters quoted are:

Virginia Historical Society, Richmond, Virginia
Arlington House Archives, Arlington, Virginia

Eleanor S. Brockenbrough Library
Museum of the Confederacy, Richmond, Virginia

Leyburn Library
Washington and Lee University, Lexington, Virginia

Virginia State Library and Archives, Richmond, Virginia
Manuscript Division

Library of Congress, Washington, D.C.

Other sources:

Allen, Juanita E. "Lee's 'Gentle Annie.'" *The United Daughters of the Confederacy Magazine* 58, no. 3 (March 1995): 12f.

Anderson, John Q., ed. *Brokenburn: The Journal of Kate Stone 1861–1868*. Baton Rouge: Louisiana State University Press, 1955.

Andrews, Matthew Page. "Appomattox: As Viewed by Mrs. Robert E. Lee." *The Southern Magazine: Virginia Number* 2, no. 3 (June 1935): 25–6.

Anthony, Susan B., et. al. *The Official History of Woman Suffrage.* Rochester, New York: Susan B. Anthony, 1900.

"Arlington House: The Robert E. Lee Memorial." National Park Service brochure, 1999.

Burks, Judge Martin P. E. Pendleton Tompkins, and John D. Letcher, comp. *The Beginning of the Protestant Episcopal Church at Lexington, Virginia.* 1930.

Callaway, James. "Character of Robert E. Lee Defamed, by Susan B. Anthony...." Richmond, Va.: Eleanor S. Brockenbrough Library, Museum of the Confederacy.

Chase, Enoch A. "George Washington's Heirlooms at Arlington." *Current History* 29, no. 6 (March 1929): 972f.

Chesnut, Mary Boykin. *A Diary from Dixie.* Cambridge, Mass.: Harvard University Press, 1980.

Coleman, Elizabeth Downey. "Mary Custis Lee's 'Arlington.'" *Virginia Cavalcade* 3, no. 3 (Winter 1953): 17f.

Congressional Record. "A Petition by Mary Anna Randolph Custis Lee...." January 22, 1872.

Connelly, Thomas Lawrence. *The Marble Man: Robert E. Lee and His Image in American Society.* New York: Knopf, 1977.

Coulling, Mary P. *The Lee Girls.* Winston-Salem, N.C.: J.F. Blair, 1987.

Craven, Avery, ed. *"To Markie:" The Letters of Robert E. Lee to Martha Custis Williams.* Cambridge, Mass.: Harvard University Press, 1934.

Custis, George Washington Parke. *Pocahontas, or The Settlers of Virginia: A National Drama, in Three Acts.* Philadelphia, 1830.

Custis, George Washington Parke. *Recollections and Private Memoirs of Washington.* Washington, D.C.: W.H. Moore, 1859.

Cuthbert, Norma B. "To Molly: Five Early Letters from Robert E. Lee to His Wife, 1832–1835." *Huntington Library Quarterly,* (May 1952): 257 ff.

Decker, Karl and Angus McSween. *Historic Arlington.* Washington, D.C.: The Decker and McSween Publishing Company, 1893.

DeButts, Mary Custis Lee, ed. *Growing Up in the 1850's: The Journal of Agnes Lee.* Chapel Hill, N.C.: University of North Carolina Press, 1984.

Dowdey, Clifford. *Lee.* New York: Bonanza Books, 1965.

Dowdey, Clifford, ed. *The Wartime Papers of R. E. Lee.* Boston: Little Brown and Company, 1961.

Earle, Peter. *Robert E. Lee.* New York: Saturday Review Press, 1973.

Eicher, David J. *Robert E. Lee: A Life Portrait.* Dallas: Taylor Publishing Company, 1997.

Fischer, David Hackett. *Albion's Seed: Four British Folkways in America.* New York: Oxford University Press, 1989.

Flood, Charles Bracelen. *Lee—The Last Years.* Boston: Houghton-Mifflin, 1981.

Fox, Larry. "The House That Custis Built." *Weekend* (26 May 1989).

Fox-Genovese, Elizabeth. *Within the Plantation Household: Black and White Women of the Old South.* Chapel Hill, N.C.: University of North Carolina Press, 1988.

Freeman, Douglas Southall. "Lee and the Ladies: Unpublished Letters of Robert E. Lee." *Scribner's Magazine* 78, no. 4 (October 1925): 339f.

Freeman, Douglas Southall, ed. *Lee's Dispatches: Unpublished Letters of General Robert E. Lee, C.S.A. to Jefferson Davis and the War Department of the Confederate States of America 1862–1865.* New York: G. P. Putnam's Sons, 1957.

Freeman, Douglas Southall. *R. E. Lee: A Biography.* New York: C. Scribner's Sons, 1934–35.

"Funeral of Mrs. G. W. P. Custis and Death of General R. E. Lee." *The Virginia Magazine of History and Biography* 35, no. 1 (January 1927): 22f.

Garrison, Webb. *Amazing Women of the Civil War.* Nashville: Rutledge Hill Press, 1999.

Hendrick, Burton Jesse. *The Lees of Virginia: Biography of a Family.* New York: Halcyon House, 1937.

Hyman, Sidney. "Washington's Negro Elite." *Look* (6 April 1965): 60f.

Jones, J. William. *Life and Letters of Robert Edward Lee: Soldier and Man.* Neale Publishing Company, 1906; reprinted Harrisonburg, Va: Sprinkle Publications, 1986.

Jones, J. William. *Personal Reminiscences of General Robert E. Lee.* Baton Rouge: Louisiana State University Press, 1994.

Jones, Katherine M. *Ladies of Richmond.* Indianapolis: The Bobbs-Merrill Company, Inc., 1962.

Kane, Harnett Thomas. *The Lady of Arlington: A Novel Based on the Life of Mrs. Robert E. Lee.* Garden City, N..Y: Doubleday, 1953.

Kennedy, Roger. "Arlington House, a Mansion That Was a Monument." *Smithsonian* 16, no. 7 (October 1985): 157f.

LaCavera, Tommie. "Lee, Jackson and Maury: The Women in Their Lives." *The United Daughters of the Confederacy Magazine* 54, no. 10 (November 1991): 8f.

"Lafayette's Visit to Fluvanna County." *The Bulletin of the Fluvanna County Historical Society,* no. 1 (September 1965): 1f.

Larner, John B. *Records of the Columbia Historical Society.* Washington D.C.: 1930.

Lee, Captain Robert E. *Recollections and Letters of General Robert E. Lee.* Garden City, N.Y.: Garden City Publishing Co., Inc., 1904.

Lee, Edmund Jennings, ed. *Lee of Virginia: 1642-1892.* Philadelphia, 1895.

Lee, Fitzhugh. *General Lee: A Biography of Robert E. Lee.* De Capo Press, 1994.

Lee, Mary Custis. School Notebooks. Unpublished documents in the Library of Congress Manuscript Collection, 1823.

Lee, Mary Custis. Prayer Journal. Unpublished manuscript in the Virginia Historical Society Archives, 1830–1838.

Lee, Robert E. Jr. *My Father, General Lee.* Garden City, N.Y.: Doubleday & Company, Inc., 1960.

Lossing, Benson J. "Arlington House, The Seat of G.W. P. Custis, Esq." *Harper's* 7, no. 40 (September 1853): 433f.

Luraghi, Raimondo. *The Rise and Fall of the Plantation South.* New York: New Viewpoints, 1978.

MacDonald, Rose Mortimer Ellzey. *Mrs. Robert E. Lee.* New York: Ginn and Company, 1939.

Miller, T. Michael. "'My Dear Louisa'...: Letters from Mrs. Mary Custis Lee to the Snowden Family of Alexandria, Virginia." *The Fireside Sentinel* 5, no. 6 (June 1991): 69f.

Mitchell, Patricia B. *Confederate Home Cooking*. Chatham, Va.: Sims-Mitchell House Bed & Breakfast, 1991.

Mitchell, Patricia B. *Cooking for the Cause*. Chatham, Va.: Sims-Mitchell House Bed & Breakfast, 1988.

"Mrs. Lee—The Arlington Estate." *Alexandria Gazette* 74, no. 128 (12 June 1873).

"Mrs. Lee's Claims." *Alexandria Gazette* 74, no. 131 (16 June 1873).

Muhlenfeld, Elisabeth. *Mary Boykin Chesnut: A Biography*. Baton Rouge: Louisiana State University Press, 1981.

Nagel, Paul C. *The Lees of Virginia: Seven Generations of an American Family*. New York: Oxford University Press, 1990.

Nelligan, Murray H. *Old Arlington: The Story of the Lee Mansion National Memorial*. Unpublished manuscript in the Arlington House Archives, 1953.

Nelson, Sallie. "Aftermath." *Taylor Trotwood Magazine* (January 1909).

Osborne, John Ball. *The Story of Arlington*. Washington, D.C.: Press of John F. Sheiry, 1899.

Power, J. Tracy. *Lee's Miserables: Life in the Army of Northern Virginia from the Wilderness to Appomattox*. Chapel Hill, N.C.: The University of North Carolina Press, 1998.

Purdue, Ida Pace. *Papers Pertaining to the Confederacy*. Howell Purdue, 1961.

Reed, Sarah A. *A Romance of Arlington House*. Boston: The Capple Publishing Co., Ltd., 1908.

Rose, Ruth Preston. "Mrs. General Lee's Attempts to Regain Her Possessions After the Civil War." *The Arlington Historical Magazine* 6, no. 2 (October 1978): 28f.

Smith, Gene. "General Lee's Daughters." *American Heritage* 47, no. 4 (July/August): 110–1.

Taylor, John M. *Duty Faithfully Performed: Robert E. Lee and His Critics*. Brassey's, 1999.

Templeman, Eleanor Lee. *Virginia Homes of the Lees*. Annandale, Va.: Charles Baptie Studios.

Thomas, Emory M. *Robert E. Lee: A Biography.* New York: W. W. Norton & Company, 1995.

Thomas, Emory M. *Robert E. Lee: An Album.* New York: W. W. Norton, 1999.

Van Auken, Sheldon. "A Century of the Southern Plantation." *The Virginia Magazine of History & Biography* 58, no. 3 (July 1950): 356f.

Williams, John Hoyt. *A Biography of the Father of Texas.* New York: Simon & Schuster, 1993.

Wood, Leonora W. "Today's Homes on Eastern Shore Are Built on Old Custis Grants." *Norfolk Virginian-Pilot*, 3 June 1951, pt. 5, p. 4.

Woodward, C. Vann, ed. *Mary Chesnut's Civil War.* New Haven, Conn: Yale University Press, 1981.

Woodward, C. Vann and Elisabeth Muhlenfeld, eds. *The Private Mary Chesnut: The Unpublished Civil War Diaries.* New York: Oxford University Press, 1984.

Young, James Capers. *Marse Robert, Knight of the Confederacy.* New York: Rae D. Henkle Co., Inc., 1929.

Zimmer, Anne Carter. *The Robert E. Lee Family Cooking and Housekeeping Book.* Chapel Hill, N.C.: The University of North Carolina Press, 1997.

The quotations from the *National Intelligencer* are all found in Nelligan, *Old Arlington.*

In addition to these sources, there are various files containing numerous clippings and articles without dates or attributions.

INDEX

"John Perry is an excellent writer whose work is consistently both entertaining and insightful. I highly recommend him as an author."

—Arkansas Governor Mike Huckabee

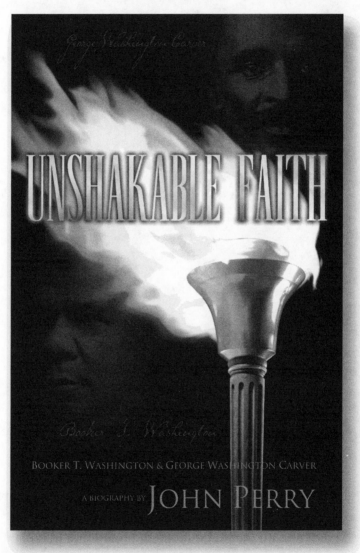

Through an abiding faith in Christ and a sense of divine appointment, Booker T. Washington and George Washington Carver, children of slaves, quietly proved their oppressors wrong. Along the way, they made remarkable discoveries and contributions that have inestimably benefited mankind to this day. A fascinating true story!

ISBN 1-57673-493-5